Managerialism

D0221832

ECON   2-17-94   16⁸⁵ P
Ⓝ

Managerialism

*The Emergence of a
New Ideology*

Willard F. Enteman

The University of Wisconsin Press

The University of Wisconsin Press
114 North Murray Street
Madison, Wisconsin 53715

3 Henrietta Street
London WC2E 8LU, England

Copyright © 1993
The Board of Regents of the University of Wisconsin System
All rights reserved

5 4 3 2 1

Printed in the United States of America

Library of Congress Cataloging-in-Publication Data
Enteman, Willard F.
    Managerialism: the emergence of a new ideology /
Willard F. Enteman.
        272 p.   cm.
        Includes bibliographical references (p. 255) and index.
        ISBN 0-299-13920-4 (cl.)   ISBN 0-299-13924-7 (pbk.)
        1. Management.   2. Ideology.   3. Right and left
(Political science)   I. Title.
    HD31.E654   1993
    658.4—dc20   93-7444

To KFE
In appreciation

Contents

Preface

In his recent translation of Aristotle's *On Rhetoric,* George Kennedy appropriately employed the subtitle *A Theory of Civic Discourse.* [1] An important purpose of this book is to expand contemporary civic discourse about political, social, and economic theory, which I have chosen to call ideology.

During most of the twentieth century, ideological debates and discussions, especially in advanced industrialized nations such as the United States, have been restricted to a narrow set of forced choices. Participants in the discussions have accepted presumptions of the debate uncritically. Two of those presumptions are that, first, democracy is the only rationally defensible political alternative and, second, there are only two economic alternatives, capitalism and socialism. Thus, all parties to the discussion agree that every society which is not totalitarian must choose between democratic capitalism and democratic socialism.

Given this basis, the parties adopt a common rhetorical strategy. The supporters of democratic capitalism only need persuade themselves and others that democratic socialism is faulty in order to establish democratic capitalism conclusively. Likewise, the supporters of democratic socialism only need persuade themselves and others that democratic capitalism is faulty in order to establish democratic socialism conclusively.

Since it is easier to cast doubt than it is to demonstrate the credibility of a theory, the advocates of the contrasting positions expend their efforts arguing against the position they oppose rather than articulating carefully the position they wish to uphold and marshaling support for it. Furthermore, both sides follow similar approaches to establish their negative conclusions. First, each tries to show that the opposite position is logically inconsistent. Democratic socialists argue that democratic capitalism is a contradictory view, and if the capitalism is retained, the society will necessarily devolve into totalitarianism (i.e., fascism). Democratic capitalists argue that if the socialism is retained, democratic socialism will necessarily devolve into totalitarianism (i.e., communism). Second, each side argues that its ideological opposite is internally incoherent and will fail whether or not it is linked to democracy. Unfortunately, there would appear to be just enough confirmatory evidence to keep both of these negative arguments alive and make them influential. When the debates move beyond academic to popular discourse, their negative tone increases in intensity and also reinforces the tendency of politically motivated debaters to fall into name calling and ad hominem arguments.

I suggest that we should return to first principles in an effort to understand the intellectual foundations of these ideological choices. Such a return means looking to the intellectual architects of the ideologies and, on the assumption that they would not make obvious errors, developing a sympathetic understanding of their most important positions. That approach yields some surprising results: we discover, for example, that the ensuing debates have been largely irrelevant to the industrialized world as it developed. Since capitalism and socialism are nineteenth-century ideologies, the fact that their architects did not foresee what would unfold a century or more later should neither surprise us nor make us lose our respect for them.[2] What is surprising is that we have clung so long and so tenaciously to these ideologies and have allowed ourselves to be dragged into pointless debates. In the context of the reality around us, we could do so only by massive distortion of the ideologies. Thus, the return to first principles is difficult for us in the late twentieth century because we have to suspend beliefs caused by illusions.

As a professor, I confess to a considerable amount of joy in teaching new generations of students about these intellectual architectural giants in the history of thought. While there is a lively debate in academic circles about what belongs in the so-called canon of great works and what belongs out, I would be glad to argue that people like Adam Smith and Karl Marx belong in any sensible listing of great authors.[3] If we were to leave them out, I am not sure I would know what is meant by *the canon* or by *great authors* anymore. In spite of my joy in discussing these authors and their works with students, and in spite of the students' evident willingness to engage the theories, it has been my students more than any other people who have forced me to raise doubts about the received presumptions of contemporary ideological debates. Initially I, like my professors before me, confidently referred to contemporary situations in order to exemplify the ideological perspectives under discussion. However, students often persisted in their questioning and forced me to realize that my examples either were not representative of the world in which we live or were not applications of the ideological theories. For instance, I increasingly lost my confidence in supporting the popular view that the United States either exemplifies capitalism or is headed toward socialism.

Even though I had to abandon conventional wisdom, it still was much easier for me to say what was not the case than to decide what may be the case. My resistance to the notion that neither the United States nor any other country is capitalist or socialist or even democratic was overcome only after considerable effort born of a natural scepticism.[4] My strongest presumption was that what I and my fellow students had been taught and what my fellow professors were teaching students must be right and that we all have to make some decisions in the face of those forced choices. As my doubts were raised, however, I began to suspect that one of the reasons current commentators occasionally refer to our ideological debates as sterile is not that ideology itself is sterile but that the ideological debates we have been engaged in focus on ideologies which are without issue in reality. The question became one of asking not so much which of the two alternatives is wrong, but what would follow if both are wrong, in the sense that neither corresponds with reality. As I began to doubt the prevailing ideologies, however, I was not content merely to bring forward negative theses.

In my classes, I had argued that every society must have an ideology whether or not it is explicit. Since I thought I was capable of dethroning one set of beliefs, I decided that I had a responsibility to articulate an alternative set which might succeed where the others had not. Disclosing an operative ideology, however, turned out to take more time and effort than I originally imagined. As this book will show, the search involved the historically philosophical task of questioning unexamined assumptions. It was necessary to challenge not only surface theories but also the foundations on which those theories depend.

While eschewing the notion that I could discover *the* alternative to the prevalent ideological formulations, I set about attempting to discover at least *an* ideological alternative which would help us come to grips with the world in which we live. For reasons which will become clear, I decided to call that ideology *managerialism*. I do not put this alternative forward apodictically. If the articulation of managerialism serves to open civic discourse and remove it from the cul-de-sac in which we find it, an important result will have been achieved.

Part of the reason it has taken me so long to articulate managerialism as an alternative ideology is that I had been accustomed to thinking that one who articulates an ideology should also hold it in high esteem. I could not bring myself to that position with regard to managerialism, though others may be able to do so. Like St. Paul, I find myself in this world but not of it. If the discourse is opened, however, I would hope we might find the articulation of another ideology which is simultaneously relevant and morally defensible. That is more than I expect, but it is not beyond dreaming.

While this book will be perhaps irritatingly abstract and theoretical to some people, I have tried to write it for a number of audiences. I have, of course, attempted to address my scholarly colleagues in the relevant disciplines. I also have been anxious to speak to intellectuals in general, because the interest in ideology seems to be coming from many quarters, not the least of which is that of scholars who are interested in literary theory. I have also wanted to speak to managers who are willing to think about the enterprise in which they are engaged. The view of some academics that all managers must be intellectually vacuous is simply a prejudice which is not supported by the facts. Finally, one of my fondest hopes is to be able to reach the frequently mentioned well-educated laypersons. I hope that anyone who will put the effort into reading the book can find something interesting, if not necessarily convincing, in it. Thus, I set myself the difficult task of writing with multiple audiences in mind. It is up to others to determine the extent to which I succeed.

In 1992 I published a book which dealt at length with the conditions of retirement for college and university faculty and academic staff. I said that that work represented a combination of apparently disparate interests in my life, and I hoped to complete another volume which would combine those interests in a more theoretical way. This volume is the one to which I referred. Some people may ask about connections between the two books. I would caution against making too much of the presence or absence of such connections. The first book grew out of my profound respect and concern for faculty and academic staff, especially as they face the new conditions of the management of their pensions. It also grew out of my own personal and professional interest in management in general and the financial world in particular. I find finance exciting because of the extensiveness of data and the capacity to use them to test theories. My concerns for faculty and academic staff have to do with the application of all of that to their lives. My concerns with ideology have to do with the foundations of the theories which we use to understand the world in which we live.

In regard to further work, the arguments of this book have implications both in the direction of deep theory and in the direction of practical applications. In the future, I intend to explore those implications. In the final chapter of this book, I suggest that we need to revise radically the foundations of what is seen as mainstream economic theory today. I suggest that on a theoretical and analytic level, much that has been considered outside the mainstream of economics needs to be more systematically developed and brought into the mainstream. Perhaps this volume helps open the way by suggesting that moving beyond the mainstream does not imply moving into socialism. Discourse in economic theory itself has been severely constrained in past years, and yet we know that the received theory has failed as a predictor of economic events.[5] In that respect, I draw attention to problems without being able to supply an alternative.

I would like to explore new alternatives in economic theory in an effort to find a more satisfactory solution. Beyond theory, I want to look toward application also. The final chapter suggests that substantial changes need to be made in the practical view of organizational life. For example, I think that we may need to revise both strategic planning and management education, and we may be able to recast the enigmatic topic of business ethics, which has still not found a comfortable home in business or the academy. In my view, further conceptual changes should be made in developing practical applications of managerialism. I hope to explore those changes in another volume. Perhaps once that is accomplished, we can hope to find a discipline of business ethics which will become something more than an addendum for a business or philosophy curriculum.

Throughout my life, I have been blessed with people who have understood my apparently disparate interests and have encouraged me in spite of the scepticism of more conventional people. Much of my intellectual life began in discussions with Siegfried Gable. I was an immature adolescent, and he was a brilliant and highly cultured person. Looking back on it now, I realize how much I was in over my head, but he was never condescending. Those deep and all too brief discussions awakened my interest in theory and persuaded me to adopt his faith in the pursuit of rigorously honest thinking. From that beginning, I turn to more formal schooling and express my gratitude to Casmir France of the Pingry School; George Van Santvoord and Richard Gurney of the Hotchkiss School; John William Miller, Frederick Rudolf, and John Chandler of Williams College; Chaffee Hall, George Albert Smith, and John Matthews of the Harvard Business School; Richard Millard, John Lavely, and Milič Čapek of the philosophy department at Boston University; Holcombe Austin and Paul Helmreich of Wheaton College; Sven Peterson and Harold Martin of Union College; John Donovan and Edward Pols of Bowdoin College; and David Sweet, Carol Guardo, and Thomas Howell of Rhode Island College. All of these people, and others whom I am sure I have inadvertently left out, have at various times encouraged me to follow my own muse rather than accepting the common view that an interest in theory and an interest in practicality are inherently inconsistent. In this context, I want to take special note of two people. Jan Ludwig of Union College and Richard Pearce of Wheaton College have been not only intellectual mentors but also friends in the deepest sense of that term. They have agreeably put up with my all too argumentative questioning and maintained our common commitment to careful thinking. They also decided we could continue to be friends even when I wandered into administration.

As I said in my previous volume, my indebtedness to many faculty is deep and profound. Faculty bashing is something of a sport now among those who seek political gain, but in the end, as a society, we shall reap what is being sowed. The evidence I can see from having returned to the trenches of teaching is that the faculty bashing is having an effect, though it may not be the one which the politically motivated say they want. The real effect is to persuade many of the best and brightest students that they do not want to become professors and be target practice for the powerful. The results of such short-term political behavior are near at hand. It is time for those of us who have been touched and measurably improved by our teachers from kindergarten through graduate school to stand up and say thank you. There can be no doubt that there are some bad apples in the barrel which holds all teachers, but the majority are good. I cannot remember one who did not make me a better person for being in his or her presence. I wish I could say that of all professions.

Once again, I want to express my appreciation to my colleagues in the philosophy department of Rhode Island College. Professors Thomas Donaldson of Georgetown University, Norman Bowie of the University of Minnesota, Clarence Walton of American College, and Michael Hoffman of Bentley College were early supporters of this project, and I appreciate their guidance. Professor Albert Anderson of Babson College and Professor George Lodge of Harvard Business School have done me the honor of reading the entire manuscript in an earlier draft and giving me the benefit of their insights. For this volume, as for the previous one, Patricia Marzzacco has been a careful reader and friendly critic. She read the material in numerous drafts, and she supported the effort even when my confidence flagged. If this volume achieves its goal of reaching as broad an audience as I hope, it is in no small measure as a result of her patience and persistence. I also want to express my appreciation to the University of Wisconsin Press and especially to Barbara Hanrahan. The press has been willing to venture into the unknown first with the book on retirement and now with this one. Their commitment to the life of the mind gives me hope for the future of an endangered species: the university presses. I also wish to thank readers who reviewed the manuscript, whose suggestions were most helpful. I suspect that where I have not followed them, I may wish I had.

Finally, I want to express my deepest appreciation to my family. In a time when the notion of a true and loving family threatens to be trivialized by manipulative politicians, mine has been a source of understanding and support even when I doubted that this material would ever see the light of day. My wife, Katie, has been my companion and best friend for over thirty wonderful years. She has had to make many sacrifices when I was absorbed with this project, and she has had to tolerate my bad moods when I was stuck on some aspect I could not resolve. Her constancy and love has sustained me throughout. This book is dedicated to her because, without her sacrifices and support, it would not exist.

Managerialism

1 Ideology
Definition, Comparisons, and Defense

A Map for the Journey

The mathematician and philosopher Alfred North Whitehead titled one of his last books *Adventures of Ideas*. [1] That is an appropriate designation for much of our systematic thinking. Through the ages and across many cultural boundaries, authors have been adventurers in the world of ideas. This book stands in that long tradition. It is self-consciously an adventure which invites readers into its world of ideas and encourages them to explore those ideas as well as their own. The ideas here have practical implications, since they are about the social, political, and economic order in which we live. The book speaks to scholars, academics, and intellectuals about theories and abstractions and about their responsibilities in the world of ideas. It also speaks to practical people, especially administrators and managers, about their responsibilities and the principles upon which their actions may be based.

In concluding his *General Theory*, John Maynard Keynes said: "The ideas of economists and political philosophers, both when they are right and when they are wrong, are more powerful than is commonly understood. Indeed, the whole world is ruled by little else. Practical men, who believe themselves to be quite exempt from any intellectual influences, are usually the slaves of some defunct economist. . . . I am sure the power of vested interests is vastly exaggerated compared with the gradual encroachment of ideas . . . soon or late, it is ideas, not vested interests, which are dangerous for good or evil." [2] These words bring some comfort to people like the author of this book, who are interested in both the practical and the theoretical worlds. While Keynes accepted the common view that all extant economics would be found in some variety of capitalism (which he sought to save) or some variety of socialism (of which he was contemptuous), an argument of this book is that both those ideologies are defunct and that they are being replaced by a different economic and political philosophy.

3

In this book, however, there is something of a reversal of the order Keynes contemplated. Keynes thought that practical people were the slaves of defunct economics and political philosophy. He was correct, especially in regard to their public rhetoric about economics and politics. Nevertheless, we should also recognize that political philosophers can be enslaved to economic theories and political philosophies of defunct thinkers. In this book, we shall see that while practical people continue to speak as if they believe the defunct economic theories and political philosophies, they act on the basis of a theory and political philosophy which is quite different. Of course, the practical people have not debated the new theory. That is not their job. At the same time, economists and political philosophers have not taken notice of the theory either, preferring, instead, to build on the foundations of the defunct theories. The implicit theory on which practical people actually operate has been in the process of development long enough that it can be explicated and both theoretical and practical implications can be examined.

The social reality which exists today in advanced industrialized societies simply does not correspond to the reality described by accepted theories. Historically, when theories did not correspond to reality, theoreticians at first tended to blame the reality. After a while, however, theory must change in accordance with new realities or the theory will be in danger of becoming an empty intellectual exercise. Political, social, and economic reality has changed. It is time for political philosophy, social principles, and economic theories to change. This book is about those changes and about theoretical and practical consequences which might flow from the changes. It is an adventure into ideas about our world. Before the adventure begins, it may be helpful to readers if they have some idea of the twists and turns of the path ahead.

The book has three basic purposes: to show that the common ideological assumptions we believe we share are no longer relevant, to articulate the implicit ideology upon which society operates so that it can be examined and discussed, and to explore some of the theoretical and practical implications of the new ideology.

Following this section, the remainder of the chapter will deal with some preliminary issues crucial to the rest of the book. *Ideology* will be used as a term designed to capture the meaning of more cumbersome phrases such as *political philosophy, social principles,* and *economic theories.* Consequently, we will examine some definitional issues with regard to ideology. Following that discussion, a brief defense of ideology as an enterprise will be offered. The chapter will conclude with a response to some concerns which may bother readers from the outset and throughout the book.

Chapters 2 through 6 provide an extensive examination of the kind of ideologies to which Keynes referred: capitalism, socialism, and democracy. In each case, the examination will lead us back to first principles in an attempt to discover the central commitments of the ideologies and the warrants for those ideologies. It may surprise readers to hear that these ideologies are defunct. The real surprise, however, is that we should expect ideologies born of the eighteenth and nineteenth centuries to have lasted through the substantial changes of the twentieth century and into the twenty-first.

Numerous people regularly provide rhetorical reinforcement for these ideologies. If anything, the proponents, especially of capitalism and socialism, seem to have grown even more strident recently. In that regard, as in many others, democracy will prove to be something of an exception. While intellectual interest in democracy increased considerably in the eighteenth and nineteenth centuries, the concept has been discussed as a political philosophy at least since Plato. In addition, while democracy has many proponents, it has few overt critics. The fate democracy will suffer may not be a fate of rejection so much as a fate of suffocation. *Democracy* has achieved the status of being an almost exclusively positive term. Having been embraced by almost everyone, the word itself is threatened with losing a distinctive meaning. We shall have to work even harder to recover its first principles from those who claim to be its friends but are in fact antidemocrats.

Chapter 2 develops organizational distinctions among atomistic, organic, and process approaches to ideology. Those distinctions should provide some context for considering the specific ideologies in later chapters. Throughout, the effort is to place debates in a broader context and to encourage an opening of the discourse about ideology. The distinctions lead to a final section in the chapter in which some logical points are made about discussing ideology. Those points will also provide grounds for expanding ideological conversations.

Chapter 3 discusses an ideology in the atomistic tradition: capitalism. We return to the father of capitalism, Adam Smith, and examine carefully his vision for capitalism and the basis for its justification as he saw it. The fundamental basis of capitalism is to orient the society around consumer needs, wishes, and desires. Since we are all consumers, capitalism is justified on the basis of providing for all of us insofar as possible. We shall see that, while numerous people claim to believe in capitalism, the ideology of the United States and other advanced industrialized societies is not based upon the fundamental defining principles of capitalism. In addition, we shall see that when Adam Smith speculated about the conditions which would lead to the ideological structures of the United States and other advanced industrialized nations, he disapproved of them because he believed they violated the fundamental principles of capitalism. We shall also see that the failure to implement foundational first principles of capitalism carries with it a loss of the moral justification for our contemporary structures.

Chapter 4 examines socialism and communism, using Marx as the primary representative. Socialism is presented as the predominant example of an organic approach. Its fundamental purpose is to satisfy the needs of workers as a unity. Since we are all part of that unity, socialism's justification springs from the satisfaction of the needs of the totality. We see that circumstances envisioned by Marx have not been created and that the fundamentals of socialism are not being followed. As with the case of capitalism, it is clear that the failure to adopt the fundamentals of socialism means that the justification of socialism is lost also. One of the favorite arguments of self-described capitalists is that all modifications to capitalism ipso facto move us closer to socialism. The chapter concludes with a section on logic.

Chapter 5 examines democracy as a prime example of the process approach. No single figure represents democracy in the way that Smith and Marx represent capitalism and socialism. Nevertheless, some fundamental democratic principles are suggested. Following Abraham Lincoln's felicitous phrase, democracy is understood as a process which exists "of the people, by the people, for the people." That, too, provides the moral basis for the justification of democracy. Following a discussion of some difficult and unresolved problems within democracy, we will closely examine democratic theory as presented by some of the foremost democratic theoreticians. We will discover that none of them really support democracy.

Chapter 6 discusses issues associated with combining democracy with capitalism or socialism. Both sets of claims are examined closely and found to be without merit. The end of the chapter returns to the logical questions once again, and an attempt is made to identify all the ideological possibilities in order to place those ideologies which have been examined in a systematic context.

Chapter 7 turns to an effort to describe in some detail the ideological principles on which the economic, social, and political order of advanced industrialized societies is actually based. The name given to that ideology is *managerialism*, in recognition of the fact that managers constitute the central figures in the ideology. The concept of management and managerialism leads naturally to an examination of the organizations which are managed. A contrast is made between the theory of the firm as developed by economists and the concept of the corporation as developed in this book. Discussion of the concept of the corporation leads naturally to a discussion of conflicting views about the nature of the corporation.

Chapter 8 is both retrospective and prospective. It uses the developments of the book to suggest new directions for ethics, economics, and business, with special reference to business ethics. As an ideology, managerialism sheds light on numerous issues in these areas, and it helps us recognize the necessity for fundamental changes in the way the issues are treated. While the study of business ethics has become more vigorous and active in the past two decades, it continues to lie at the margins of philosophy and business studies. An active and very talented group of people has been at the center of the movement to develop business ethics. However, they are not seen as part of the core of either area. Some suspect that the philosophers do not respect business ethics because they are suspicious of business itself. Others suspect that business professors and business executives are suspicious of business ethics because it has the potential for embarrassing them. There is perhaps a modicum of truth in both claims—just enough to sustain them. My suspicion is that the studies have not gone deep enough. Instead of doing what they are prepared to do—examine theoretical structures in depth—the philosophers see business ethics as a kind of applied ethics and simply reproduce the conflicts of normative ethical theories with simplified, if not simplistic, examples from business. In my view, the first task of a philosophical approach to business ethics should be to understand the deep theoretical foundations of business. When the philosophers of business ethics do that, they usually fall back on conventional economic theory and unexamined platitudes about capitalism. One hope for this book is that it will encourage a deeper examination of unexamined assumptions, so that business ethics can find its location as part of the core of philosophical studies. In addition, my hope is that in the search for solid theoretical foundations, references to business practices will be less superficial and less easily dismissed by business professors and business executives as irrelevant.

The theoretical and the practical are united in managerialism, and the inadequacies of the other approaches are transcended. While a fundamental justification for managerialism can be stated, however, that justification is not capable of giving sufficient intellectual warrant to managerialism. Finally, while business ethics encompasses problems not solved in this book, we do take a step in the right direction by locating where and how it might be exercised.

With our path now before us, we will turn to some definitional issues.

The Definition of Ideology

In order to avoid problems associated with equivocation, scholars often find it necessary to define central terms carefully at the outset of their works. That is doubly important with the word *ideology*. It has had such a long, troubled, and conflicting history that, perhaps more than most words, it needs to be treated with some specificity. The place to start, as Alice said, is at the beginning. Unless we know what we are talking about, we cannot hope to make much sense.

The word *ideology* has been suffused with ambiguity and confusion since its origin. It has been, at once, a term of praise, a term of scorn, a vague description of a (vague) epistemology, and an excessively general description of thoughts, attitudes, and approaches. We dare not, as the Queen said, make words mean anything we wish. We want to communicate with other people. The historical incongruities surrounding *ideology* resonate even today, and they are responsible for many of the current responses we witness.

Ideology was born as a rhetorical device, and we have not removed it entirely from that domain. It does identify something important, however, and we should save it if we can. The task will be to see if we can capture the important core of past meanings while leaving behind mere attitudinal responses to the word. If so, it can stand for something first, and after that people can respond positively or negatively to what it stands for. Such an analysis should take away some of the equivocation and some of the emotionality. Once that is done, we shall find that *ideology* stands for something which is general enough to be interesting but specific enough to be an object of careful analysis.

In the modern United States, ideology is often an object of ridicule, as it was for Marx. Ironically, the criticisms are similar. The self-defined practical people in the United States portray ideologues as stubborn people more concerned with promoting their own outlooks than with accepting practical responsibilities. Simultaneously, the term *ideology* has acquired two apparently contradictory connotations: one referring to otherworldly impractical debating and the other to something dangerously about this world. In a sense, both aspects are correct. Ideology is theoretical, but it also involves theory which is decidedly relevant to the world we inhabit. The ambiguity is part of the tension in the quotation from Keynes earlier in this chapter.

I suggest that we consider the ideology of a society to be that set of principles upon which the political, social, and economic order of the society is based. Ideology in general is, then, all possible such principles.

The Debate about the End of Ideology

In the section on semantic history later in this chapter, we shall see that the word *ideology* originated in France in the early nineteenth century, around the time of Napoleon. From Napoleon to Marx and on to Daniel Bell and other twentieth-century social scientists, people have persistently attempted to declare an end to ideology.[3] All their efforts have been based on the same mistake, which is, at its base, a definitional one. They examined specific ideologies which they argued were wrongheaded. They were not consistent with each other about what the offensive ideologies were or why they were offensive. They then identified ideology in general with the specific ideology or ideologies they rejected. Since they believed those ideologies were pointless, they concluded that ideology itself must be pointless. The conclusion simply does not follow from the premises. Even if we were to grant that false ideologies exist—after all, that is a central thesis of this book—it does not follow that all ideologies are false.

It is a matter of some historical irony that just about the time Bell and other social scientists were declaring an end to ideology, interest in it was being revived in some unlikely quarters. For university students in the 1960s, many of whom were in some personal danger, the war in Vietnam and human rights became subjects of intense debate. Those debates were first and foremost ideological. Shortly thereafter, some works in political science took up, again, the cudgels for ideology as an important topic. For example, in 1971 Kenneth and Patricia Dolbeare published a pioneering book. From a most unusual quarter, George Lodge, a professor at Harvard Business School, began lecturing and writing articles on ideology. That material became the centerpiece of an important work: *The New American Ideology.* [4]

The recent turmoil in the Communist and formerly Communist worlds has revived an interest in ideology on the part of people in those countries without reviving much interest in any of the ideologies which have been offered since the industrial revolution. When the most scholarly leader of a newly freed country, Václav Havel of Czechoslovakia, turned to the American rock star Frank Zappa for ideological and cultural guidance, we have some idea of how much philosophy and other intellectual disciplines have failed to say anything interesting to those groping for order in what threatens to be uncontrollable chaos. What we know from eastern Europe after 1989 is that whatever direction it wishes to go is not outlined by the present alternatives in practice or in theory.

After the revolutionary events in eastern Europe, many capitalist apologists comforted themselves by quoting the eastern Europeans as saying that whatever ideology they would adopt, it would be "not-socialism." Since those apologists assumed that only two alternatives existed—socialism and capitalism—they concluded that the eastern Europeans were choosing capitalism. However, the eastern Europeans said with equal force that whatever ideology they would adopt would also be "not-capitalism." Journalists have been the most persistent in promoting the notion that these societies are becoming capitalist. Recognizing the loss of faith of people in centralized totalitarian (and, typically, corrupt) control, the journalists have assumed those people became "born again" capitalists. However, all of that rests on the rather shallow assumption that people who reject socialism must be in favor of capitalism and vice versa. Similar comments can be made about the so-called Third World societies. Thus far, they have not so much found an ideological approach which makes sense for them as they have found the alternatives offered by others to be inadequate.

Those who have tried to end ideology by declaring its death have been partially right. As we shall see, what ended was not ideology itself, but particular ideologies. The traditional ideologies do not correspond with reality and are in that sense false. The resolution of the debates between the ideologists was not—as each side dearly wished—the victory of one side over the other. It was, rather, the demonstration of the irrelevance of both sides. Those who pronounced the end of ideology were, then, half right, but that means that they were also half wrong. Ideology had not died. Unless society is without any order, ideology cannot come to an end, because every society must operate on the basis of some social, political, or economic principles. The job of the intellectuals is to articulate those principles. When the conventionally articulated principles are inadequate, the task becomes one of listening, learning, articulating, and revising in the face of analyses, arguments, and debates. That is the task attempted here.

The Proposed Definition

There is nothing shocking or erudite about the definition of ideology which was suggested earlier. It does not commit us to more than that which is functional. Etymologically, *define* comes from the Latin *definire,* which means limit. The word *define* shares a common root with the word *definite*. One important function of a definition is to place definite limits on the appropriate use of a word. A definition which does not delimit is functionless. The proposed definition of *ideology* fulfills the task of delimiting. Many activities—even intellectual activities—are left out of the proposed definition. Ideology is not the same as religion, art, or science. Using this definition, we cannot meaningfully apply *ideology* to something other than a society.

It would be foolish for me to request status as a czar of the word *ideology*. There are more extended uses of the term. I once heard a critic refer to the ideology of a symphony. It is possible to guess at what he meant, but his use of the term extends it beyond what is helpful, at least for this book. At the same time, it would be a mistake to make the definition too limiting. In specifying that ideology applies to a society, there is no implication that it only describes existing societies. Ideology may refer to nonexisting societies or even imaginary societies, whether or not the author thinks they should exist.

Comparisons

Now that we have a working definition of *ideology* and some basic understanding of it, we will examine our proposed definition by comparing it with other suggestions. By clarifying what implications are intended and what ones are not intended, the process of comparison should aid us in further understanding what is meant by *ideology*.

Semantic History

The *Oxford English Dictionary* identifies the origin of the word *ideology* with the French thinker Destutt de Tracy, who in 1796 read a paper about the thought of Etienne Bonnot de Condillac. Tracy used the word *ideology* to describe Condillac's thought. Interestingly, Tracy did not discuss Condillac's political and economic views in his paper. Tracy recommended using the term *ideology* for the identification of Condillac's views about how humans have ideas which relate to the external world.

Tracy's suggestion was a bit disingenuous. In his *Traité des sensations,* published in 1754, Condillac struggled with an epistemological problem which has haunted philosophers for centuries. That question may be put most simply by asking how we can prove what few people doubt: that there is an external world independent of our sensations.[5] Tracy wanted to count Condillac, who was widely respected at the time, on his side in the dispute. Tracy believed that the external world could not be proved. From that he concluded (erroneously) that its existence must be doubted. Condillac had been much more careful. Condillac had established such a high standard of proof—mathematical proof— however, that his program was essentially doomed before it started. Condillac died in 1780, so it was not difficult for Tracy to take advantage of Condillac's inability to advance a convincing mathematical proof of the existence of an external world and argue that since the only reliable knowledge we can have is of our own ideas, that is all we can say exists. The view that there are only ideas is what he identified with the term *ideology,* using the semantic heritage of *ideas.* Thus, *ideology* was born in confusion and imprecision. We shall see in the paragraphs below dealing with synonyms for *ideology* that this sense of ideology has remained even to the present.

If the subject of ideology had remained in that portion of the intellectual world known as epistemology, it would not have been brought into the domain of practical affairs. For that transformation we are indebted to Napoleon. In 1776 Condillac published a piece on economics and government, "Le Commerce et le gouvernement considérés relativement l'un à l'autre," in which he argued that agriculture is the fundamental source of wealth. That was a view held by the economists known as physiocrats and is nationalistic enough that it would not have irritated Napoleon.[6] Condillac also argued for free trade (an unusual position for a physiocrat), and ever faithful to his admiration for mathematical reasoning, he argued for the use of rational discourse to arrive at civil laws which would solve social and political problems.

Napoleon was too impatient to wait for the lengthy process of debate and dialogue which such an approach implied. He successfully played on the anti-intellectualism which dismissed the epistemological issues discussed by Condillac so that he could dismiss Condillac's economic and political views as either foolish or dangerous. Napoleon branded the followers of Condillac *ideologues,* and that term, along with *ideology,* continues to carry the connotation of irrelevant intellectualizing or dangerous political propagandizing.[7] Napoleon saw Condillac and his followers as a threat to his own dominance, and he closed their university center.

A few decades later, Karl Marx reintroduced the term. Like Napoleon, he ridiculed those he identified as interested in ideology. Marx argued that ideologies are conceptual structures created by ruling classes to justify their position. Marx dismissed ideology because he said it was an instrument for dominance by the ruling class over the working class. Curiously, later Marxists would come to align ideology with Marx's constructive views and assert that only those theories which could successfully deal with class distinctions could be called ideologies. Of course, those theories, by definition, were all variations on Marxism, since a criterion of *successful,* on those marxists' terms, is an accepted treatment of classes.

As has been indicated, the term *ideology* will be used in this book in a more neutral sense than some of the semantic history would suggest. Certainly, one may wish to respond to particular ideologies negatively, but in this book, the general term will be used without the negative connotations it has had. The proposed definition was designed to give the term a neutral standing.

People often wonder why philosophers and other scholars frequently discuss definitions at great length without turning to an obvious source: the dictionary. The response depends considerably on an understanding of the nature of dictionaries, but explaining that would probably take longer than turning to dictionary definitions, and the question is not as irrational as scholars sometimes suggest. The complete definition of *ideology* as it appears in the third edition of *Webster's New International Dictionary* is as follows:

> Ideology
>
> 1 a: a branch of knowledge concerned with the origin and nature of ideas.
>
> b: a theory in philosophy advocated by Destutt de Tracy (1754–1836): ideas originate from sensation.
>
> 2: visionary speculation: idle theorizing; *often:* an impractical theory or system of theories.
>
> 3 a: a systematic scheme or coordinated body of ideas or concepts especially about human life or culture.
>
> b: a manner or the content of thinking characteristic of an individual, group, or culture ⟨bourgeois *ideology*⟩ ⟨medical, legal, and other professional *ideologies*⟩ ⟨kept his *ideology* inviolate⟩.
>
> c (1): the integrated assertions, theories, and aims that constitute a sociopolitical program ⟨a national *ideology* that was not static but altered with altering circumstances⟩.
>
> (2): an extremist sociopolitical program or philosophy constructed wholly or in part on factitious or hypothetical ideational bases.[8]

An examination of a number of dictionaries would give us a list of suggested synonyms for *ideology: beliefs, doctrines, teachings, tenets, convictions, credo, canon, creed, principles, rules, dogma, doctrine, standards, postulates*. No one of them carries the meaning suggested in the definition adopted for this book, and even collectively they are inadequate. However, they do contain a core of the meaning. They refer to some fundamental principles about something. The synonyms are not clear about what the something is, and they seem even less clear about whether the principles need to be explicit or whether they could be implicit. In this book, *ideology* refers to the total, complex social, political, and economic order of a society or societies. By way of contrast, while examples from science and religion may be used to illustrate points about ideology, it is a mistake to refer to scientific theories or religious doctrines as constituting an ideology. For example, Einstein's theory of relativity is not an ideology, though it states some important principles. Similarly, the religious doctrine of the divinity of Christ is not an ideological doctrine, as important as it may be in establishing differences between religions. Thus, the synonyms listed above need to be qualified as referring to the social, political, and economic order.

The word *order* has consistently appeared as part of the suggested definition. Someone might ask whether a theory which held that there is no order, just endless chaos, in the social domain might qualify as an ideology. The answer is that such a position needs to be confronted if it can be given some reasonable articulation but that even when so articulated, it is not an ideology. It might be described as the refutation of ideology, just as a demonstration that Jesus of Nazareth was not the Christ might be a demonstration of the impossibility of Christianity without being called a Christian religious theory. It seems that Christian religious theory must depend on the acceptance of Jesus as the Christ. If that much cannot be accepted, no matter how important the religious theory, it cannot be called Christian. Similarly, if it can be shown that there is no social order at all, then the impossibility of ideology will have been shown, but that view is not itself an ideological theory. Thus, ideological theories must be about some social order. This leads, then, to the conclusion that *ideology,* as used here, is the fundamental principles of the social, political, and economic order of society.

Conceptual Issues

A number of conceptual issues are important to consider in understanding ideology and its definition. These are not, as some may think, merely semantic issues. They deal with important conceptual dimensions, and unless we are careful about them, there is a danger we shall apparently solve problems but will have done so only because of equivocations about the conceptual backdrop of the terms. Since George Lodge has been almost single-handedly responsible for reviving an interest in ideology and since he and I both suggest that there is a new ideology, let us start with an examination of his definition of the term.

Lodge gives us two definitions of *ideology:*

> An ideology is a collection of ideas that makes explicit the nature of the good community.

> The concept of ideology assumes that a community is an organic whole influenced largely (although not necessarily exclusively) by a dominant set of coherent ideas.[9]

While these two definitions are not equivalent, they raise three important conceptual issues which need to be pursued: about the necessity of an ideology's being organic, about the necessity for coherence, and about the necessity that all ideologies must have some influence on the course of human events. Let us take them in order.

It is important to avoid importing more into the word *ideology* than is necessary. Lodge seems to want to restrict ideologies to those which conceive of society as an organic whole. We shall discover, however, that the issue of an organic versus a nonorganic nature of society is central to ideology itself. We shall see later that the concept of organic whole is by no means transparent, and we shall see that there are ideologies which assume societies are not organic wholes and should not be organic wholes on any acceptable definition of that elusive term. Our use of *ideology* does not limit it to conceptions of communities which are organic wholes. Lodge's own ideology is an organic one. Managerialism is not. On Lodge's definition, an ideology for which society is not an organic whole would be a contradiction in terms—like female peacocks—and could not exist by definition. The definition suggested for this book allows the expression *nonorganic ideology* to have meaning and not to be eliminated merely by definition. We do not want to win our debates about ideology by definitions of terms, or the greatest fears of Condillac's irrelevancy will be borne out. Thus, the definition of *ideology* suggested here is broader than Lodge's.[10]

In the first definition cited above, Lodge talks only about a "collection of ideas." The second definition commits him to a "set of coherent ideas." The latter more closely delimits what might count as an ideology, and it requires a definitional discussion to ascertain whether the ideas of some putative ideology are coherent. That is quite unfortunate, since one of the criticisms made of some ideologies, especially by adherents of other ideologies, is that the disputed one is incoherent. For example, Milton Friedman has argued that democratic socialism is an incoherent ideology. By Lodge's second definition, if Friedman is correct, it would not make sense to say that democratic socialism is an incoherent ideology, since if it is incoherent, it cannot be an ideology.

Lodge's first definition, which only requires a collection of ideas, is more appropriate. Democratic socialism is an ideology. It may be an incoherent one. Even if we could show that it is incoherent, however, that would not eliminate it from the class of ideologies. It would put it into a class called incoherent ideologies, and that class should not be made empty by definition. Democratic socialism certainly is a collection of ideas. Furthermore, it is a set of principles upon which the political, social, and economic order of some (perhaps ideal) society may be based. Thus, it fits with the definition of an ideology.

In Lodge's second definition, he says that there is an assumption that society is influenced by ideology. For definitional purposes, we should leave this question open. It is the verb *influenced* to which attention should be drawn here. We may be able to articulate the principles of a society without showing whether those principles have any influence on the society. C. Northcote Parkinson teaches lessons through the use of humor. In his generally serious book *The Evolution of Political Thought,* Parkinson has a delightful passage in which he pokes considerable fun at the notion that political theory has any importance at all or any influence on anyone except professors of political theory. He concludes: "The student who is advised to read drivel should at least be warned that it is drivel he is being asked to read." [11]

At some points, Marx takes a similar view of ideology: that it is a consequence of, not a cause of, something that happens in society. Marx had to deal with the classic question of how something which is entirely without physical properties—thoughts—could have an influence on anything material. He concluded that it could not and that only material things could be causal agents. Thus, Marx argued that ideology expresses fundamental conditions of a society and that it has no influence on the society. In modern terminology, we might say that Marx's view was that ideology is a by-product of social activity. It is not influential. We should not eliminate such views by definition. Even though we may disagree with both Parkinson and Marx as well as others who have held similar views, the argument, not the definition, is important.

As we can see from the definitions offered, Lodge also wants to commit ideology to discussing the nature of the good community. There would seem to be some confusion in regard to this commitment. On the one hand, it seems safe to suggest that the ideology of a society functions to legitimate that society on its own grounds. If that is what Lodge means by committing ideology to discussing the nature of the good community, we can readily accept his suggestion. However, if he means that it describes the good community in some reasonable and defensible way beyond mere parochial rationalization, then he would seem to be mistaken in confining the use of the word so severely. I shall try to show that capitalism, socialism, and democracy are ideologies which provide principles for a good community in the second sense, of nonparochial principles based on good reasons. The fact that they do so gives them reason to command our respect, but it does not warrant the conclusion that any ideology, by the very definition of the term, must develop principles for the good community in the second sense of *good*. After all, one could describe the ideology of apartheid or of "Communist" China without wanting to be committed to the view that either ideology describes a good society (in the second sense). In short, the class of ideologies which make explicit the nature of a bad society should not be made empty by definition. In addition, a class of ideologies that make explicit the nature of a society which we are not yet prepared to conclude is either good or bad should not be made empty by definition.

Nevertheless, Lodge has done a great service in raising the topic of facts and values in regard to ideologies. Apart from the semantic exercise we just went through, the topic in general is so important that it deserves a more general and extended treatment. In offering his definition, Lodge surely was not trying to dispense with this topic, because it must be faced directly by anyone who proposes to write about ideology. We should take the time to examine the theoretical arguments carefully.

Briefly put, the issue we face is whether ideology is merely descriptive or also evaluative. Let us put that in the form of a question: In constructing ideologies, are we solely describing an ideology—imaginary or real—or are we also evaluating the ideology? The issue is an important one to resolve at the start so we know how to proceed and so we know what comments might stand as sources of agreement or disagreement with a particular ideology.

For example, one could attempt to describe apartheid and the way in which it is or is not practiced. If that is all ideology is committed to, then it would not make sense to say in refutation that apartheid is wrong. By contrast, some adherents of apartheid believe it is right (whether or not it is practiced). If we took the view that ideologies are only evaluative, it would not be a legitimate criticism to point out that apartheid does or does not exist. We are, then, at the doorway of an issue that has vexed modern thought, and it is important to understand the view expressed in this book. Some historical background may be helpful.

In a desire to gain the respect accorded to the physical sciences, social scientists of the late nineteenth and early twentieth centuries developed an argument that social science, like physical science, should be "value-free." There is a tendency to trivialize that view, but we should resist that tendency. Only a brief glance into history will demonstrate how attempts to impose values on science proved disadvantageous to its development. Darwin is, perhaps, the clearest example we can cite. He was attacked from many quarters for his scientific conclusions. Undoubtedly, if some churches could successfully suppress his views even today, they would do so. Science had to emerge from that religious stifling before it could develop useful knowledge. The social sciences, because of their less secure theoretical foundations, were more likely to be subjected to the successful imposition of values on research. Social scientists struggled for years to overcome these frustrations. They saw the emerging success of the physical scientists and argued for that route for themselves. Much social scientific research has been advanced as a result of that development. At the same time, what should have begun as a heuristic—separating facts and values— became a dogma and lost its rootedness.

Thus, the concept of value-free investigation was used and advanced as part of the definition of social science. Without this approach, there could be no knowledge of the human condition. Having sundered facts and values, social scientists found it almost impossible to bring them back together again. In arguing for the separation, the methodologists had asserted that in the realm of facts we could have knowledge, whereas in the realm of values we could only have opinions, biases, and prejudices. That meant that all opinions were of equal warrant. We were left with the strange situation, then, in which one could say, for example, that women were or were not—as a fact—capable of the same intellectual achievements as men, and one could develop reliable theories about that situation. However, when it came to the question of whether it was appropriate to exclude women from opportunities to develop their intellects, each person's opinion was considered as good as any other person's opinion.

We have located, then, the sundering of facts and values in the social sciences, as well as social scientists' suspicion of ideology and consequent distancing from it. The social scientists were concerned—with good reason— that if they had to check their scientific ideas with the nonscientific authorities, they would never be able to make any progress in advancing knowledge. So, without negotiations, they made a deal: as scientists, they would offer no opinions which had any claim to validity beyond personal prejudice, and then they would be free to investigate areas previously closed to them, because their investigations would have no impact on areas treasured by the authorities—the values.

Ideology cannot make such a deal. Let us turn to a practical example to see why. In this case, the question will not be whether some theories can be free of value commitments, but whether some institutions can be free of value commitments. The issue itself became a burning one when universities were dragged into debates about the war in Vietnam in the late 1960s. Some of the lessons learned from those debates have relevance to the question of institutional neutrality (as it was called), and that may help shed light on the issues of theoretical neutrality in regard to values. It is something of an oversimplification to see the situation divided into three categories, but that will help us to understand the point, and it is not an egregious oversimplification.

There were conservatives who were quite consciously in support of the prosecution of the war by the government of the United States. There were radicals who were strongly opposed to the prosecution of the war. The radicals were by and large more vociferous than the conservatives, and the life-styles of both sides tended to imitate their political views. Between these extremes were people who identified themselves as moderates. Both the radicals and the conservatives sneeringly called the moderates "liberals" also.[12]

The radicals wanted the colleges and universities to throw their weight behind the effort to stop the war by refusing to support it and by taking other actions which would frustrate government agencies intent on prosecuting the war. These actions would include rejecting research funding tied to corporations profiting from the war efforts, not permitting such corporations to recruit on campus, shutting down the Reserve Officers' Training Corps, and preventing agencies of the federal government from recruiting on campus.

When they bothered to involve themselves in the campus debates, the conservatives argued that they saw nothing wrong with having the university support the country's efforts in these ways. After all, they said, those who pursued the war policies were duly elected officials of the government, and if the radicals could muster a majority, they could vote them out or pressure them to reverse their positions. In any event, the conservatives believed that the policies of the government were correct.

Then there were the moderates. Many had a difficult time identifying their personal views on the war, and even more could not bring themselves to countenance the passion with which the radicals were pursuing their objectives. Beyond that, the moderates argued that the university should take no position on social or political issues. They argued that the university was a place which should maintain a position of value neutrality in regard to such issues.

Some courageous college and university presidents, to the anger and dismay of many of their board members, tried to blunt the thrust of the radicals' anger by announcing publicly their personal opposition to the prosecution of the war. At the same time, however, they made it clear that the views they expressed were their own and did not reflect the views of the university. The university, like a machine, had no moral views to express, because universities are not the sort of creatures that have morals.[13] The moderates were, in general, older than the radicals, and they remembered painfully the frightening experiences of the early 1950s, when Senator Joseph McCarthy had shown the same contempt for value neutrality that the radicals were showing in the late 1960s. The university moderates saw in the radicals a threat to the neutrality of the university different in focus but not different in kind from the threat of the early 1950s. They reasoned that the circumstances called for the same kind of courage the best universities had shown in the early 1950s. What they viewed as their courageous stand was buoyed by an ideological principle of value neutrality: it was a fundamental principle which was held to be common in the academic society. The radicals would have none of what they saw as merely evasive arguments. This time the moderates had to deal with articulate, if equally uncivilized, people within the university.

Professor Robert Paul Wolff, a self-identified radical and one of the radicals' intellectual heroes, stepped in to give some intellectual warrant to what was largely an emotional outpouring. In 1969 he published a book, *The Ideal of the University,* which was the result of some talks he had given. No one was surprised when, after some analysis, he concluded:

> As a prescription for institutional behavior, the doctrine of value neutrality suffers from the worst disability which can afflict a norm: what it prescribes is not wrong; it is impossible. . . .
>
> No institution can remain politically neutral either in its interaction with society or in the conduct and organization of its internal affairs.[14]

This view was general enough to be called philosophical, and yet one hardly needed a course in deductive logic to discern that the university was one of those institutions which could not be neutral.

What was surprising was the conclusion Wolff moved to next. Having found that in all honesty he could not show that the university was neutral, he then said:

> However, the honest and consistent course is not always the best. . . .
>
> . . . I would urge both students and professors to hide behind "lehrfreiheit" [freedom of teaching] and "lernfreiheit" [freedom of learning], and give up the attempt to politicize the campus.[15]

Only the source of radical intellectualism could have taken this position without inducing an explosion. Now that those times are behind us and we can contemplate them with some equanimity, it may be amusing to reflect on what the radicals might have said if moderates had argued that they understood that the doctrine of neutrality is a lie but that they were persuaded of the importance of perpetuating the lie. Perhaps the moderates were not sufficiently artful to arrive at such a formulation.

The point of this story is to bring home a clearer understanding of the implications of value neutrality. Social scientists sought the refuge of value neutrality precisely because they wanted to pursue research that could not be pursued otherwise. They did not consciously engage in deception, as Wolff would have us do. No doubt many believed in the value-neutral position they took, both in regard to the social sciences and in regard to universities. If we are to evade the Wolffian suggestion that we pursue a dishonest and inconsistent course, however, we have to acknowledge that in matters of ideological theory, there is no value neutrality, just as there probably is none in matters of institutional behavior. Perhaps with hindsight, we can now say that what should have been said was that the university does subscribe to values and that it is by no means value neutral. We can say that among those values are the value of truth seeking, the value of the promotion of learning, the value of the freedom of speech for all. We might quote Aristotle, who said that he loved Plato but he loved the truth more. Acknowledging that the university necessarily stands for values might spark a grander campus debate about what values staff, faculty, students, administrators, alumni, and board members think they have in common. Those principles would then constitute some of the ideology of that society.

The principles mentioned in the proposed definition of *ideology* may have elements of facts and values about them. Ideology may seek to describe the principles on which the economic, political, and social order is based. It may also be normative about that order. Frequently it will not be clear which is operative, because often that is not clear in reality. As the analysis of this book develops further, it will be important to describe as dispassionately and as clinically as possible the ideology of our society. There is nothing in the definition of *ideology,* however, which will prevent those principles from having both a value and a factual base. The word *principles* has been consciously chosen because of its ambiguity.

In defining ideology, Kenneth and Patricia Dolbeare say: "For our purposes, it is enough that an ideology be held by some segment of politically active people and that it have the potential of gathering support and affecting American politics." [16] The Dolbeares' direct interest was in the United States and ideologies in that context. Our concerns here reach beyond those geographic boundaries, though it seems reasonable to pay special attention to the United States. The question of whether or not the principles of an economic, social, and political order must be explicitly stated and held by some segment of society in order to qualify as an ideology is a particularly important one for this book. I shall be arguing that an identifiable ideology operates in the United States and elsewhere but that the ideology is not stated, understood, or held by any segment of politically active people, though unknowingly we act on the basis of that ideology. Theologians have argued that all people have a religion whether they know it or not. That implies that some people may act on religious premises without knowing what they are. In this book, we shall see that an analogous situation exists in the political, social, and economic realm. Decision makers in our society operate on the basis of an identifiable ideology even though they do not know either that they are doing so or what that ideology is.

The modern mind hears about ideology and thinks naturally (and appropriately) about theories such as capitalism, socialism, and democracy. That natural response may be a result of the influential book written by the economist Joseph Schumpeter.[17] While the argument of this book departs from that of Schumpeter's, this work owes an obvious debt to him. His view that capitalism, socialism, and democracy are the ideologies which need to be examined was accurate in the 1940s and remains accurate today. They are discussed as the ideological possibilities for advanced industrialized societies as we look to the twenty-first century. We think of them as articulated and explicit views which are more or less closely applied.

It may seem curious to the modern mind to think of the possibility of an implicit ideology, one that is operative but not articulated. Historically, however, that has been the case as often as not. Theories, especially social theories, often lag behind reality. Aristotle's *Politics,* for example, is in many ways an explication of what Aristotle found already in existence. In that sense, Aristotle tried to correct Plato's attachment to ideas by requiring a return to the empirical world and to an examination of things as they are. Aristotle looked closely at the world around him and, on the basis of his observations, developed principles which covered the instances he saw. He is said to have acquired 150 constitutions of various Greek city-states. His *Politics* was an attempt to develop general principles based on that collection and on other observations. Aristotle enunciated the principles he thought he found already implicit in society.[18]

Following the example of Aristotle and recognizing that many others could be identified, we should accept the view that ideology may be implicit or explicit. At times, the actual ideology of a society may be explicit: the members of the society may acknowledge and understand the ideological basis of the society. In those times, one need only read the documents which explain the ideology of the society and listen to those who represent the leaders of the society as they explicate its meaning. At other times, the actual ideology of the society may be implicit, even though other ideologies may be discussed and declared to be the basis of the society. A society in which the explicit ideology is substantially different from the implicit ideology does not lack ideology. It lacks congruence of its explicit and implicit ideologies.

The Importance of Ideology

Too many people would disagree with the rather definite statement of Keynes quoted at the beginning of this chapter for us to avoid discussing the issue of the importance of ideology entirely. The basic argument here is fairly simple. All societies must be based upon some set of political, economic, and social principles. In that sense, the analogy to religion is apposite. Following the earlier discussion of implicit and explicit ideologies, we may say that sometimes the ideology a society follows is the same ideology that is acknowledged and discussed and at other times it is a quite different ideology. In analyzing the nature of the ideology of society, it is equally important that we understand both the explicit ideology and the implicit ideology if we are to understand the society.

The ideology of a successful and functioning society is the common economic, social, and political principles on which social interaction is based. That ideology may be celebrated on appropriate occasions, but in the smoothly functioning society, the ideology is not typically the subject of sustained or serious debate among members of the society. When the ideology becomes the subject of debate, there is some reason to believe that the principles are no longer commonly shared. Ideology provides the context in which daily life proceeds. In that sense, ideology is like good eyesight. It functions most effectively when it is noticed least. As soon as it becomes the subject of attention, there is evidence of a breakdown.

A useful analogy from the history of science will illustrate this point. The scientific historian Thomas Kuhn argues that science normally proceeds by operating within what he calls a paradigm.[19] The scientific paradigm comprises a set of common principles held by the practicing scientists. Most of the science we know about and observe falls in the class of what Kuhn calls normal science, which is that science based upon the common principles shared by the community of scientists. Practicing scientists assume that those principles are not a fit subject for scientific discussion. Kuhn argues that the existence of paradigms is important for the progress and development of science. He says that when a dominant paradigm exists, scientists agree on the rules for conducting science. In addition, they agree on what constitutes evidence, what constitutes discovery, and what constitutes progress.

In this regard, a paradigm is for science what ideology is for society. Practicing scientists cannot afford to be distracted by examining closely the assumptions and fundamental premises of science. That would lead them into philosophy, and if they went there, they would threaten the consensus. Similarly, decision makers cannot afford to be distracted by examining closely the principles of the society in which they operate. Ideology is as important to society and its decision makers as the fundamental scientific principles are to science and scientists.

Practicing scientists are usually impatient with the probing questions of philosophers. They want to get on with the development of science and their own experiments. They hope to make discoveries, and they hope to make progress in the context of the consensus. Similarly, people confronted with the need to make decisions are understandably impatient with philosophers' questions.

People who must make decisions typically do not want to discuss the principles of society. They need to get on with making decisions.

Kuhn says that in science occasionally the dominant paradigm breaks down and is replaced by another. When that happens, radical changes occur in science. He points out that during such times even the notion of the existence of a scientific community is under strain. Kuhn's approach to the history of science was pathbreaking and is still the subject of some controversy. While some pedagogical purpose is served in understanding the analogy between paradigms and ideology, it is a mistake to equate them, and it will be helpful to turn to someone who has written perceptively about social developments so that the reasoning can be direct.

In 1969 the management theoretician Peter Drucker published a book titled *The Age of Discontinuity*. [20] In that book, Drucker argues that typically society is reasonably stable and what change there is occurs well within the context of shared assumptions. Sometimes, however, the society proceeds through periods of what he calls discontinuities. During those times, the commonly accepted assumptions break down, and the consensus upon which they were built is lost. In the periods of discontinuity, the assumptions themselves become the subject of debate, and the debate grows increasingly acrimonious, because the society does not have shared assumptions which might be used to help resolve the debate. Drucker says that discontinuity will continue until a new set of shared assumptions is adopted (whether explicitly or implicitly). Drucker went on to argue that industrialized society in general and the United States in particular was going through such a period of discontinuity (or at least he believed it was as of 1968).

With the benefit of hindsight, we can see that Drucker was largely correct and that he was more prescient than people knew at the time. We shall see later in this book that the fundamental principles which were used to understand social development since the industrial revolution are no longer the rules guiding society. In Drucker's terms, we were and are living through a period of discontinuity. The breakdown and our failure to see our way out of it may account in part for the difficulty our society has in making substantial progress on a number of fronts. During a period of discontinuity, there is no consensus about what might constitute an acceptable way out of social dilemmas. In fact, the discontinuity may be so severe that the members of the society may not agree that the society is in a period of discontinuity.

It is possible that one of the reasons public debate seems to have become so acrimonious is that we are living through a period of discontinuity and hence there is no consensus about accepted rules which might take the place of the dying ideologies. We are without an accepted set of principles about social and public life. Extremists have more opportunities in such times because they are not pestered by the requirements of careful thinking. They appeal to a natural human desire for stability and predictability. Extremism tends to raise the heat of the debates without increasing the light.

In a period of discontinuity, people cannot accept even the appropriate rules for the discussion. As a consequence, they cannot agree on solutions. The circumstances of the current situation may have caused the increase in litigiousness. Courts are the place of last resort for disputes among people in our society. When people can no longer agree on what is right and proper, they turn to a judicial system which at least has a process for resolving disputes. The common response to what is perceived as an affront is to sue the other party. Both legally and administratively, however, the courts are not up to the task. That is not their fault: they were not designed to shoulder the burdens given to them. The judicial system is designed to deal with behavior which falls beyond limits which the society can accept. There should always be actions which are allowable under the law but recognized as wrong by the society at large. The *de minimus* approach which must be taken by the courts does not provide sufficient ground for an ideology.

In a sense, we should have been able to see this social breakdown in the one social science which had serious justification for declaring itself to be a science: economics. It is instructive to reread American economics texts from World War II to the late 1960s. They are written in a self-satisfied tone, as if economists possessed the laws of the economy as much as physicists possessed the laws of physical matter. For some period of time economists confidently talked about fine-tuning the economy so that they could play off employment and inflation within tenths of a percentage point. Since the mid-1960s all that has come apart. The wags like to quote George Bernard Shaw, who is credited with saying that if we laid all the economists end to end, they still would not reach a conclusion.

Apart from economics, it seems that a breakdown in the conventionally accepted ideologies has occurred and that we are living through the later stages of that breakdown. This book attempts to describe the emerging ideology which will dominate our society for a period of time until it too experiences a breakdown. The point of view presented arises from close observation of and involvement in the world in which we live. Prior societies had their ideologies, and we may safely presume that future societies will have theirs. Taken collectively, all those ideologies are mutually inconsistent. Given all we know about historical developments, it would be an act of supreme arrogance to think that one could discover the eternal ideology. It is arrogant enough to think that one can articulate an ideology as yet unrecognized, but if we are in the later stages of a period of discontinuity, perhaps we can begin to see how we shall emerge.

Social progress can only be made when a strong consensus exists about what constitutes progress, what is proper, what is to be accepted, and so forth. If a society is going to make any significant progress, it will need a paradigm. That paradigm, that consensus, that commonly held set of political, social, and economic principles, is called an ideology. Social progress depends upon the existence of an ideology. Through the remainder of the book, we shall examine first those ideologies which are said to characterize the principal alternatives for advanced industrialized societies. They will be shown to be inaccurate, and their failure underscores Drucker's insight into the social breakdown. Another ideology has been emerging in the wake of their breakdown, but it has remained implicit. The task of the final chapters of the book will be to explicate that ideology so that we can understand it and its implications.

Responding to Scepticism about Conceptual Purity

Many readers may feel a particular sort of scepticism as they read this book, and it will be helpful to deal with it at this point. The critical portion of the book proceeds by developing the fundamental principles of proclaimed ideologies and showing why they are defunct. Some readers may be concerned that the treatment of those principles rigidly insists upon their purity, and that having found that they are not applied in the pure sense, I conclude that they are defunct. The most impatient readers may declare it all to be a semantic exercise (perhaps they will say: a typical philosophical semantic exercise) which plays word games but comes to no substantive end. This view deserves to be taken seriously.

It is true that we shall search for the fundamental aspects—the first principles—of the ideologies examined. It is true that I shall argue that abandonment of those fundamentals means essentially abandoning the ideology itself. It should be remembered, however, that each ideology may have numerous variations which would not necessarily entail the abandonment of the ideology itself. Thus, we can acknowledge that variations on all these ideologies exist and that in practical application, life is messy and few things are as clear as our theories seem to imply.

At the same time, our words must have some definite limits. If not, they can mean anything at all, and there is no difference, for example, between capitalism and socialism or between democracy and totalitarianism. The concern here is not merely with the words themselves, but with the underlying concepts which they express. Our task will be to articulate the underlying conceptual meaning of these ideologies. When there is significant deviation from that conceptual meaning, the ideology no longer belongs to that class. Certainly there are difficulties with drawing lines, and a person who had lived through each of the historical modifications of the ideologies might not recognize how substantially the fundamental conceptual meaning had been lost. Admittedly,

it is often difficult to accept arguments which insist upon sticking to fundamental standards. In the next few paragraphs, however, we shall examine a
fascinating example from another domain—religion—to illustrate the point
that fundamentals are important.

Andy Warhol said in 1968 that, in the future everyone would get fifteen minutes of fame. The city of Pawtucket, Rhode Island, has had two such moments
in the sun. Its first was when it became the cradle of the industrial revolution in
the United States. The second occurred in 1983, when it took a landmark case
to the United States Supreme Court. The case involved the Christmas season.
The municipal authorities in Pawtucket decided to erect a crèche on the property of Pawtucket City Hall. Predictably, some people objected, arguing that
the separation of church and state meant that public authorities could not show
publicly supported favoritism for any religion. A case was filed in court, and
it eventually went to the United States Supreme Court, which agreed to hear
the case, presumably because the Court had something it wanted to say on the
subject.

The Supreme Court rendered a decision favoring the city of Pawtucket and
permitting the display of the crèche. For the purposes of illustration here, let us
concentrate on the reasoning of the majority.[21] It was as follows: The crèche has
over time become a secular symbol without significant religious import. Therefore, displaying the crèche does not violate the separation of church and state,
since the scene is not a religious symbol. It is, rather, a symbolic representation
for the entire secular celebration of the Christmas season. Thus, the majority
of the Court argued that the public authorities of the city of Pawtucket were in
the right when they allowed the construction of the crèche on city property.

Faced with a Solomon-like decision, the Supreme Court managed to split
the baby by rendering a politically clever ruling which was, nonetheless, religiously bankrupt. The crèche, symbolizing the birth of Jesus Christ, is probably
one of the two most important symbols binding the Christian community. The
crèche, with its remembrance of the star, of the angels and the shepherds, of
the wise men, of the Virgin Mary, of Joseph, and of the appalling conditions
imposed by secular authorities is a symbolic representation that "God sent his
only begotten Son into the world, that we might live through him." [22] What else
sensible could the crèche be said to symbolize? Does it symbolize the birth
merely of an important or interesting or persuasive or thoughtful or amusing
person? Not for a Christian. The Supreme Court, in rendering a politically
correct decision, stripped the crèche of its religious importance and left it in
the class of objects commemorating merely historically important events. No
good Christian should have accepted that political deal with the secularists.

A person who believes that God intervenes in our lives might have supposed
that God was testing Christians when he caused the Pawtucket municipal au-

thorities to construct that crèche. God was, perhaps, testing to see whether Christians really had taken the Christ out of Christmas. If God was conducting such a test, the Christians failed. Our believer in divine intervention might imagine that God was so disappointed that he decided to test the faithful again. Later, at Easter, in a town not far from Pawtucket, it was discovered that a cross had been erected on municipal property. Our believer might have assumed that God thought that this would be an easy test for weak humans. God might have decided that even they would not convert the cross into a secular symbol. He might have reasoned, further, that since they could not ignore the Christian significance of the cross, perhaps they would also recognize the mistake they had made in regard to the crèche.

Almost as soon as the objections to having the cross on public property were raised, people began dragging out and dusting off the earlier Pawtucket arguments and suggesting that the cross is not a Christian religious symbol but a secular symbol about the coming of spring! Shortly thereafter, in a bizarre turn of events, someone cut down the cross and hid it where it was not found for a considerable period of time.[23] By the time it was found, the controversy had died down, and no one seemed much interested in pursuing it. Our believer in divine intervention might conclude that God had decided to test humans the second time with an easier test but that once it appeared they might fail that test also, rather than letting the Supreme Court secularize the cross, too, he decided to stop the test before it was completed.

The story raises a question: When do modifications to Christianity become so substantial that what is left is no longer Christianity? I would suggest that the line is crossed when the modifications alter fundamental principles of Christianity. At that point, they have modified it out of existence. Certainly there are a number of issues, such as church governance, on which Christians can disagree while remaining within Christianity. However, there must be limits, too, or being a Christian means nothing. For example, it would seem to make sense to say that the issue of the divinity of Christ is of deep importance to Christianity. It seems reasonable to say that the person who does not believe in the divinity of Christ simply is not a Christian. When the Court decided that the crèche was secular, it did a tremendous disservice to faithful Christians. We can have no idea what the Court would have done if the case of the cross had come before it, but a good Christian can only worry and suspect it would have found the cross to be secular display also. If the Court had so decided, what it would have been saying is that there is no essential difference between Christianity and other religions or nonreligions, and the Christian religion would, from that perspective, have lost its distinctive meaning. In that case, of course, the crèche and the cross could have remained on public property, but they would have been merely secular symbols like Christmas trees and the Easter Bunny. Any good Christian should resist such an interpretation of the meaning of Christianity. Christians should rather say that there is something fundamental about Christianity. Belief in the divinity of Christ and the symbols of that divinity are among those things.

It is possible for someone to say that anyone who insists on a belief in the divinity of Christ as essential to Christianity is only talking about pure Christianity and that there are other variations on Christianity which are acceptable but do not depend upon adherence to the divinity of Christ. It is difficult, however, to see how those people are talking sense. The doctrine of the divinity of Christ is a fundamental defining characteristic of Christianity. Interestingly, it is also what gives Christianity its moral warrant. It is precisely because Christians believe in Christ that they accept the moral lessons of Christ. Christians do not believe we should love our neighbors as ourselves merely because some historical figure said we should. They believe it because they believe the Son of God said so.

Leaving aside religious implications, we shall be looking for similar foundational principles for the ideologies we examine. We want to know what the principles are without which the ideology does not exist. There may be many variations on the implementation of those fundamental principles, but once the principles themselves are abandoned, the ideology in question has been abandoned no matter how laudatory the other proposed objectives might be. We shall also be looking for the principles which give each ideology its moral warrant. As the ideologies are examined, it will be up to the reader to decide whether the fundamental principles have been developed. That determination can only be made after examining the analyses.

Thus, the argument will be that the fundamental principles of capitalism, socialism, and democracy can be identified and that they do not correspond to the actual conditions of society. Rather, those ideologies have been displaced by an ideology which has its own principles. Therefore, it is not simply that the principles of the others have been abandoned, but that a new ideology—managerialism—has emerged. Managerialism is an ideology with its own principles which are substantially different from the fundamental principles of the other ideologies. If we are to understand the world in which we live, we need to understand that new ideology and the ones from which it springs.

2 Approaches to Ideology and a Logical Point

In this chapter we will accomplish two tasks. First, the chapter will provide some intellectual organization which will be useful for the remainder of the book. Its purpose is to aid readers who are unfamiliar or uncomfortable with extensive theoretical discussions. The second part of the chapter will discuss a purely logical point which will be important for the remaining chapters. It is important to recognize what is and what is not implied in the first part of the chapter. I shall divide the field of ideology into three broad approaches. I have selected the categories primarily for purposes of organization and as aids to later understanding of the theories themselves. The identification of the different approaches should not be confused with ideological theories themselves. The ideological theories need to stand or fall on their own, not because of their organizational proximity to these approaches. The approaches provide a means for constructing an understanding of the theories. They are not theories themselves. It may be useful to think of the selection of the categories as similar to the ways in which colleges and universities divide the intellectual domain into departments, divisions, and schools. While those designations have some intellectual merit and while it would be wrong to see them as a merely arbitrary or capricious organizational structure, it would also be mistaken to treat the designations as warranted on the basis of some deep theories. In general, physicists have more in common with other physicists than they do with, for example, sociologists. That does not mean that physicists and sociologists have nothing in common, nor does it make clear a priori where an individual course offering should be lodged. A course dealing with the social origins of physics may be constructed in the context of sociology quite as much as in the context of physics. The professor who is substantially ignorant of either probably has no business offering the course. When students start to question the logic of the organizational categories, we know that the categories have served their purpose and the students need to concentrate, rather, on the topics taught within the organizational units. Similarly, if readers find themselves debating the intellectual merits of these organizational categories, they may decide that the categories have served their purpose and they are ready to move on to examining the ideological theories themselves. Obviously, those readers who are already sufficiently aware of ideological theory to find these categories distracting can move on without being distracted further.

This same point can be made in a nonmetaphorical way which conforms more closely to the demands of analysis. The description of the different approaches does not provide premises for valid arguments about the theories. Establishing the basis of the different approaches is not a necessary step in the argument of the book. By way of contrast, the theories, when developed, do provide premises for further arguments. For example, even if we should decide that some ideology is best characterized as atomistic, nothing of importance can be derived from that fact. If it were found that some claim of an author did not conform to what might be expected of an atomistic approach, that would not be a criticism of the theory. It would be a criticism of our classification of the theory. However, if a person claimed to be a capitalist and claimed also to believe in government support for cartels, we would be correct in asserting that the person was not advocating, supporting, or expressing a capitalist approach.

The first two approaches I describe here carry with them substantive notions of what society is like and how people relate to it. The third approach, instead of attempting to answer substantive questions about the nature of society, emphasizes procedures for resolving disputes in the society and for establishing social policy in general. In the final section of the chapter, which examines the bifurcation fallacy, I do make some points which are important for the argument of the book. The fallacy is more easily explained after the development of the different approaches, because they can then be used as examples. One central argument of the book is that the bifurcation fallacy is committed regularly in ideological discussions. In fact, I believe it is committed regularly in other debates also, so its importance lies beyond ideology. Ideological debates seem particularly susceptible to this fallacy, however, and by identifying it early, I hope to avoid it myself and to be able to alert readers to cases in which it is committed.

Following some historical tradition, I label the first approach we consider atomism, the second organicism, and the third process. In the description of these approaches, many ideological issues will become apparent. Having explored the three approaches to ideology, we naturally ask how those approaches are related to each other.

Atomism

In atomistic social theories, society at large is conceived to be nothing more than the aggregation of its individual elements. For purposes of illustration, a comparison might be made to a pile of leaves which is understood as nothing more than a collection of individual leaves in a particular cubic area. Since the leaves are all in that area, they are in a form we call a pile. If we are asked to move the pile, we move the leaves to the new place. After we have moved all the individual leaves, we do not return to the original place and get something called "the pile" which is separate from the individual leaves and then move that to the new place so the complete pile can be said to have been moved. The complete pile is moved when the individual leaves have been moved. Thus, the pile of leaves equals the totality of individual leaves. The pile is nothing more than the individual leaves in a specific configuration. One can talk about the pile as a whole, and one can even discuss changes in it, but we make those general references only for the sake of our convenience and the convenience of our listeners. If we were pressed to do so, and if we had enough time and energy, we could explain changes in the pile by explaining changes in each leaf. The numerous individual explanations would, when taken together, make up a complete account of the pile itself and its changes.

A term for the general perspective which has just been described is *reductionism,* and it comes in two different forms. The first and most rigorous form has to do with knowledge. It is said that all knowledge of the pile can be reduced to knowledge about each leaf. The second form, which is less rigorous but still very interesting, has to do with the question of what exists. In that form of reductionism, one would say that the pile does not exist apart from the individual leaves. There is nothing called "the pile" separate and apart from each individual leaf. References to the pile are simply shorthand for the aggregation of the individual leaves.

While the example of the pile of leaves may seem mundane, an important and deep issue in the foundations of science is directly related to this question of atomism. Science seeks to develop explanations for phenomena and to suggest what we should suppose exists. The scientific atomist assumes that explanations of large-scale phenomena can be constructed completely and accurately by reference to individual parts. The term *atomism* is used in this context because the fundamental parts were once considered to be atoms and, in Greek, *atomon* means indivisible. Physicists now believe that atoms themselves are complex objects composed of subatomic particles. However, they still believe that finding explanations for those subatomic particles will yield explanations for atoms, which, in turn, will yield explanations for larger phenomena. Further, they assume that the larger phenomena are nothing but the subatomic particles in a specific configuration and, in general, that all phenomena are composed of different arrangements of fundamental particles. The assumption of atomism is an important one, because if it is true, once scientists acquire explanations of the activities of particles and the laws which govern those activities, they can be assured that they have gained all the understanding possible and needed for explaining all phenomena of whatever scale or size.

The belief that the laws governing the activities of the fundamental particles will one day prove sufficient to predict and explain all behavior, however, does not imply that scientists will stop thinking about or discussing the larger phenomena. In the first place, it should be recognized that the effort which has been described is an ideal one and that, while considerable and impressive progress has been made on the basis of the atomistic assumption, at this time this scientific program is by no means complete. Scientists do use laws on a larger, macro scale in order to have explanations for that macro scale, while remaining convinced that eventually the macro-scale laws can be reduced to smaller, micro-scale laws. In addition, even if the atomistic scientific program were completed, as some believe it essentially has been in regard to chemistry and physics, it would still be convenient to refer to some phenomena directly on the larger scale.

Let us explore an example of the utility of larger-scale principles which are, nonetheless, based on atomistic assumptions. In all likelihood, it will always be easier for the auto mechanic to use large-scale understandings of how cars operate than to look at chemical and physical laws and move up from there. The presumption remains, however, that the automobile is nothing more than a collection of parts and that understanding each part and the ways it interacts with other parts is sufficient for understanding the operations of the automobile.

The scientific approach of atomism is at least as old as Democritus (circa. 460–ca. 370 B.C.), and it has enjoyed periods of greater and lesser popularity. It is not surprising that social analyses have looked to scientific analyses for their inspiration, especially in the case of atomism. If a comprehensive program of atomism is correct, then human actions, like those of piles of leaves, can be explained by reference to the atomic and subatomic particles which make up human beings. Each person has his or her own special configuration of atomic and subatomic particles, just as each pile of leaves has its particular arrangment of leaves. In atomistic analyses of human behavior, it is believed that understanding the whole person involves only understanding the parts of the configuration. Just as we concluded that there is no separate thing called "the pile" apart from the collection of leaves, so there is no separate thing called "the person" apart from the aggregation of the subatomic particles. Extension to society, then, is natural and easy for the atomist. For the social atomist, societies are composed of people, and once we gain an explanation of individual humans and the laws which govern their actions, we shall have a complete explanation of all social phenomena.

Consider, for example, a group of people gathered around a gate at an airport waiting to board the plane. Imagine that they are moving around, occasionally getting in line, and so on. In order to understand the behavior of that group (for example, to explain why they suddenly line up with their boarding passes in hand), we need only understand the behavior of each of the individual people. There is nothing more to be added to the explanation. In this sense, social atomists assume that in principle a thorough understanding of social phenomena can be gained from an understanding of individual actions and behaviors.

Practicing atomistic social scientists may be prepared to concede that it will always be convenient to refer to large-scale phenomena on a large-scale level and to have laws which govern them on that level, just as surgeons do not cloud their minds with the physics of patients' bodies. Similarly, if economists want to determine the likely consequence of a short supply of some commodity, they might be content to use general laws and general analyses to explain that phenomenon. Nevertheless, that general gross-level analysis does not contradict the assumption that the reactions in the economy are an accumulation of the reactions of individuals in the economy. Economists try to understand pricing structures by using laws of supply and demand, but the laws themselves are shorthand summaries and generalizations about numerous individual decisions and behaviors.[1]

In atomism, the actions of individuals are responsible for the actions of the economy. There are no more fundamental economic explanations than those describing how individual people make their decisions. For example, the presumption in economics is that the Gross Domestic Product (GDP) consists of the individual purchase and sale decisions of the individual units in the society. Those individual phenomena are aggregated to arrive at the GDP. Similar observations can be made about the other measures of the economy. They are atomistically derived as an aggregation of individual phenomena. The laws of economics are presumed to explain the larger phenomena, but they do so only because they are generalizations about individual actions.

For the economist, individuals seek to maximize their utility, and firms seek to maximize their profits. The results of the individual efforts are aggregated to arrive at the result for the economy at large. Reality for the economist is the actions of the individuals, and while larger-level laws may be used, they are used as mere conveniences. What the economy at large does is the direct consequence of what is occurring on the disaggregated level. In this context, we might say that it is assumed that macroeconomics can be reduced to microeconomics. By that it is meant that explanations on the macroeconomic level are in principle logically and mathematically derivable from explanations of microeconomic phenomena.

A similar atomistic approach may be taken in seeking to understand political structures, especially in what are called democratic societies. The conclusion of an election is the result of the addition and comparison of the votes. If there are two candidates, after the citizenry votes, the ballots will be tallied and compared, the winner of the majority of votes will be determined, and the "will of the people" will be announced. There is no "will of the people" distinct from or different from the majority vote in the balloting. The desires of the society are thus presumed to be the aggregation of the desires of the individuals, and that is all. Just as in moving the individual leaves in order to move the pile, we did not have to go back and move something called "the pile," so in counting the ballots, we have a social decision in a democratic society, and we do not have to go back and find what "the society" wants which might be distinct from the results of the balloting.

The atomistic ideological approach presumes that the society is nothing more than the accumulation of the decisions of the individuals in that society. There is no country or state apart from its citizenry. To recall the leaf example, there is no pile distinct from the aggregation of leaves. As we shall see in the next chapter, capitalism is an example of the atomistic approach to ideology. In a sense, the capitlist view is based upon an assumption about individual behavior: that it is egoistic (i.e., that all people always attempt to do what they think is in their own best interests) and that what the society wants is what results from the interactions of these individuals.

Capitalism itself is both descriptive and prescriptive. It says that in fact people act as it presumes, and it says that interferences with such actions are disadvantageous and will lead to less than what the society (the aggregate of the individual people) want. The view is also compatible with what might be called a perspective of moral neutrality or moral relativism. If the society decides that it wants to have some legislation enacted or some products sold, the society has a right to that result. There is, in this view, no legitimate right to override the aggregate desires of the people. Moral relativism, egoism, and atomism all line up to support one another in describing society and in offering prescriptions for society.

Capitalism is not the only possible atomistic approach. Thus, it is important to make a distinction between atomism as an approach and capitalism as a specific ideology. As indicated, I have used atomism as a general organizational category. Capitalism is a specific ideology with its own fundamental principles. Even if one were to find aspects of capitalism which are not atomistic, that would not constitute a refutation of capitalism. As an ideology, capitalism should be evaluated—descriptively and prescriptively—on its own merits, irrespective of whether or not it is in all regards an instantiation of atomism. We shall discuss capitalism at much greater length in chapter 3.

Organicism

It is helpful to begin consideration of the organic approach by thinking about human beings and by contrasting the organic and atomistic approaches on the level of individual humans. As we have seen, the atomistic approach presumes that the human being is nothing more than an aggregation of subatomic particles. The organic approach with regard to individual humans denies that the atomistic view is complete. It does not necessarily say that the atomistic approach is wrong, as far as it goes. While the atomists express a desire for a comprehensive program, the organic approach insists that even though the atomistic approach may provide a partial understanding of individual humans in principle, it will never be able to provide a comprehensive account. The organic approach presumes there is something more to the human than an aggregation of subatomic particles. No matter how thorough and complete atomists might ever be in their description of a person, they would necessarily miss the totality of that person. An organicist might suggest that, having missed the totality of the person, atomists also miss a most important aspect of the person. The assertion of the organic approach is that the program associated with the atomistic scientist can never be carried out completely, because by definition it ignores some realities about individual people: those attributes which make them distinctively human and make all of them the persons they are. The term *organic* is used to capture the meaning of the view in order to point to the notion that the person is an organic whole, not just an accumulation of biological entities (cells) or chemical and physical entities (subatomic particles).

Throughout history, numerous attempts have been made to capture and describe the organic difference on the individual human level and to describe the organic aspect. Sometimes words like *self* and *soul* have been used to make that distinction in regard to individuals, and such references occur in literature and in other attempts to understand people. None of these terms have proved entirely satisfactory or persuasive. Nevertheless, whatever name is ascribed to the totality, the organic approach presumes that the whole of the human is greater than the sum of its parts and that to be forced to ignore that whole reality is to be forced to miss some significant portion of reality itself. Many people resist strongly the effort to reduce them and understandings of them to mere biology. Sometimes the organic view is coupled with what is called a view of emergence. The view of emergence holds that in the complex interaction of the physical properties of the individual human, something emerges. That something which emerges on the organic level has been the subject of attention for the organic approach.

A difficulty with the organic approach is that its adherents are not clear in describing precisely the attribute identified in referring to humans as organic and not merely atomistic. Language which refers to *souls* or *selves* is notoriously vague, and it is never clear how one might go about determining whether there is a soul, for example, or what it is like and what it does. Presumably we can understand what the heart does, what the liver does, and so on, and if there should be a difference of opinion between people about what those parts do, there are ways to resolve the disagreements. Furthermore, in cases in which the disagreements cannot be resolved, scientists would agree to suspend judgment until agreement is found.

What can be said, then, about the soul or the self or even the unnamed je ne sais quoi which is attributed to the human? Can there be a dispassionate and unbiased way to determine whether such a reality exists and, if so, what it does? People who adopt the organic approach are not usually very helpful in this regard. Their claims are often accompanied with considerable passion, and one is left wondering whether their passion is meant to compensate for weak arguments. Nevertheless, it would be difficult to dismiss casually the centuries of history in which people have held organic views about individual humans, and it would be difficult to ignore entirely the testimony to an organic nature which seems to arise in diverse cultures and circumstances.

Thus far, we have concentrated on the level of the individual human with regard to the organic view. That was introduced by way of approaching the social level. Let us turn to that larger level and attempt to understand the organic perspective with regard to society. If we keep the individual human example in mind, we may be able to understand what an organic view of society would assert. The organic social thinker believes that society is not merely the aggregation of the actions of individual members of the society. For example, Socrates argued for the recognition of a difference between a herd and a polis. A herd is a gathering of people without common purpose and common values. The people of a polis have something in common which gives them a quality greater than a herd. Socrates' search for an understanding of that distinction gave rise to I. F. Stone's accusation that Socrates was antidemocratic.[2] Almost surely Socrates did not favor democracy, but the issue is a descriptive, not a prescriptive, one. Stone's dispute with his reconstructed Socrates is, at its base, a dispute between Stone the committed social atomist and Socrates the skeptical social organicist. Socrates held society—the polis—to have organic charactertistics and to operate as a whole.

One argument frequently presented in favor of an organic approach is that we can never understand what is going on in a society or why a society is moving in the direction it is unless we understand the society as a whole. The sociologist Emile Durkheim stated the organic view by using the expression The whole is greater than the sum of its parts. By that Durkheim meant that in order to understand the development of a society, one could not merely understand it as a sum of the actions of individual members of the society but must also understand the whole of the society, which is more than the mere aggregation of the parts.

We might understand the organic view more completely by thinking about the academic disciplines of psychology and sociology. We might think of psychology as the study of individual humans and sociology as the study of humans in groups. The organic view would hold that no matter how thorough and complete psychology is, it will not be able to explain all human activities, because some human activities come about as a result of organic operations of the society in which particular humans exist. By contrast, the atomistic view of social psychology holds that all social activities can be explained ultimately with a complete understanding of the actions of each individual person in the society and that all sociological explanations can be derived from psychological ones. To return to our earlier language, the presumption of the social psychologist is that all sociological laws can be reduced to psychological laws.

The organic approach does not necessarily presume that all social groups develop organically. Some groups may remain merely atomistic, and the example used earlier of the crowd of people gathered around the gate at the airport may be a good case of such a group. Nevertheless, the organic approach suggests that sometimes the organic perspective is the only one which can explain fully the actions which are to be investigated.

For example, consider a well-prepared and successful athletic team. The members of the team may be operating because of self-interest, but almost invariably, when the team is performing at its best, one will find actions occurring which evade explanation by reference to individual members alone. During those times, athletes speak of the presence of team spirit. Such a phenomenon may be intangible, but the players who have experienced it may say that it is a necessary ingredient for a complete explanation of their activities.

A close-knit family may offer another helpful example. People in a close-knit family frequently do things they would individually like not to do and refrain from doing things they would individually like to do. When they reflect on their reasons for what they did, they may say it was for the sake of the family. Numerous other examples could be used. In all such cases, the organic approach presumes that some real phenomena cannot be completely dealt with using the analytic powers of atomism alone.

We may have some understanding now of how the organic view operates on a descriptive ideological level: it simply disagrees with the atomistic view that society is made up only of individuals, and it presumes that on some occasions society is, as Durkheim said, greater than the sum of its parts. It may be useful at this point to ask how organicism operates on a prescriptive level. For these purposes, consider a nation as an organic social entity. The nation may have a destiny and a direction greater than the collective ambitions of citizens. Under the organic view, the present citizenry may be reasonably asked to sacrifice for that future and that destiny. In this regard, the philosopher Jean-Jacques Rousseau made an interesting distinction between what he called the will of all and the General Will. The former, he believed, was the will and the desires of the people atomistically conceived (as one might determine it, for example, by polling). The latter referred to the will of the nation at large. In Rousseau's view, there was no reason to believe that the will of all and the General Will should always indicate the same social actions. Rousseau argued that whenever the will of all and the General Will were divergent, the legislature or the government should follow the dictates of the General Will.

Both the strength and the weakness of the organic view are illustrated by the General Will. The strength is that on a factual and descriptive level, there does seem to be something to the view that some societies are more than the simple sums of their parts. The weakness is that it is very difficult to identify what that something more is or what it should demand. This problem is analogous to the one discussed earlier about the individual human and the soul or self. There is no reliable way to determine when what is being recommended comes as a result of the General Will (or whatever name is used for identification). In practice, in circumstances in which organic ideologies predominate, it is usually the leaders who claim to know what the General Will is, and they argue that they have a right to make decisions based on their reading of that Will. That poses a significant problem. If the leaders are the ones who must read the General Will and if their readings always eclipse expressions of the will of all, then we have set the conditions for dictatorship and, more dangerous, totalitarianism. Totalitarians from Adolf Hitler and Benito Mussolini through Joseph Stalin and Fidel Castro to the Ayatollah Khomeini and Saddam Hussein have all claimed knowledge of an organic nature which could not be checked by the people they claimed to serve.

The fact that totalitarians have taken advantage of the organic perspective for their own purposes, however, should not blind us to the possibility that the organic perspective may be correct both descriptively and prescriptively. Consider, for example, the matter of pollution. It is quite conceivable that if individuals were asked to decide whether it is in their interest to avoid polluting the environment, the majority would decide that it is not and would vote to do little about pollution. It may be that when the longer view of the society is taken into account, however, it is in the interest of the society to avoid pollution. Thus the immediate personal interests of the population should be sacrificed to the longer perspective of the society. The example is chosen advisedly. In the past, it is clear that people and businesses did not concern themselves much with the fact that in many instances they were spoiling the environment which would be inherited by their children and grandchildren. They treated the environment as a place to be used without concern for the future. It was not that they did not have the ability to understand the devastating effects their actions might have on the environment. They were obviously smart enough for that. It was simply not in their individual self-interests to make the determinations and to exercise caution about polluting. In addition, it certainly was not in their best interests to have legislation which would maintain a clean environment. The environmental problems would not be obvious until distant generations had been born, and thus, they had little impact on the interests of the present generation. Cost-benefit analyses always concluded that nothing should be done about the environment, because costs are immediate and benefits are only for future generations.[3]

Socialism is an example of an organic approach. For socialists, the individuals of a society may be reasonably required to sacrifice personal interests in the name of the advancement of the society as an organic whole. What is best for the society at large may not be what each member of the society would vote for if he or she were given the choice. The leader of the socialist community is supposed to understand the overall interests of the society and to act in accordance with those interests. Socialism is not the only possible organic approach any more than capitalism is the only possible atomistic approach. Nevertheless, those two broad alternatives are the substantive ideological possibilities discussed for modern industrialized life. Chapter 4 offers a more detailed discussion of socialism.

Recently, some attempt has been made to develop a new perspective called communitarianism. The sociologist Amitai Etzioni has led this development because of his concern with an excessive individualism which he fears has swept the United States. At one academic conference, I heard communitarianism referred to as a combination of communism and unitarianism. The speaker's obviously amusing identification had a ring of truth about it. Etzioni and his followers want to blunt the excesses of atomistic individualism (thus, the reference to unitarianism) with an organic commitment to community (hence, communism). I should point out that the communitarianism of Etzioni postdates Lodge's efforts to develop an ideology he labeled communitarianism. While the two versions of communitarianism share some common elements, Lodge does not confine his articulation of communitarianism merely to a commentary on activities in the United States. He intends that it be understood as a new ideology rather than a reactive perspective. It is a little difficult to believe that Etzioni did not know about Lodge's earlier use of the term (they were on the same university faculty for a period of time), and it is difficult to know why he decided to use the word. We will consider Lodge's development of communitarianism more extensively later in this book.

Beyond approaches of atomism and organicism, it is useful to identify a third general approach, which attempts to evade the conflicts inherent in atomism and organicism by concentrating on procedures for the process of social decision making. We will call it the process approach.

Process

The frustrations of substantive ideology sometimes lead to proposals for an ideology which limits itself to specifying a process for resolving disputes and conflicts. The desire for process may be linked to an attempt to find a value-free position. If a process can be adopted, then the dispute can be referred to the process for resolution, and there is no prior commitment to the outcome.

For illustrative purposes, consider the debate about abortion which has proved so frustrating to both participants and bystanders. Each side seems entrenched in its own position and feels it cannot yield to the other side. Each side has a problem with its own slippery slope. Thus, the abortion debate devolves into a debate in which two different sides take two opposing positions. Compromise seems impossible, because compromising on one side potentially yields too much to the other side. In 1973 the Supreme Court, in the *Roe* v. *Wade* decision, tried to find a compromise, but the compromise was not fully satisfactory to either side (though it has been accepted more by one than the other). The Court tried again in 1989, in the *Webster* v. *Reproductive Health Services* decision. Once again, its ruling was not satisfactory to either side (though it has been accepted more by one than the other). Thus, substantively, there does not seem to be much room for compromise or for resolution.

In an article titled "Neutral Dialogue and the Abortion Debate," William Galston, a philosopher who has joined the communitarian effort led by Amitai Etzioni, showed how people have tried to move the debate onto more productive footing by asking that we discuss the general rules and procedures for debate and for governing society, apart from our particular views on a topic such as abortion.[4] The hope is that we can come to some agreement about rules for civilized social, political, and economic procedures for making decisions and that if we can agree on procedures, we have a better chance of finding a way out of the substantive debate. In short, we invoke the agreed-upon procedures and then commit ourselves to living with the outcome of the substantive issue, no matter whether that conforms to what we thought when we entered the procedure. Such rules are analogous, for example, to Robert's Rules of Order or any other rules for order in a debating forum. The rules should be agreed to before the debate starts, and they should be followed rigorously during the debate, with the result that some decision or other is made. At the conclusion of the debate or discussion, whichever side "wins" or whatever compromise is reached, everyone is supposed to leave satisfied that his or her position was well represented and resolved.

Galston is quite pessimistic about the possibility of finding a neutral procedure which would solve the debate about abortion. He makes the point that some position or other would be slipped in under the guise of procedural neutrality. That seems a serious problem, especially in a situation in which there is little room for compromise. In other cases, the procedure often moves toward something like splitting the difference between the two sides. There is no difference to be split in the abortion issue. If having an abortion is an act of murder, then the state has a substantial interest and, under criminal and moral codes, should take strong action against the perpetrator. Surely no one advocates killing young children when parents find them inconvenient, even if as the result of some apparently neutral procedure that should be the decision of the society.

Although Galston is not optimistic that the procedural approach will resolve the debate over abortion, it may be clear what is meant by the process approach to ideology. Some processes are agreed upon, and substantive decisions arise in the context of the operations of those processes. We shall see in chapter 5 that democracy is a specific ideology which can be identified as representing the process approach. In democracy, what is most important is the process for making social decisions. Presumably there is no prior commitment to outcome on the part of the system. Of course, each person in the democracy may have a personal commitment, but the process itself creates the social decision by determining what the majority desires. While democracy is an important example of a process approach to ideology, it is not the only case possible. Finally, in order to avoid confusion, it is important to point out that atomistic and organic ideologies often have strong procedural components. Those procedures, however, are not substantively neutral but are designed to advance the principles of the ideology in question.

Bifurcation Fallacy

Logic has a double reputation. On the one hand, people admonish each other to be logical. This would seem to mean that they respect logic. On the other hand, discussions of logic are often viewed as sterile. Logic does not deserve the latter reputation. It can be made both exciting and extremely informative. For example, Raymond Smullyan wrote an instructive and entertaining book on logic which is quite accessible.[5] This section will not have the good humor of Smullyan's book, but the point made here should be useful for application beyond the confines of ideological arguments.

It will be necessary to introduce a special phrase as a shorthand reference for more extensive points. This bit of jargon should function like a nickname. One should always be able to substitute the formal name for the nickname without changing the truth values of what is said. The formal name is what is contained in this section. The nickname is *bifurcation fallacy*.

Later in the book, it will be clear that jargon can have a form of rhetorical power and that it is important to know the origins of the terms thus employed. Some explanation of the origin of this phrase is appropriate. The term *bifurcation* is taken from Whitehead, who talked about the bifurcation of nature by the classical (i.e., Newtonian) scientists. Whitehead did not speak of a bifurcation fallacy, and his concerns about bifurcation are not those raised here. Like the bifurcation Whitehead identified, however, the bifurcation mentioned here functions as an inaccurate conceptual imposition on the reality supposedly observed and reflected to us. Both bifurcations function like eyeglasses. They may help us see better, but they may also distort. If we forget the latter, we shall be led to draw inaccurate conclusions.

The term *fallacy* is taken directly from logic. A fallacy is an illusion of reasoning. A fallacy appears to be using valid reasoning but in fact uses a reasoning form which is invalid. In our case, the bifurcation fallacy occurs when it is mistakenly supposed, based upon some proffered evidence, that a bifurcation exists. Identifying the fallacy should be enough to convince rational people to stop committing it. In the case of ideology, however, the commission of the bifurcation fallacy has become so routine and so pervasive that there is no recognition that a fallacy has been committed and, as a consequence, no realization that anything like it should be given up.

The fallacy should be explained before we directly address its ideological applications. In order to do so, let us turn to literature, which is intrinsically interesting. In this case, the stories of *Gulliver's Travels* will be more instructive than even Jonathan Swift would have suspected. When Swift wants Gulliver to have an adventure in which he will face ideological issues, we are taken to a land inhabited by reasoning horses, the Houyhnhnms. The Houyhnhnms believe the world is divided into two parts: themselves and the Yahoos, a brutish, human-like race. The Houyhnhnms are rational, honest, and socially cooperative. The Yahoos are lustful, licentious, and selfish.

It is reasonable to suspect that Swift himself accepted a dualistic view of society, because Gulliver retains the conceit even after he returns to England. A considerable time after his return, Gulliver remonstrates with his cousin for persuading him to allow his travels to be published. In addition, in spite of the fact that Gulliver very much wanted to stay with the Houyhnhnms, he had to leave because they decided he was a Yahoo. The Houyhnhnms concluded that the kind treatment of Gulliver given him by his master violated reason and nature. Initially, some Houyhnhnms argued that all Yahoos, including Gulliver, should be killed. Fortunately, that proposal was defeated and was replaced, instead, with a resolution allowing each Houyhnhnm to retain two Yahoos in a slavelike status. Since the Houyhnhnms believed Gulliver was somewhat more capable of reasoning than other Yahoos, however, they decided he was a great danger to Houyhnhnmia, and his master was exhorted to banish him from the country.[6]

The Houyhnhnms' decision that Gulliver, in spite of obvious physical and mental differences from other Yahoos, was nevertheless a Yahoo came from simple logic: There are only Houyhnhnms and Yahoos. Gulliver is not a Houyhnhnm. (This can be shown most easily by physical differences: Houyhnhnms have four legs and hooves and talk through their noses.) Thus, Gulliver must be a Yahoo (perhaps of a somewhat different variety than the familiar kind).

Gulliver himself accepted this logic. He personally found the judgment of the Houyhnhnms that he be banished a little harsh, though he admitted that his defective reasoning is what led him to hope for a less onerous judgment. He never questioned the logic of the Houyhnhnms. In fact, when he returned to England, he concluded that since the people of England were obviously not Houyhnhnms, they were Yahoos, though he knew full well they really were not. He had accepted the Houyhnhnms' view completely: he could not stand the sight, sound, or smell of his wife, and he was disgusted to think that he was responsible for the conception of his children.

The entire imbroglio remains unresolved by Swift, and to the end it evades the obvious resolution: reconsidering the oversimplification. The problem is a logical one. With the acceptance of the bifurcating premise that only two possibilities exist, the conclusion follows. Of course, if the bifurcation premise were not accepted, then the conclusion would not follow. The thoughtful reader of *Gulliver's Travels* must know that there are more possibilities for rationality in the world than what is accepted by the Houyhnhnms. Indeed, Gulliver's wife might provide one of those alternatives.[7] Gulliver's problem is built into the logic of categorization and classification.

We need to exercise some caution at this point. Since we saw the results of bifurcation, we may be tempted to abandon classification and categorization completely. Some of both, however, is probably essential to knowledge. If we were to treat everything in its full individuality (and, of course, everything is, in some sense, unique), then we could make no generalizations, and finally we would lose even the capacity to say that everything is different from everything else. Having avoided the one extreme of universal uniqueness, we should also caution ourselves against the other extreme of universal oneness. It is just as dangerous to gloss over differences which actually exist as it is to make too many discriminations. Treating the universe as one undifferentiated blob will also stymie attempts to gain knowledge. We must be careful to make both important discriminations and important conjunctions.

Gulliver was so entranced by the bifurcation of the Houyhnhnms that he ignored what he had already learned as a result of his travels: that there are more legitimate categories than Houyhnhnms and Yahoos. On his first journey, he had discovered that the Lilliputians, too, accepted a dualistic account of the world. They believed there were only Lilliputians and their enemies, the Blefuscuians. Surely Gulliver, even with his "diminished" reasoning ability, should have been able to conclude that the Lilliputians and the Houyhnhnms could not both be right. The kind of false dual categorization which the Lilliputians and the Houyhnhnms accepted is what will be called the bifurcation fallacy.

Somewhat more technically, the bifurcation fallacy is committed when one suggests dividing a domain into two categories without recognizing that there are cases which do not fit in either category. The common motivation for bifurcation is to identify some existence negatively. Apparently, it was difficult for the Houyhnhnms to identify positively the exact characteristics of a Houyhnhnm or a Yahoo. Negative classification is generally easier than positive classification: in general, it is easier to say what something is not than to say what something is. Thus, it was much easier for the Houyhnhnms to identify Gulliver as a non-Houyhnhnm than to identify him as a Yahoo. But if their bifurcating premise is accurate, then a non-Houyhnhnm is by definition a Yahoo, and no further investigation need be followed.

There is a logical way out of the bifurcation problem. If the classes are, in fact, logically exclusive, then there is no fallacy. If, for example, the Houyhnhnms had been truly rational and identified the two categories as Houyhnhnms and non-Houyhnhnms, then they would not have committed the bifurcation fallacy, because everything is either X or non-X. Notice, however, that their problem—what to do about Gulliver—would have been more difficult to resolve. Gulliver would have belonged to the non-Houyhnhnm class along with the Yahoos, but he would not necessarily have been a Yahoo. Treating him as if he were a Yahoo without defining further what a Yahoo is would have been irrational (and Gulliver tells us that the Houyhnhnms embody rationality).

What makes the logically proper bifurcation work is dividing the domain into two mutually exclusive and collectively exhaustive classes (for example, Houyhnhnms and non-Houyhnhnms). Whatever belongs to one class cannot belong to the other class, and everything in the domain must be in one class or the other. We make an illegitimate bifurcation when we divide the domain into two nonexclusive classes or into two classes which are not collectively exhaustive.

We shall see that the bifurcation fallacy has haunted ideology at least since the industrial revolution. The tacit assumption that all substantive ideologies must be either capitalist or socialist has led to all too many pernicious conclusions. The defenders of capitalism act as if anything which modifies capitalism must be socialist and must be taking the society toward socialism. Just as the Houyhnhnms defined Gulliver as a Yahoo simply because he was not a Houyhnhnm, so the capitalist apologists define anything which they believe to be noncapitalist as socialist. Similarly, the socialists have identified modifications of socialism as "concessions to the capitalists." The distortions of those lenses of bifurcation have led not only to bad arguments but also to a failure to understand what is fundamental about the positions and what alternatives may exist. If, like Gulliver and the Houyhnhnms, one commits the bifurcation fallacy, then it follows that there are only two possibilities in total.

Through the rest of this book, we shall be on the alert for commissions of the bifurcation fallacy. That will have some fortunate consequences. It will cause us to examine closely the first principles of capitalism, socialism, and democracy. It will not be sufficient to assume they have been adequately defined by a negative definition. It will also cause us to be open to the possibility that some ideologies are outside the bifurcating classes and, in fact, are not even contemplated by the categories of the bifurcating classes. One such ideology, called managerialism, will be articulated. Until we can shed ourselves of the distortions of the bifurcation fallacy, however, we cannot contemplate managerialism. Since the industrial revolution, many influential ideological conclusions have been tacitly based on the bifurcation fallacy. Understanding the fallacy will enable us to discover more possibilities in the world.

3 Atomism Applied
Capitalism

Pure Capitalism: Freedom from Values?

Economists, especially in the United States, are fond of the notion that capitalism is an economic system only and that it has no connection to political or social ideologies. That notion is often supported by the view that two forms of economics exist: positive economics and normative economics. It is supposed that positive economics addresses only scientific issues and implies no commitments to values. It is supposed that issues can be resolved on the basis of facts and logic and that value-laden issues should not be introduced. In normative economics it is supposed that issues of value arise and that those issues cannot be resolved on the basis of facts and logic but only on the basis of the specific tastes and values of the proponents and opponents.

Milton Friedman has, perhaps, put the case most forcefully in the title essay of his book *Essays in Positive Economics*. He starts by reaching back a century to John Neville Keynes's book *The Scope and Method of Political Economy*. He quotes Neville Keynes as saying that political economy has three distinct aspects: it is a body of systematized knowledge concerning what is, a body of systematized knowledge discussing criteria of what ought to be, and the art of a system of rules for the attainment of a given end.[1]

Actually, Friedman goes further than Neville Keynes, for he even denies any sensible notion of knowledge about what ought to be. Friedman says pointedly:

> Positive economics is in principle independent of any ethical position or normative judgments. . . . In short, positive economics is, or can be, an "objective" science, in precisely the same sense as any theory of the physical sciences. . . .
>
> I venture the judgment, however, that currently in the Western world, and especially in the United States, differences about economic policy among disinterested citizens derive predominantly from different predic-

tions about the economic consequences of taking action—differences that in principle can be eliminated by the progress of positive economics—rather than from fundamental differences in basic values, differences about which men can ultimately only fight.[2]

In the first chapter we examined the distinction between fact and value. That section was presented in order to respond to the increasingly popular view that the distinction is so foolish as not to be worthy of consideration. In 1953, when Friedman published his *Essays,* it was a mark of scientific sophistication to declare that an absolute distinction existed and that knowledge could be achieved only in positive science (in this case, economics). It was asserted that normative views could only yield opinions which could not be rationally disputed and, as Friedman says, finally could yield only to the extreme symptom of irrationality: might makes right.[3]

Leaving aside the historical and institutional reasons suggested earlier for the absolutist view of a distinction, that is a serious and important position with regard to the logic of science. This view will not be addressed directly at this point, because so much of this book addresses it, especially as it might apply to social, political, and economic principles constituting an ideology. It should be understood, however, that views like Friedman's successfully suppressed serious academic interest in ideology because they required ideology to be involved in what ought to be as well as what is. In regard to what ought to be, they argue, reasoning is ultimately functionless, and we can only fight.

Incidentally, Neville Keynes did not accept the distinction drawn by Friedman. Keynes was interested in the old-fashioned notion of political economy, which is closely related to ideology. He thought one could have knowledge in all three domains, though the nature of the knowledge might differ.

The Adam Smith Problem

This strange phrase applies to a number of issues which are directly relevant to the question of the relationship between facts and values in capitalism. The issues are often intermixed and confused with one another in discussion and presentation. This book is not the place to examine all the dimensions of this so-called problem, but some aspects are particularly relevant for our investigation. The first set of issues arises directly from the fact we have already noted that many economists want to divorce facts and values entirely. Smith is a bit of an embarrassment for the advancement of that agenda. Before publishing *The Wealth of Nations* in 1776, he published a widely successful book titled *The Theory of Moral Sentiments.* That book, first published in 1759, established Smith as an important moral philosopher. As the title indicates, *The Theory of Moral Sentiments* explores moral issues. It represents Smith's efforts to ground morality on a suitable understanding of psychology. Had Smith published no other works, he would have been a respected moral philosopher in his time and would have remained so, at least among philosophers, until today. *The Wealth of Nations,* though, is the book that made him even more famous among intellectuals as well as more practical people. It has made his name well known even to the present day. That book, primarily about economic topics, laid the intellectual foundations for capitalism.

From the early nineteenth century forward, writers have occasionally attempted to explain the fact that Smith wrote both books. Thus, one aspect of the Adam Smith Problem is dealing with Smith as a person who was both a moral philosopher and the principal architect of modern economics but who apparently misunderstood the importance of separating facts and values in order to construct economics as a science. In this respect, the Adam Smith Problem becomes essentially Adam Smith's problem, and scholars make an effort to interpret his writing so that they can save him from himself. I refer to this aspect as the scientific economic aspect of the problem.

At some points, economists and others caught with trying to solve the Adam Smith Problem have seen it as an even deeper problem than one threatening the basis of scientific economics, one of logical inconsistency on crucial issues between *The Theory of Moral Sentiments* and *The Wealth of Nations.* It seems that people have felt that if they could only show that *The Theory of Moral Sentiments* and *The Wealth of Nations* are logically inconsistent in important ways, then reasonable people would have to choose *The Wealth of Nations,* and *The Theory of Moral Sentiments* could be ignored as an instance of youthful indiscretion on the part of Smith. This is what I call the logical aspect of the Adam Smith Problem, and it leads to an even more threatening version of Adam Smith's problem.

Finally, a more intellectually constructive aspect of the Adam Smith Problem is based on the presumption that Smith knew how to avoid logical inconsistencies and knew what he was doing in developing economics. The question raised is: How are we to interpret *The Theory of Moral Sentiments* and *The Wealth of Nations* so that they can be understood as an integrated whole rather than as separate documents with little in common? I have labeled that the philosophical aspect of the Adam Smith Problem. I might have as easily called it the historical aspect. I chose the word *philosophical* because the issue is, at its base, a philosophical one.

Scientific economic aspect of the Adam Smith Problem.
We have already noted the effort to separate positive and normative economics as well as the explicit understanding that there is no knowledge to be gained in normative economics, whereas knowledge can be gained in positive eco-

nomics. This point has been put most aggressively by economists who identify themselves with capitalist economics, so it is relevant to ask about Smith's views on these issues. On the surface, it would appear that Smith did not agree with the separation. He never denounced or retracted either *The Theory of Moral Sentiments* or *The Wealth of Nations*. He made no explicit distinction between the level of knowledge (or the absence thereof) in one as compared with the other. By all appearances, Smith himself believed that such a thing as knowledge in regard to moral matters existed, as he believed that knowledge existed in regard to economic matters. Scientific economists feared that, since there is in principle no rational way to resolve normative disputes, if economics as a science were to enter into moral territory, it would be in danger of being bogged down hopelessly, and the agenda of scientific economics could never be advanced. As we saw in considering Friedman's view, science can make progress; morality cannot. In principle, at least, the scientific economists believe that scientific investigations can yield answers which are agreed to and which have demonstrably false contradictories. The scientific economists also believe, however, that a similar claim cannot be sustained for morality. They believe that, while values are the kinds of things about which opinions can differ, they are not the kinds of things about which some people can be right and other people wrong. This radical a priori separation of facts and values is rooted in the development of science, at least as these people see it.

In order to maintain their a priori position, the scientific economists had to treat *The Theory of Moral Sentiments* as if it were inadequate and misguided. The earliest nineteenth-century attempts to solve this part of the Adam Smith Problem in essence dismissed *The Theory of Moral Sentiments* as secondary to and even inconsistent with *The Wealth of Nations*. The problem, then, is solved, because *The Theory of Moral Sentiments* is the work of Smith in an early prescientific phase when he lacked the scientific insight he gained by the time he wrote *The Wealth of Nations*. In this interpretation, *The Theory of Moral Sentiments* is a product of early youthful exuberance and speculation, while *The Wealth of Nations* is a scientific treatment.

In its most extreme forms, the position was a bit difficult to maintain, because *The Theory of Moral Sentiments* is a strong book and contains numerous insights which Smith maintained in *The Wealth of Nations*. For example, one of the critical turning points for Smith's thesis in *The Wealth of Nations*—the famous argument of the invisible hand—is tried out in different guises in at least four different places in *The Theory of Moral Sentiments*.

In the twentieth century one of the most sophisticated historians of economic thought, Jacob Viner, continued the discussion of the Adam Smith Problem. Viner was a careful scholar who recognized the extremes to which earlier efforts had gone. He also recognized that it would be difficult to maintain a complete divorce between *The Theory of Moral Sentiments* and *The Wealth of Nations*. Viner's explanatory image was one of maturation rather than radical change. Viner gave Smith credit for writing a strong book in *The Theory of Moral Sentiments*, but he found *The Wealth of Nations* a more mature book which reflects the development of a scientifically oriented scholar. In the introduction to his recent book of collected essays by Viner, Douglas Irwin summarizes Viner's considered views on the Adam Smith Problem:

> Viner attributes the divergence of the two books to their fundamentally different purposes. *The Theory of Moral Sentiments* was a philosophical book, in which, "failing to compare his conclusions with facts, [Smith] saw no necessity for qualifying them." *The Wealth of Nations,* by contrast, was written with an eye to the real world, where blemishes in the order appear: "The apparent discrepancies between *The Theory of Moral Sentiments* and *The Wealth of Nations* mark distinct advances of the latter over the former in realism and in the application of the saving grace of common sense." For this reason, Viner believed *The Wealth of Nations* to be the better of the two books.[4]

In this one passage, we can see two themes neatly brought together: first that philosophical thinking is nonfactual, and second that *The Wealth of Nations* represents a more mature Smith. On these grounds, the a priori thesis of the separation of facts and values can be maintained in spite of Smith's apparent refusal to agree. Even the considerable sophistication of these themes at Viner's hand, however, fail to account adequately for some recalcitrant empirical facts.

Perhaps the most embarrassing fact is that after completing *The Wealth of Nations,* Smith returned to *The Theory of Moral Sentiments* and revised it considerably. Unfortunately for the scientific case, the revisions did not deal with the issues which would bother the scientific economists. Even in its substantially revised versions, *The Theory of Moral Sentiments* remained a book decidedly in the tradition of moral philosophy at that time, and Smith made no effort to distinguish facts from values.[5] Facts and values permeate both books.

A second recalcitrant fact comes from a recognition of the historical and intellectual context in which Smith wrote both books. Much of *The Theory of Moral Sentiments* is written in a spirit closely related to what we today might identify as developmental psychology as practiced by psychologists such as Jean Piaget, Erik Erikson, Lawrence Kohlberg, and Carol Gilligan. Recognizing that historical fact, however, does not help the case for making a distinction between a scientific base of *The Wealth of Nations* and a fact-free base of *The Theory of Moral Sentiments,* because the former has a strong dose of moral psychology in it also. An important psychological idea in *The Wealth of Nations* is the assumption of self-interest. Smith does not elevate that notion to the status of universality, nor does he make it part of irrefutable dogma in either volume. However, it is a view which, in one form or another, is typically assumed by the scientific economists.[6] In a sense, then, both volumes directly involve presumptions of moral psychology. Surely this is not a conclusion which would satisfy the efforts of scientific economists to divorce the two radically or to establish one as immature and the other as mature.

A third fact that the thesis of the scientific economists fails to consider is that Adam Smith himself never recanted the major points of *The Theory of Moral Sentiments*. They are left, then, with the fact that the man Fritz Machlup once suitably described as the adam and the smith of economics apparently did not recognize this most elementary and fundamental distinction.

Finally, we have good reason to believe that Smith understood the arguments for the distinction between facts and values, and thus, it cannot have been out of ignorance of the issues that he failed to accept what the scientific economists consider an appropriate distinction. We know that David Hume drew the distinction most clearly and forcefully in his own *Treatise of Human Nature*, published twenty years before Smith's *Theory of Moral Sentiments*.[7] There is an abundance of historical evidence that Smith was very familiar with Hume's works and with Hume himself. We may conclude quite confidently, then, that Smith's failure to agree to a distinction between facts and values was conscious and considered.

Thus, whether we accept the earlier, more radical interpretation of the Adam Smith Problem or the later, more sophisticated version, it is clear that the problem is not Smith's but that of the scientific economists. Either they should substantially qualify their reverence for Smith as the principal architect of scientific economics, or they should revise substantially their notion of the relation between facts and values in scientific economics.[8]

Logical aspect of the Adam Smith Problem.
A logical search for discontinuity between Smith's two books would be the most lethal if it were successful. Scholars have attempted to show that the two books are inconsistent in some important ways. There is some surface plausibility to the notion that they might be inconsistent. *The Theory of Moral Sentiments* seems to celebrate benevolence as a fundamental moral and psychological principle, whereas *The Wealth of Nations* seems to celebrate self-interest as a fundamental principle. It is easy to exaggerate the extent to which those celebrations in fact occur. Smith was so careful and scholarly in his writings that it is difficult to find unqualified dogmatism in any of his works. Over the years scholars have been unable to point to important statements in one work which are in fact contradicted by important statements in the other work. Such inconsistency, which might be extended to logical antecedents or conse-

quences, simply has not been shown, in spite of what seems to be the surface inconsistency.

The scientific economists, who might like most to find such an inconsistency, have put their case at a serious disadvantage in this regard. By consigning *The Theory of Moral Sentiments* to moral discourse and by concluding that moral discourse is neither true nor false, they leave themselves with the positivists' conclusion that moral sentences are cognitively meaningless and, as a consequence, cannot stand as an element in a logical analysis. Thus, while in their methodological view, sentences of *The Theory of Moral Sentiments* cannot be shown to be consistent with sentences of *The Wealth of Nations*, they cannot be shown to be inconsistent either. This aspect of the problem, deceptively tempting as it is for their case, then, actually cannot be part of it.

We need to be careful in drawing our conclusions about the logical aspect of the issue. Smith's books are big and sprawling volumes which range over a number of topics and subtopics. While we know that Smith taught both logic and rhetoric, it is still possible that sometime someone will be able to establish an inconsistency which has not yet been noticed. If that inconsistency were significant for Smith's arguments, then the Adam Smith Problem would legitimately become Adam Smith's problem, and we would have good reason to make the distinction. At this point, however, no such contradiction has been found, and the larger presumptive contradiction cannot be sustained.

Philosophical aspect of the Adam Smith Problem.
After examining these failed efforts, we must ask whose problem the Adam Smith Problem is. It would seem that the problem is much more one of the commentators than one of Smith's. Some commentators tend to bring to a reading of Smith's work such a strong bias in favor of divorcing facts from values that they impose that conclusion on the books before examining them closely. As a result, they conclude that Smith has a problem. It is as if we were to listen to two works of the composer Edward Kennedy ("Duke") Ellington, for example, the raucous and rowdy "Cottontail" (at least as interpreted by Ella Fitzgerald when she sang with Ellington's orchestra) and Ellington's pensive and ponderous *Black, Brown and Beige,* and decide that the two compositions are so different that they could not have been written by the same person. We might then conclude that there is a Duke Problem, which we would reinterpret as the Duke's problem. The problem, of course, would not be the Duke's at all: it is our problem if we cannot understand how those two works fit into a coherent whole. Similarly, the interpretaton of the Adam Smith Problem is a problem of the interpreters, not of Smith. Dismissing one side or the other in the name of solving the problem may solve the interpreters' problem, but it does not solve the Adam Smith Problem. To paraphrase Wittgenstein, having created the problem, the commentators should solve it.

We are led, then, to a constructive version of the Adam Smith Problem. It is the most interesting from an empirical point of view. In this construction, the commentator, perhaps a historian or a philosopher, assumes that *The Theory of Moral Sentiments* and *The Wealth of Nations* as well as Smith's other works are part of a whole and then accepts the task of determining how the pieces fit together.[9] In a particularly exciting version of addressing the Adam Smith Problem, Patricia Werhane has recently published an important book developing a coherent interpretation of Smith's entire corpus.[10] She recognizes the other aspects of the problem I have characterized, but she proceeds primarily in the spirit of this third aspect. She modestly refuses to suggest that she has found the final solution to all the issues, but her conclusions are rich and interesting. She argues that we have concentrated too much on the dichotomy between self-interest and benevolence. She believes both approaches can be joined more sensibly by recognizing that neither of them was Smith's fundamental principle. She suggests, rather, that both were derived from his deeper commitment to justice. Werhane's new way of understanding the Adam Smith Problem is fully consistent with the argument of this section: capitalism as an ideology combines both facts and values, and it has done so since Smith first designed capitalism.

Capitalism as an Ideology for Business

The attempt to divorce capitalism from its broader ideological base has led people to confuse the fundamental principles of capitalism with its derivative principles. While capitalism is often invoked by apologists and lobbyists for business enterprises, it is important to understand that the fundamental purpose of capitalism is not to defend business or its activities. Contemporary business apologists tend to quote Smith selectively, and it has become something of a fad among some of the supporters of business in the United States to wear neckties with a likeness of Adam Smith. However, Smith was not an apologist for business or business people. As we shall see, Smith could be trenchant in his criticism of business. He believed that the wisdom behind his approach was that it would curb the excesses of business without invoking government. Smith did not seek to put business people in charge of the society or the economy. He was smart enough to recognize that no one could sustain such a proposal either logically or morally and that it would merely give one group of people hegemony over another. He did not expect business people in general to act out of any interest other than their own, and he believed that it would be naive to expect otherwise.

Consumers

Far from putting business people in charge of the economy, Smith wanted to put consumers in charge. He believed that if the consumer were really in charge, the rapacious temptations of business people would be curbed by the operations of the economy and by their selfish desire to serve the consumer.[11] Smith believed his view did not force a choice among the interests of merchants, laborers, and landowners. Capitalism required them all to serve the interests of an aggregation: consumers.

From Smith's perspective, placing service to the consumers at the center of the economy was morally permissible, because the aggregation of consumers includes all people. It is possible to be a merchant and not a laborer; it is possible to be a landowner and not a tenant. However, it is impossible not to be a consumer, especially as Smith saw the development of what we call the industrial revolution. In many regards, Smith had a reasonably accurate sense of what was ahead for society after the industrial revolution. Smith himself had persuaded the University of Glasgow to make a home for James Watt, the inventor of the steam escape mechanism essential to harnessing steam power. While we should not claim perfection for Smith as a fortune-teller, he was remarkably prescient and saw with considerable accuracy how society would develop in the future. His later works were devoted to those developments.

Thus, while one can imagine an argument to the effect that people who live on self-owned farms and, perhaps, extraordinarily wealthy people living on their inheritances need never be consumers, they would not constitute a significant portion of society in the future as Smith saw it, and even they would increasingly have to become consumers.[12] One of Smith's dominant messages, whether on the national or the individual level, was that we could no longer be isolated. Consumers were the only all-inclusive group, and Smith argued that an economy which serves the interest of consumers will automatically be an economy which serves everyone.

Consumer is King

Thus, the fundamental assumption of capitalism can be summarized by the expression Consumer is king. A capitalist economy is an economy which provides consumers with the greatest range of goods and services possible at the lowest possible price. The fact that everyone is a consumer provides both the economic basis of capitalism and the moral justification for it. To paraphrase the famous expression of Abraham Lincoln, capitalism is an ideology of the consumer, by the consumer, and for the consumer. The fact that we are all consumers gives capitalism its moral foundation, just as the fact that we are all people gave Lincoln's expression moral justification for democracy. Without that moral foundation, capitalism would be a free-floating economic ideology with no sensible basis. On those grounds, capitalist arguments could be used selectively for propaganda on behalf of business interests. That is not what Smith meant or said, however, and it is difficult to know why such a value-free ideology would be interesting for a society, since society at large cannot evade value issues, no matter how much some economists might like to think it can.

Economically and ideologically, capitalism should create a market economy in which firms adjust rapidly to changing consumer needs and demands. In capitalism, each firm operates on the basis of its owner's self-interest. The label *profit maximization* has been given to that goal, but the expression has its foundation in Smith and in capitalist economics. It is from the self-interest of the owners of the firms that consumer needs are to be met, not from a hope for concern for the community on the part of people who own businesses. The market is supposed to supply the discipline which will make the firms produce and sell what consumers want, and the market will keep firms from selling what the consumers do not want.

Capitalism and Social Freedom

In this regard, capitalism is morally tied to social freedom.[13] In that context, capitalism provides the greatest amount of social freedom by giving the greatest choice possible to the consumer. The expression *the greatest choice possible* is used for two reasons. In the first place, capitalism does not supply consumers with whatever they may desire. If, for example, consumers want automobiles priced below cost, the market will not be able to provide for them without frustrating the desires of other consumers. Of course, the economy could be put under regulatory demand to market such automobiles, or automobiles could be subsidized to such an extent that consumers would believe they were able to purchase one below cost. In order for that to happen, however, a reallocation of the demands of the economy would be necessary, such that the objective could be met. Then other consumer desires would not be fulfilled. Thus, although it would appear that the economy had met a consumer desire, in fact, overall it would have frustrated the aggregated totality of consumer desires. Second, no economic system can produce the impossible. If, for example, using current technology it is impossible to cure cancer, then no matter how much consumers may wish for that, a cure cannot be produced. On the other hand, capitalists would quickly insist that capitalism lowers the price of automobiles as far as possible and provides the most hopeful conditions under which a cure for cancer may be found, consistent with the other desires of consumers.

Survival of the Fittest

At this point, it is helpful to invoke another principle which will link the "Consumer is king" principle with the operation of firms. That principle can be summarized by the expression *survival of the fittest*. It may seem strange to invoke an expression which we associate with Darwin and the theory of evolution, since Darwin's *Origin of the Species* was not published until seventy

years after Smith's *Wealth of Nations*. However, the notion of the survival of
the fittest was not new with Darwin. It had been part of intellectual life since
the early Greek philosophers. The concept was invoked in Smith's time. Im-
manuel Kant, for example, used it to support a critical stage in his argument
designed to show that the utilitarians were wrong in thinking that happiness
is the end of mankind. More than twenty years before the publication of *The
Wealth of Nations,* Hume used the concept in order to argue for eliminating
nationalistic barriers to international trade. Darwin's grandfather, a contemporary of Smith's, had articulated a version of the survival concept in his own
biological writings. Darwin himself acknowledged Smith's successor, Thomas
Robert Malthus, as a source of inspiration for the application of the survival
principle, and Malthus got the notion from Smith. Thus, we should not be surprised that Smith used the concept in developing his ideas about the operations
of an economy. At the same time, we should be careful. The fact that the concept was well known does not in any sense diminish the credit which should be
given to both Smith and Darwin for its use and application. Smith and Darwin
presented empirical and analytic evidence in a systematic way which gave support and credibility to the view that the principle applied to the separate areas
they chose to study. Darwin's was the more difficult task, not only because he
had to overcome centuries of religious prejudice, much of which he originally
endorsed, but also because he was suggesting that the principle was operative
in a world beyond thinking creatures. It is one thing to suggest that humans
should arrange their affairs in order to have only the strongest survive. It is quite
another thing to suggest that the lives of birds also conform to such principles.
Since Darwin could not ask birds what motivated them, it was difficult to find
the appropriate explanation. At the same time, even though it was arguably
easier for Smith to imagine the broad application of the concept in economics,
his perspicacity is certainly admirable.

Firms compete with one another in supplying consumers with goods and
services. Those firms which provide goods and services at a price consumers
are willing to pay survive; those firms which fail to provide goods and services
at a price consumers are willing to pay disappear. If some goods cannot be supplied at a price which a sufficient number of consumers will pay, those goods
will not appear in the economy. If one firm puts a price on some product and
another firm can sell the same product for less, the second firm will survive,
and the first will fail, unless the first brings down its price. In either eventuality,
the consumer wins by getting the product at the lowest price possible. If a firm
puts a price which is too low on the product—if the revenue does not cover
the costs—then that firm will go out of business. The firms which remain in
business will be those firms which are pricing products in order to cover costs
and nothing more.

It is important to understand the reasoning behind this assertion. If the firm charges anything more than cost, its action will encourage another firm to enter the market and offer the product at a lower price. If some element of the price is still above cost, a third firm may enter the market, the first may drop its price to meet the competition, or the second may drop its price to thwart potential competition. In any event, the market mechanism will force the price down to the cost. If the price falls below cost, the firm will be losing money and will go out of business. Because of the principle of the survival of the fittest, the only firms left in existence will be those which are offering goods at cost. Thus, the consumer is able to purchase at cost all those goods which can be produced successfully.

The economists' insistence on the centrality of the principle of profit maximization and the stories from the financial press about the profitability of companies leave the impression that firms actually gain a profit. They do not and cannot in a capitalist economy, because the profit is eliminated by the market mechanism. The accountant's use of the term *profit* is particularly misleading in this context. Packed into that is a return to the entrepreneur for a salary equivalent, sometimes a return for the use (i.e., replacement) of capital, a return for the use of land, and a return commensurate with the risk which has been undertaken by the entrepreneur.[14] In addition, sometimes an element of that profit is a return which comes about when the market is not perfect. Under capitalism, as long as the government and its agencies stay out of the economy, such conditions, called disequilibria, should be short-lived and can be safely ignored.

What could be a more efficient system for delivering goods and services at minimal cost to all of us? It is impossible for the goods and services to cost less (though artificial mechanisms may cause specific ones to be priced lower or higher), and it is impossible to have better distribution, since capitalism is the system which is most responsive to our desires.

In order to have the capitalist economy work, there must be no barriers to entrance into business and no protection for exit from business. It must be easy to start producing goods and services, and it must be easy to go out of business. Any other condition causes disequilibria. If, for example, the government were to pass a law which said that in order to start a business, the entrepreneur had to file an application a year ahead of time and had to put money in escrow, then that would restrict entry into the market, and existing businesses would know that they could survive, while maintaining higher prices, until competition could overcome that barrier. Similar results would come from protecting certain businesses. Thus, anything which interferes with the survival mechanism of the market economy either drives up prices or removes choice from people. It is in this context that the capitalist strictures about government interference in business make sense. If the government is involved at all, that involvement will necessarily cause either higher prices or restricted choice. Either result prevents the consumer from being king.

These twin principles lie at the foundation of capitalism. Other assumptions, implications, and suppositions have been identified with capitalism, but none of them are fundamental. Once we are clear about the foundational moral commitment of capitalism—an ideology of, by, and for the consumer—we can see how these principles are both critical and adequate. Because of other claims about capitalism, however, it will be wise to look more closely at some of the assumptions, implications, and suppositions often associated with capitalism.

Assumptions of Capitalism

Physics and Atomism

Smith wrote "The Principles which Lead and Direct Philosophical Enquiries: Illustrated by the History of Astronomy" and counted that material among the few documents he believed worthy of publication after his death. In it, Smith shows that he had a close and careful understanding of Newton, and he argues that Newton is the culmination of astronomical and physical thought. While we have no direct testimony from Smith, it seems reasonable to suppose that the economic system which Smith developed was modeled on the classical physics which Smith knew well and which was already achieving considerable practical and theoretical success. It makes sense to think of firms as economic atoms. Each is imagined to be very small relative to the whole, and each is presumed individually to have essentially no impact on the whole. Just as a chair is nothing more than an aggregation of a large number of atoms arranged in a certain manner, so an economic condition is the aggregation of a large number of firms and individuals arranged in a certain manner. The system is atomistic in the sense used in chapter 2, since the presumption is that the whole is nothing more than the aggregation of its parts. The economy expresses the interests and needs of all people, and the economy finds a way of addressing the maximum number at the lowest cost. There is no social need over and above the aggregated needs of the people.

In this system, it is critical that the firms remain small, with no impact on the overall economy. In addition, the firms must be free to enter into business when sufficient demand exists and to go out of business in the absence of sufficient demand. If there is any resistance to the rapid establishment and dissolution of firms, then the consumer's interests will not be served. Thus, rapid entrance and exit is of critical importance to capitalism.

Economic atoms and physical atoms both operate in accordance with laws, and it is the task of the scientist to discover those laws. Smith wanted to discover the fundamental laws of economics as Newton had for physics.

Teleology

Bernard de Mandeville's *Fable of the Bees,* produced in 1723, was well known to Smith. In that work, Mandeville described individual bees going about their separate tasks without intending positive collective results. When the individual bees fail to carry out their special roles, the colony vanishes. The philosophical issue faced here is known as teleology. The question is whether what occurs does so because the participants (or, in the extreme, God) designed or intended the ends or whether the occurrences came about as a result of other forces which did not intend those ends but simply operated on the basis of other nonteleological factors. Newton had successfully made teleological analyses unnecessary in physical sciences.[15] Smith's friend and colleague David Hume had constructed powerful arguments apparently refuting the teleological argument for the existence of God, which states that since there is design in the universe which cannot be accounted for as the result of human efforts, there must be a designer of the universe, and that designer is God. Thus, the religious teleologists had argued that God does intervene in the activities of the world. The economic theoreticians known as the mercantilists, against whom much of Smith's economic theory was written, had declared that intervention in the economy had to occur if it was to operate effectively. Smith understood his great success to be that he demonstrated not only that intervention was not required but also that where intervention occurred it would result in harm to the economy: it would reduce the supply of goods and services to the consumer, or it would cause the price to the consumer to be unnecessarily high, or both. Smith believed the principle of survival operated in conjunction with the principle of the consumer as king to make the economy operate as effectively as possible.

Purposes and Human Motivation

Thus, capitalism is an ideology created quite consciously on the model of the physics of Smith's time. Operations are lawlike and atomistic and do not have a need for teleological assumptions. In addition, capitalism dispenses with a need for discussing purposes or intentions of the major actors. The owner who fails to price properly will go out of business. For example, even if some owners wanted to be generous and pay their employees higher wages than the competition, they would soon find that the price they were required to charge for their products in order to pay for payroll expenses was so high that they would not have enough sales. Thus, the owners' intentions or desires are really quite irrelevant. Friedman makes this point most forcefully:

> Unless the behavior of the businessmen in some way or other approximated behavior consistent with the maximization of returns, it seems

unlikely they would remain in business for long. Let the apparent immediate determinant of business behavior be anything at all—habitual reaction, random chance, or whatnot. Whenever this determinant happens to lead to behavior consistent with rational and informed maximization of return, the business will prosper and acquire resources with which to expand; whenever it does not, the business will tend to lose resources and can be kept in business only by the addition of resources from the outside. The process of "natural selection" thus helps to validate the hypothesis—or, rather, given natural selection, acceptance of the hypothesis can be based largely on the judgment that it summarizes appropriately the conditions for survival.[16]

The so-called market mechanism will take care of all inefficiencies and will force the economy—through no intention of producers or government agents—to produce at the most favorable level possible for the consumers.[17]

Smith was not an extremist on this topic or any other. He did not really believe that people act without motivations. Since he wanted to be realistic, he believed that the most reliable assumption of the motivation of owners was self-interest. Each owner, seeking to satisfy self-interest, would be forced by the nature of the economy to satisfy the interests of the consumer. Essentially, owners had no choice in the matter. If they priced or produced improperly, they went out of business, no matter how honorable their intentions might have been.

Implications of Capitalism

Determinism

Smith's system, like the physics of his time, was deterministic. The parts of the system interacted in ways prescribed by economic laws, and the results came about because of those economic laws. Whatever choice we might imagine participants thought they made would be effectively trivial. This is an important point to emphasize, for it would become a common assumption of mainstream economics in the so-called capitalist societies. Notice that in the quotation cited in the previous section, Friedman indicates that the motivation of the businessman makes no difference. The results are all that matter. In fact, it makes no difference to economic theory whether or not the businessman has any motivation at all.[18]

The economics of capitalism in general remains deterministic. Economists want economics to be a deductive science in which results—output—can be deduced from input. That means that the participants in the process have no effective discretion. The participants may think they make choices in setting prices, for example. However, if they make the wrong choice, they will be like the wild animal which "chooses" to eat poison—out of business. In a capitalist structure in which prices instantly clear the market, in which there is perfect information, in which bankruptcy and entrance occur without delay, and in which the individual investor has the same access to capital as the firm, the individual actors could exercise no effective discretion.

Participants may insist that they do make choices. Business executives certainly think they choose inventory levels, pricing structures, personnel policies, marketing strategies, capital plans, and so on. The executives think they are decision makers. They labor over decisions because they think they have some effective discretion. They even think that they are justified in being paid handsomely for exercising that discretion properly. Under the economic view of capitalism, however, they are wrong on all counts. Their sense of choice is mere illusion. Actually they have no choice, and the capitalist says that we recognize that fact when we step back and take an overall economic view.

Without referring to economics in his example, the rationalist-deductivist philosopher Spinoza made a similar point most dramatically. In defending his own determinism, he said that if a rock rolling down a hill were self-conscious, it would think it was making all the twists and turns out of its own choice. We, of course, know better. Spinoza argued that people think they make genuine choices because they are self-conscious, but like the rock, they do not really make such choices. Spinoza's analogy extends appropriately to economics in capitalism. The owners of the firms are self-conscious, and that makes them think they are making choices as they conduct their business. When the economists step back, however, they can see that owners have no effective discretion. If they did, there could be no economic laws which would provide the deductive schema for predicting the course of the economy.

Suppositions Claimed Necessary for Capitalism

The Hypothesis of the Rational Person

Some people have argued that a fundamental principle of capitalism is that human beings are rational creatures making economically calculated decisions. Actually, as we have seen, in capitalism there is no need to assume that humans are rational. Even though the notion of the rational person was popular in Smith's time and even though later commentators on capitalism liked to have us envisage the economic man who makes rapid calculations of his economic interest and rapidly responds to the circumstances, Smith resisted all those temptations and quite explicitly denied that he believed people were rational and would act in a rational way in the economy.

Following Freud at least, a substantial body of evidence would seem to suggest that people are not rational. Humans do not make rational decisions always or perhaps even frequently. Many purchases are made on the basis of fads, whims, or perhaps even suppressed sexual impulses. Fundamentally speaking, capitalism should be silent on the rationality of consumers. The economy is to produce goods and services irrespective of the rationality of the consumers. In general, some people, such as business school professors, may find it convenient to assume that firms run on rational grounds will probably survive. That is at best a generalization, however, and as we learned from Friedman, it has little to do with actual business decisions in a capitalist economy. Furthermore, there is no guarantee that rationality will produce survival. Capitalism depends on the existence of numerous firms which are producing goods and services in competition with one another. Thus, the supposition of the economic man, while featured centrally in writings defending or criticizing capitalism, is actually irrelevant.

Private Property

Perhaps the assumption most widely supposed to be associated with the definition of capitalism is that of private property. In his *Dictionary of Economics and Business,* Erwin Esser Nemmers defines capitalism as "an economic system which permits private ownership of the means of production. However, such a definition would also apply to other forms of organization. The distinguishing facts in modern times are (1) large amounts of capital used in production, (2) relatively great freedom of economic activity, and (3) in recent times, the great importance of the corporate form of business."[19] This multipart definition has some interesting aspects which we will do well to note. The first sentence embeds the notion of private property deeply in the heart of capitalism. Some people will be surprised that I have not included private property in my definition of capitalism. The topic deserves further analysis.

There is no doubt that Smith and later capitalist economists recognized the importance of private property—in some form—to capitalism. Smith's treatment of private property, like his treatment of the associated labor theory of value, however, is restrained.[20] He did not give the same attention to private property that he gave to the functioning of the marketplace or to the division of labor, for example. In *The Wealth of Nations,* Smith directly refers to private property fewer than a half dozen times. Those references are, in general, positive, though some indirect references, such as to primogeniture, are much less consistently favorable. Smith was aware of the temptations for abuse by people who held property, and he favored moderating actions, including those of government.

It would be wrong to argue that Smith opposed private property, as the socialists would. He was, however, by no means an unqualified advocate of it. His central interest was reserved for the market and the positive effects it could achieve. No doubt he would have accepted the view that in general private property would aid the operations of the market, because he believed people would never be as attentive to other people's money as they would be to their own. Thus, in arguing for an economy which should be immediately responsive to the consumer, Smith recognized the important role that private property would play. Nevertheless, the central emphasis is the responsiveness to consumer desires at the lowest possible price and with the widest possible range of goods and services. Private property was at most a means to an end for Smith; it was not a central definitional condition.

By and large, people have followed Smith's lead in this regard. Something of a split is discernible. When people who support capitalism concentrate on its economic basis, they also concentrate on the market mechanism. By contrast, when people who support capitalism concentrate on broader social, political, and ideological issues, they concentrate on ownership of private property. A technical reason explains this differentiation. Recalling that the capitalist economists strive to create a deductive system, we should recognize that in the equations, whereas the market mechanism has a central role, private property has no deductive role. The equations of capitalist economics would hold or not hold with or without private property. Thus, popular suppositions to the contrary, Smith did not give a central defining role to private property, and others have followed that tradition. Capitalist economists qua economists emphasize the marketplace. Capitalist apologists qua ideologists emphasize private property.

We can make these points more clear by looking further at Nemmers' definition. In the first sentence, he declares that capitalism *permits* private ownership. He does not suggest, as others do, that it *requires* private ownership. Thus, he does not believe that private property is a necessary condition of capitalism. The second sentence may have been included to leave room for his treatment of fascism, which he suggests also permits private property.

Nemmers' third sentence makes three distinct points. The first point, identifying a need for large amounts of capital to be used in production, cannot be a central part of the definition of capitalism unless we are ready to dismiss Adam Smith and others from the ranks of capitalist theoreticians. Production in contemporary society is certainly capital-intensive. That, however, is an historical accident, not a defining characteristic. The second part of the sentence is so ambiguous that it is not at all helpful. Its meaning turns on definitions of *relatively great* and *freedom*. The former is, by nature, imprecise. The latter is part of what the debate is all about. As we shall see, socialists would argue that the freedom for individuals to be without provision of minimal needs, as might occur in a capitalist system, is like dropping naked people in the Antarctic and telling them they are now "free" to go wherever they wish. The third part of the sentence raises the topic of the corporate form of business, and we will discuss that at some length in the remainder of this chapter.

Granting Exceptions: The Thin End of the Wedge?

We have, then, a picture of an atomistic economy in which numerous small firms are in constant motion, competing with one another in an attempt to satisfy the desires of consumers. It would have to be easy to set up business, and it would have to be easy to go out of business. Government is the only threat to this efficiently operating mechanism, because only it has the concentration of power which would allow it to intervene. Any government intervention would necessarily either drive up prices or restrict available goods and services. Let us look at some examples.

Licensing Physicians

Consider an example which seems harmless enough and which many people would probably support: the requirement that physicians be licensed. Effectively that means that they must go to an accredited college and an accredited medical school, serve in an accredited hospital, and pass medical examinations. Presumably we support that system because we believe it helps insure the quality of medical care. Perhaps it does, but we know also that it limits the number of people who can be physicians. As a consequence, the requirement drives up the price of medical services, restricts their accessibility, or both. As the situation stands currently, the government's restrictions on medical practice make entering the medical profession very difficult and expensive. Such restrictions may be justifiable in many people's minds, but the economic consequences follow also.

Patents, Copyrights, and Trademarks

Consider two other provisions which the government makes and which most people seem to support without much hesitation: patent policies and copyright policies. Both provisions are anticapitalist in the sense that they drive prices up and/or restrict choice. Patent policies grant the right to an approved inventor to be the sole marketer of a product. Without the explicit approval of the inventor, no other person or business may produce or sell the product. The government which grants the patent also enforces it. As a consequence, inventors can restrict the supply of their products and cause prices to rise to the level which produces the greatest profit for them irrespective of consumer interests or needs. This time, *profit* is the correct word to use, because the inventor takes advantage of the government-sponsored disequilibrium. Such patent rights are clearly a case of government involvement in the economy, and the consequences are as Smith would have predicted. Similar statements can be made about copyrights. A copyright is granted by the government in order to prevent others from freely copying the material in question.

In all fairness, we should recognize that many people argue that such restraint of trade as established by the government in the case of patents and copyrights is necessary in order to encourage intellectual developments. Those people might argue also that in the long run such restraint is in the interest of the consumer, since it permits a broader offering of goods and services to come to market.

However the arguments with regard to social benefits proceed for patents and copyrights, a similar government intervention and restraint would not seem to be justifiable on the same grounds. Trademark legislation supports the business which objects to the use of its trademark by some other business or person. For example, the Coca-Cola Company can use the courts to prevent anyone from using the name or distinctive writing of Coca-Cola without permission.[21] One can even gain trademark protection on a mark which is not used and perhaps never will be used. Whereas it may be arguable that patent and copyright legislation is in the long-term interest of the consumer, it is difficult to imagine a convincing argument which would make a similar case with regard to protecting unused trademarks. It is clear why such legislation is in the interest of businesses. It is not at all clear how it is in the interest of consumers.

Privileges of Incorporation

Perhaps the provision granted by government that would have the greatest impact on society and the development of capitalism was that of perpetuity and limited liability as granted in privileges of incorporation. Historically, as firms needed capital, the protections of limited liability under incorporation became important to the owners. Incorporation limits the liability of the investors to the extent of their investment. By contrast, in an unincorporated business, the owners are responsible personally for all risks and debts of the business. Thus, the risk falls squarely on the owner-manager's shoulders. If large investments are needed and if distant investors have to be brought in to insure the accumulation of the necessary capital, then in all likelihood such investors would be unwilling to accept an open-ended personal risk for their investment. Any calculating prospective investor looks at the upside potential (the prospect for making money) and the downside risk (the potential for loss) with regard to a particular investment. It would be much more difficult, if not impossible, to get the requisite investors if their risk potential included their total personal resources.

It is one thing to attempt to persuade someone to invest in a corporation where the downside risk is guaranteed by the government and the upside is unlimited. It is an entirely different matter to ask someone to invest in a situation where both the downside and the upside are unlimited. If the downside can be protected by limiting liability while still providing for an unlimited upside, then it would be considerably easier to find investors. That is the genius of governmental provisions of incorporation. Incorporation does not quite create an anti-Newtonian world in which what goes up can be prevented from coming down. It does, however, take a large step in that direction by establishing a condition in which something can go up much further than it could come down.

Incorporation is an important protection granted by the government to the owners of the incorporated business, and they can use it to its fullest advantage. Consider the case of the Darling-Delaware Company. The precise details are difficult to obtain because the company has declared that it does not have an obligation to file quarterly results with the Securities and Exchange Commission. Apparently, in 1990 bondholders in the Darling-Delaware Company received a second-quarter report which included a footnote stating that the company did not have sufficient cash to meet an interest payment of $12.2 million, due soon after the report was distributed. In the note, the company added that it did not believe that it would be able to borrow sufficient funds to make the payment. The company reported that it suffered from a number of problems. Darling-Delaware produces tallow and bone meal from animal parts. The shipments of animal parts to its processing facilities had slowed, and federal regulators had told the company that it would be responsible for cleaning up some of its waste dumps in which it had deposited unused parts of animals. The company's stockholders are some of the most knowledgeable people in business. The *Wall Street Journal* said that they included, for example, the Bass family of Texas, Richard Rainwater, Edward W. Rose, Jr., and the Airlie Group of Greenwich, Connecticut. The debt instruments, however, were widely distributed to numerous investors by Drexel, Burnham Lambert, whose former employee was a main owner of Airlie Group. Twenty months before declaring that they could not meet their interest payment, the investors had voted themselves a dividend of $179 million.[22]

The privileges of incorporation did not develop without considerable debate and struggle in the political sphere. While interest in incorporation protections has a long history, with the advent of the industrial revolution, interest became more pronounced, especially in England. The parliamentary debates were lengthy, heated, and rancorous.[23] They were debates about the public interest. People opposed to granting privileges of incorporation argued that corporations with limited liability could not be trusted to operate in the public's interest, that they would allow the accumulation of wealth without risk, and that the incorporators intended no one's interests except their own. The people in favor of granting privileges of incorporation argued that it was necessary to grant the privilege of limited liability because without it business would not develop and the country would lose to foreign companies.

In the earliest debates, the people opposed to granting incorporation privileges were politically victorious. As business interests grew and exerted increasing power over the political process, however, those opposed were finally worn down, and the privileges of incorporation were granted. Even then, they came gradually. Ironically, they were first granted only to charitable organizations. The idea had taken root, though, and after a time the privileges of incorporation were granted to businesses also.

When we hear people argue that government should remove itself from involvement in business, we should remember that the power and privilege of incorporation is a result of government involvement in business. Without the governmentally granted protections of incorporation, the investors in the Darling-Delaware Company would be forced to use their own obviously considerable resources to make sure the contracted interest payments on debt were made.

The End of Capitalism

The development of the widespread use of incorporation may mark the beginning of the end of capitalism. Many of those who most adamantly opposed allowing government to grant the privileges of incorporation also advocated capitalism. Insofar as capitalism calls for a business sector which is forced to respond to the needs and interests of consumers and insofar as incorporation grants insulation from the vagaries of the marketplace, the privileges of incorporation and capitalism are in conflict. Adam Smith recognized the conflict, and he threw his considerable weight on the side of those opposed to what were then called joint-stock companies. Since Smith's position on this issue has not been addressed in capitalist literature and since it may come as a surprise to many people, it bears direct quotation at some length:

> It is to prevent this reduction of price, and consequently of wages and profit, by restraining that free competition which would most certainly occasion it, that all corporations, and the greater part of corporation laws, have been established. . . .
>
> . . . The pretence that corporations are necessary for the better government of trade, is without any foundation. Corporation laws, however, give less obstruction to the free circulation of stock from one place to another than to that of labour. . . .
>
> Joint stock companies . . . differ in several respects . . . from private copartneries.
>
> First, in a private copartnery, no partner, without the consent of the company, can transfer his share to another person, or introduce a new member to the company. . . . In a joint stock company, on the contrary,

no member can demand payment of his share from the company; but each member can, without their consent, transfer his share to another person. . . .

Secondly, in a private copartnery, each partner is bound for the debts contracted by the company to the whole extent of his fortune. In a joint stock company, on the contrary, each partner is bound only to the extent of his share. . . .

The trade of a joint stock company is always managed by a court of directors. The court, indeed, is frequently subject, in many respects, to the control of a general court of proprietors. But the greater part of those proprietors seldom pretend to understand anything of the business of the company. . . . This total exemption from trouble and from risk, beyond a limited sum, encourages many people to become adventurers in joint stock companies, who would upon no account hazard their fortunes in any private copartnery. . . . The directors of such companies, however, being the managers rather of other people's money than of their own, it cannot well be expected, that they should watch over it with the same anxious vigilance with which the partners in a private copartnery watch over their own. . . . Negligence and profusion, therefore, must always prevail, more or less, in the management of the affairs of such a company.[24]

If the last paragraph has a particularly modern ring to it, that is a result of the power of Smith's mind and his willingness to follow the lead of logical reasoning. He recognized the threat that incorporation posed to capitalism, and he tried to prevent it. His efforts were to no avail. The business interests in England had too much political power, and they gained the fruits of that privilege by being granted the power of incorporation.

In the modern world, the fact of incorporation is taken so much as a given that people forget that incorporation is a gift of government, granted to organizations to protect their investors and to insulate them from the demands of the market. Smith had advocated just that exposure to demands in order to make firms responsive to market forces. The granting of incorporation privileges is not a simple binary matter like determining whether or not a light is on. Incorporation laws are complex, detailed, and usually extensive. They grant legal rights and privileges to the owners and managers. They are the subject of specific actions of government agencies. They are also subject to revision and change. In the United States, various states competed with each other to see which could legislate incorporation provisions which gave the greatest advantage to investors. Delaware finally won that interstate competition. As a consequence, many major corporations are incorporated in Delaware. Delaware does not even require a corporation to which it grants a charter to do any of its business in the state of Delaware.

In the late 1980s, when managers of corporations were threatened by specialists in takeovers who wished to force managers to run their corporations more in the interest of the investors, managers looked to the state governments to help them develop legislative devices to prevent the investors from pressuring management. What had been a privilege for investors became a privilege for managers.

Smith saw the implications of incorporation privileges when he said that managers of other people's money would not give the same attention to those interests that they would give to their own and that negligence and profusion would come to dominate the operations of managers. One of the charges of the much maligned "corporate raiders" was that the managements had become lazy and careless. If the raiders took over, they said, they would run the companies more efficiently.[25]

It is important to note, however, that the privileges of incorporation played an important role in the development of many economies. They not only protected investors from potentially large liabilities but also allowed the accumulation of capital. Such accumulation was necessary for the development of the corporation's capacity for capital-intensive manufacturing. The corporation which is allowed to accumulate significant amounts of capital has two advantages. In the first place, if the accumulated capital is not economically necessary to meet competition, the corporation can use the capital base as a way of enhancing its competitive position. For example, it could consciously underprice a product, hoping to recoup a temporary loss when the competition folded. In that way, the corporation gains substantial protection from the marketplace. In the second place, if large amounts of capital are necessary for manufacturing a product, then because an accumulation of capital is necessary, the freedom of competitive entrance into the market is restricted. In short, incorporation helps retard rapid exit from a market, and it helps prevent the entrance of competition. Both conditions may have been critical to the development of economies, but they are inconsistent with capitalism.

The argument presented here does not say that the licensing of physicians, the existence of patent, copyright, or trademark policies, and the granting of the privileges of incorporation by the government are wrong or inappropriate. Rather, the argument is that such conditions violate the fundamental principles of capitalism. With the development and spread of incorporation privileges, capitalism was undermined, as Smith had recognized. Ironically, then, the end of capitalism was under way just as Smith was articulating its principles.

Peter Berger: Contemporary Capitalist Ideologist

Another irony can be noted before we turn to the next chapter on socialism and Marxism. In a recent defense of capitalism as an ideology, Peter Berger briefly refers to corporations:

> Closely linked to [the expansion of the middle class] has been the rise of the corporation as a new and immensely important form of economic organization. This, of course, has greatly encouraged the growth of bureaucracy, with all its social and social-psychological consequences, at the very center of industrial capitalism. But it has also meant a separation of property, in the legal sense, from effective economic control. . . . Many non-Marxists have maintained that this change has brought about a fundamental transformation of the class system. This, in all likelihood, is an exaggeration.[26]

Interestingly, Berger recognizes the importance of the development of the corporation and some of the impact that Smith predicted over two centuries ago. He does not think that the changes are fundamental to capitalism, however, and he never returns to the topic in his book. While, for the sake of argument, we might grant his contention that the impact of the development of the corporate structure may be insignificant from the perspective of an analyst of class, in this book we seek a conceptual base for capitalism. The rise and dominance of the corporate structure in so-called capitalist countries has undermined the conceptual fundamentals of capitalism.

Actually, Berger thinks that the development of the corporation has posed more problems for Marxism than for capitalism. He says: "Since Marxists have always placed great stress on property (necessarily so, since their entire view of capitalist society and its alleged evils is based on a theory of property and expropriation), this change has produced endless problems for them." In a note to this passage, Berger goes on to say: "It is curious that Marx believed that the emergence of 'joint-stock companies' (the British term for corporations) meant a positive progression from private to collective ownership, a sort of herald of socialism, while the corporation today is the bête noire of most Marxist analyses of 'monopoly capitalism.' "[27] I can find no passages in Marx which would support Berger's claim in the note. Marx did not spend much time discussing joint-stock companies and, as far as I can tell, never addressed the issue of incorporation. That should not surprise us, for as Friedrich Engels said in an endnote to the third volume of *Das Kapital,* "In 1865 [when Marx wrote the notes on which Engels constructed the third volume], the stock exchange was still a *secondary* element in the capitalist system. Government bonds represented the bulk of exchange securities."[28] Engels goes on to point out that at that time the joint-stock companies were basically insignificant to the overall economy. That view closely matches Alfred Chandler's view of the historical development of business, and it may only increase our admiration for Adam Smith's prescience.[29]

Marx does refer to joint-stock companies briefly in the second volume of

Das Kapital, especially in part 2, where he discusses the "turnover of capital." Marx's references are rather benign and, given his ability to rise to rhetorical heights, that may constitute a rather reserved judgment, but it does not constitute an argument for the companies as a positive progression. We are probably safe in accepting Engels' assessment that joint-stock companies simply were not economically important at the time Marx was writing. Given the importance even Engels believed they gained, that was not a particularly complimentary comment for Engels to have made about Marx, who, above all, wanted to be a scientist and to predict the future.

In some of his emendations to volume 3, Engels himself made the most extended comments on joint-stock companies. He accused them of engendering monopolies and of promoting managerial parasites: "Thus, in this branch, which forms the basis of the whole chemical industry, competition has been replaced by monopoly in England. . . . It reproduces a new financial aristocracy, a new variety of parasites in the shape of promoters, speculators and simply nominal directors; a whole system of swindling and cheating by means of corporation promotion, stock issuance, and stock speculation." [30] In the endnote, his analysis is even more trenchant:

> But with this accumulation, the number of rentiers, people who were fed up with the regular tension in business and therefore wanted merely to amuse themselves or to follow a mild pursuit as directors or governors of companies, also rose. And . . . in order to facilitate the investment of this mass floating around as money-capital, new legal forms of limited liability companies were established wherever that had not yet been done and the liability of the shareholder, formerly unlimited, was also reduced more or less. . . . The ordinary individual firm is more and more only a preliminary stage to bring the business to the point where it is big enough to be "founded." [31]

Thus, both Marx and Engels asserted that the development of stock companies was a stage in the development of capitalism, but their comments cannot be said to have been positive.

Conclusion

Let us conclude, then, by reiterating that the fundamental principles of capitalism are the demands of the notions that consumer is king and the fittest survive. Any interference in the natural operations of the economy will produce disadvantages to consumers (i.e., everyone). The economy is imagined to consist of numerous atomic economic units, none able to control markets and all subject immediately to the needs, desires, and interests of consumers. The capitalist economy operates of consumers. Through the presence and absence of purchases, the capitalist economy is ultimately operated by consumers, and given the deterministic situation of the economy, it can be reasonably said to operate for consumers. Consumers equal people. Thus, Lincoln's formula applies to capitalism.

The economy of the United States, however, simply does not correspond in a significant way to the fundamental concepts of capitalism. Symptomatically, that may be no more clear than in the fact that a consumer movement has grown in the United States, and it has grown without much managerial talent guiding it. If the United States economy were really capitalist, there should be no consumer movement at all. Capitalism is consumerism. Capitalism was designed to cause rapid reaction to consumer needs, interests, and desires.

The granting of incorporation privileges dramatically changed the rapidity of that response. Incorporation also allowed businesses to gain political power far beyond that which could have been gained by an individual or a partnership. The advantages created by incorporation were followed by numerous other devices, through which government intervened in the economy to the advantage of businesses. It should not be forgotten, however, that the privilege of incorporation alone made an enormous contribution to and change in the nature of the economy. When the Exxon Corporation's tanker *Valdez* struck a reef in Alaska, some question arose about which party had more power. At the time, on any reasonable economic analysis, the Exxon Corporation was bigger and more powerful than the state of Alaska. In fact, if we were to use annual sales as an analogy to GDP, the Exxon Corporation would be among the top two dozen countries in the world. The chief executive officer of Exxon probably has more discretion in the allocation of resources than most national leaders. That discretion and power comes in large measure from incorporation privileges and other beneficial forms of government involvement. When we hear an advocate for the business sector decry "government involvement in business affairs," we can safely translate that to mean "government involvement which I do not like." Almost surely, the advocate does not really want the government to abandon all significant involvement in business, for most businesses enjoy government involvement which is advantageous to them. If Smith is right, those advantages come at the expense of consumers. To be evenhanded, we should also mention that most businesses suffer from some government involvement which executives do not like. Again, if Smith is right, that also disadvantages consumers.

In the United States during the 1980s, one of the business groups most vocal in complaining about government involvement in business was the banking and financial community, and it was successful in pushing back government regulation while securing greater government support. At the same time that federal guarantees of the downside risks of depositors increased, the downside risks of investors remained protected. Through it all, executives were freed from prior restrictions, and they used that freedom to mismanage many financial institutions. The cost to taxpayers (not, we should note, depositors, lenders, or investors) is estimated to top a half trillion dollars, and much of it may be responsible for the recession of the early 1990s.[32]

The list of the examples of government support for business at the federal, state, and local levels is so long that it makes no more sense to detail it than it would to detail the numerous ways government detracts from business discretion. The point is not to criticize involvement on a wholesale basis. Surely by this time in history, such criticism cannot be wholesale. Few people would argue for dismantling the whole apparatus and returning to capitalist ideals. Some government intervention is probably wise and sensible; some intervention is probably foolish and counterproductive.

The fundamental warrant of capitalism, however, was not efficiency but morality. It promised a society of the consumer, by the consumer, and for the consumer, and since we are all consumers, it promised a society responsive to us. That is gone now, and whatever has replaced it does not have an articulated justification.

4 Organicism Applied
Socialism and Marxism

Both intellectually and chronologically, socialism began as a reaction to capitalism.[1] The reaction was both to the theories of capitalism and to the realities for which the socialists held capitalism responsible. No figure gained as much importance in these debates as Karl Marx. In a sense, Marx was the center to which all previous socialism was headed and from which all later socialism might emerge. While we could imagine a modern socialist ignoring almost any other single predecessor, it is almost inconceivable to imagine, even 150 years later, that someone interested in socialism would be ignorant of Marx. An understanding of Marx will guide us to understanding the fundamentals of socialism. Thus, the chapter is structured around the thought of Marx. Other forms of socialism are discussed, but Marx is the main vehicle for understanding the strengths of socialism as well as its limitations.

Marx is also a pivotal figure in much thought beyond economics and ideology. His works do not make easy reading, and they are grounded in his own experiences, both intellectual and practical. They are, however, conceptually rich and strong in their arguments. While some commentators, especially self-proclaimed Marxists, tend to treat Marx's writings in the tradition of biblical inquiry, allowing only minor questions and criticism, such an approach is not consistent with his life, spirit, and philosophy. Marx did write in an authoritative style, which he acquired from Hegel. Too often, however, supporters and detractors alike treat his style as if it were authoritarian. In addition, unfortunately, some of his disciples think they and their followers must learn to repeat the tenets of Marxism as if it were a catechism. Marx was a complicated thinker, however, and the complications are worth understanding.

According to legend, someone once confronted John Maynard Keynes, accusing him of inconsistency in some of his opinions. It is said that Keynes retorted, "When I find evidence or arguments that show my previous position to be wrong, I change my mind. What do you do?" Much the same story could have been told of Marx. Even within his magnum opus, *Das Kapital,* Marx makes substantial changes in his analysis as the three volumes proceed, and those changes are not trivial.

Here we should also say something about the terms *socialism* and *communism.* Some commentators attempt to make a distinction between them, but collectively the commentators do not agree on the elements of the distinction. Early in his political writings, Marx made a distinction relating to social developmental phases, but use of the term *communism* diminished as Marx's writings proceeded. By the end it hardly appeared at all, having been almost entirely replaced by *socialism.* By and large, throughout this chapter the terms will be used interchangeably.[2]

Utopian Socialism

The first examples of socialist thought came from what Marx and Engels would later refer to pejoratively as utopian socialism. The utopian socialists imagined a society based on cooperation, not competition. They believed that society should be sure everyone had the necessities of life. They thought that, like a united family, society should satisfy at least the minimal needs of its members. They believed that provisions should be made even for members of the family who were not able to meet the competition or to contribute as much as their needs demanded. Since the socialists were influenced by ideals of times other than our own, it may be useful to take an example from an earlier agrarian context to illustrate their point.

Imagine a family living on a farm. The healthy and able-bodied members are expected to contribute to the work of the farm in order to aid the family. If any of the members of the family should become sick, the rest of the family would take over the person's tasks in order to keep the family and the farm functioning. It would be the height of cruelty to force members of the family to compete with one another and then when some became sick to refuse to give them any help.

In understanding socialism, the analogy to the family is an appropriate one. The utopian socialists believed that a familylike relationship could exist among people of a society even though the members might not be relatives. Many of the utopian socialists put their sincere beliefs into practice: they wrote in detail about communities in which to carry out the principles of cooperation and also created such communities. In the early 1800s the United States alone had almost two hundred utopian socialist communities.

The organic aspect of utopian socialism springs from its base in the interest in the family. As we saw in chapter 2, some people think of the family as an example of a social organization which may not be entirely understandable if the analysis is confined to each of the constituent members. The family, it is thought, is something more than the mere aggregation of its members. When that view is transported to a larger social level, it is said that society—whether a small community or a country—is not merely the summation of its present members. The socialist would argue that a society has a destiny which is beyond the destiny of the individual members or even their aggregated destinies.

The notion of supraindividuality may be shown more persuasively if one looks at the difference in the "time horizon" of the individual citizens as distinct from the society itself. Presumably a country, like a corporation, is expected to have an endless life. Each individual will live for only a small portion of the life of the country. The interests of the society itself extend over a much longer term and are grander than the interests of individual members. The utopian socialists believed that if we were all confined to being atomistic seekers of our self-interests, always in competition with each other, then the larger interests of society would not be addressed. Recalling that the nature of the capitalist society forced us to engage in short-term selfish behavior, the socialists believed that it would be senseless to appeal to a more beneficent side of our nature. From their perspective, appropriate changes could be made only by a radical transformation of the conditions of society itself. They believed that transformation should enable us to construct a society based on the cooperation of its members rather than constant competition. They believed that such cooperation would help society realize its best end overall.

Utopian socialists produced extensive literature about how the socialist community will operate when it takes over from capitalism. The literature is also clear about the problems with capitalism. It is not clear, however, about how a society might move from its capitalist condition to a socialist condition. Marx sought to fill that vacuum, and the combination of his intellect and his rhetorical skills suited him well for the task.

Marx

Several facts about Marx's life are not often noted but are worthy of mention because they help us understand the brilliance of the man and his important contributions to the development of ideology in the last half of the nineteenth century and the bulk of the twentieth.

Marx started his university career as a lawyer. While the law is not taught in continental Europe in the "paper chase" fashion popular in the United States, nevertheless all lawyers learn early that it is important to attempt to get an argument structured on grounds favorable to their case. Attempting to structure an argument means controlling both the language of the argument (the terms used) and the direction of the argument (what counts as appropriate premises, as appropriate evidence, and appropriate argument form). We could make an analogy here to the control of a committee meeting. In many cases, the party which controls the agenda and the rules of procedure effectively controls the outcome. If all parties to the debate can agree to your conditions and if you are clever enough in constructing those procedures, you stand a much greater chance of having your side "win" than if someone else sets the conditions. Successful lawyers are at least equally attentive to (supposedly neutral) procedural conditions as they are to the substance of the case.

From the law, Marx shifted to philosophy, a discipline also much concerned with language and the progress of argumentation. In the United States, some people say that a major in philosophy is the best preparation for law school and for the practice of law. The current Law School Admission Test, which is required by the most prestigious law schools, has three parts: reading comprehension, logical reasoning, and logical games. The latter two sections are taken directly from logic, one of the most important parts of philosophy. Like lawyers, philosophers soon learn that terminology is important in the advancement of argument and that the structure of the argument is crucial.

Marx's first and only persistent career was as a journalist. Apparently he was so successful at journalism that he moved rapidly from being what today we would call a stringer to the position of editor of *Rheinische Zeitung*. Like lawyers and philosophers, journalists learn to be sensitive to language and to the development of argumentation. The purpose of sensitivity to language for journalists, however, is communication. In the process of uncovering complex and sophisticated attempts to miscommunicate by the people they cover, journalists learn about the importance of terms and the progress of argumentation. Thus, Marx's argumentative, communicative, and rhetorical skills were well honed, and he could put them to good use in presenting the case for socialism and communism.

Another aspect of Marx's early intellectual development is important, though also often overlooked. Marx's doctoral dissertation examined the natural philosophy of Democritus and Epicurus. By the time Marx wrote his dissertation, he was deeply influenced by Hegelian philosophy, having rejected the attempts of Kant to synthesize the rationalistic approach with the undeniably successful developments in empirically based natural philosophy after Newton and his successors. Hegel is an extreme example of an organicist: his philosophy discounts the importance of the development of atomistic science. Nevertheless, Democritus and Epicurus are two classical archetypal forbears of atomism both on a physical and a social scale. Thus, Marx understood well the allure of atomism, and he rejected it in favor of an organic approach.

With this background in mind, we are now ready to move on to an understanding of socialism and the rhetorical power it gained under Marx. Early on, Marx's fundamental debating strategy was to establish that only two mutually exclusive possibilities for industrialized society existed: communism and capitalism. We shall see that Marx made distinctions among varieties of socialism, but he contended that all varieties but communism were essentially bankrupt, however well meaning. Thus, from his perspective, communism was the only ideology worthy of consideration.

He basically argued that an objective reading of history reveals that it has been made up of class struggles. He asserted that class struggles in the industrialized world had developed into a class struggle between the wealthy capitalist and the impoverished working poor. Marx said that the capitalist puts capital to work in the marketplace in order to accumulate more capital. At the same time, workers have no choice but to sell their labor in order to make enough to survive in the world created by the capitalists. Marx argued that capitalists make their money by exploiting their positions as owners of private property and by controlling the production process.

Labor Theory of Value

In the last chapter we saw that Smith held what is called a labor theory of value but that he did not take it as a fundamental condition of capitalism. Because of Smith's attitude toward the labor theory of value, we left the subject unexplored there. We cannot slight it any longer, because, unlike Smith, Marx embraced the labor theory of value and argued that everything had value only in regard to the amount of labor which went into its production. Thus, Marx accepted both Locke's labor theory and the importance Locke attached to it. Marx argued that the capitalist attempted to sell a product at a price greater than that paid the laborer. That meant the worker's labor was undervalued in wages, for if the capitalist paid workers their actual worth, then the capitalist would have nothing left over with which to make profits.

For the sake of clarity, let us consider an easy illustration. Consider the production of a cotton sweater. In order to keep the analysis simple, assume a capitalist owns the farm, the seed, and all necessary tools and equipment. The cotton seeds have no value on their own. They are given value only because someone whom the capitalist hires plants them and nurtures them into a productive cotton plant. Again, the raw cotton on the plant has no value on its own. It gains value in the labor that someone whom the capitalist hires puts into transforming the raw cotton into thread. We can proceed similarly with the cotton thread until it is made into yarn and, once again, with the yarn until it is knit into a sweater. It makes no difference that at any point in the process the cotton could have been sold, to be completed by someone else's labor. The same principle would hold true: the value of the product equals the total amount of labor put into the product itself. Marx argued that the capitalist adds nothing of value and thus is not entitled to anything when the sweater is sold. Marx saw, however, that this ideal is not borne out in reality. Capitalists do receive something when they sell the cotton sweater. In fact, Marx suggested they receive a great deal.

Private Property

Marx asked how the case just described could come about. His answer directly approached the question of private property. Marx said that the capitalist, using the state, asserted hegemony over land, tools, equipment, and so on. Marx believed that that hegemony kept workers dependent upon capitalists. Marx argued that the difference between what capitalists charged and what they paid workers constituted a surplus value, which the capitalists in turn pocketed. That difference, said Marx, actually belonged to the workers, not to the capitalists, for the simple reason that capitalists could not increase the value of any product, because they put no labor into it. Thus, the Marxist view is that through the institution of private property, capitalists make money without working and accumulate that money to be used to extend their hegemony over more workers.[3] In that manner, they are able to increase their wealth. This wealth, Marx argued, actually belongs to the workers. It has been stolen by the capitalists for their own advantage.

It is important to recognize that in the example chosen, the farm is the private property of the capitalist only because the state has agreed to treat it that way.[4] Marx argued that nothing in nature or in the natural environment makes land the property of anyone.[5] The person who asserts ownership of land can back up that assertion only by getting the state to acknowledge that ownership. Marx said that capitalists controlled the activities of the state in order to insure their positions of ownership. That meant they kept their positions of control and, thus, their ability to reap the illegitimately derived profits.

The example of the cotton sweater may be a little distracting, because it does not relate directly to the industrial revolution, which by Marx's time had gained ascendancy. Marx argued, however, that the industrial revolution served to exaggerate the conditions outlined. He believed the industrial revolution did provide advantages of mass production. He was in no regard calling for a return to an agrarian economy as some of the other socialists seemed to be. Marx argued that the advantages of the industrial revolution accrued primarily to the benefit of the capitalist. After the industrial revolution, instead of owning a farm on which labor would be put into some identifiable product, the capitalist owned a factory and supplied the equipment, the inventory, and the eventual means for distribution. In that manner, workers became increasingly alienated from the results of their work.[6] They could have no identity with the final product because it was entirely removed from them. Consequently, workers were even less aware of the capitalist's appropriation of the value of their labor than they might have been otherwise. For Marx, however, the principle remained the same: the worker is the only person in the process who adds value. The capitalist simply takes advantage of a state-authorized position as owner of the business. We should note, in addition, that ownership of a business is an even greater abstraction than ownership of land.

Marx argued that in comparing the need for supervisors (i.e., extractors of surplus value) in manufacturing and agrarian economies, there is little need for a multitude of capitalists, because one capitalist supervising business could be responsible for much more wealth than the supervision of land would allow. Mass production meant that supervision could be maintained over much more production, which in turn meant more appropriated value. The worker who had nothing other than labor to sell would be forced to compete for employment with other workers, and that competition would, as Smith had shown, drive down the wages of labor. Marx argued that reducing the wages of labor provided even greater profits for the capitalist.

Thus, the labor theory of value was a linchpin for Marx's argument. Factories have no value apart from the labor which goes into constructing them. Machinery has no value apart from the value which goes into manufacturing it. The workers in the factory added their labor value to the implicit labor value in the machines, in the factory, in the partially manufactured inventory, and so on, to give new labor-based value to the product. The capitalist, enjoying a position granted by virtue of abstract rights of property ownership enforced by the state, charged full price for the product and only returned what was necessary to pay the workers. When they were fortunate enough to work, the workers did so at wage levels only supporting bare subsistence. The capitalist pocketed the difference as profit. In addition, Marx argued that in order to make the whole system work and yield attractive profits to the capitalist, there would have to be a reserve army of unemployed. This vast group of people would be out of work and ready to take on any job immediately. In the face of that potential, the individual worker would have to relent to the demands and avaricious penuriousness of the capitalist and would accept employment at rock-bottom wages.

There may be some skepticism about Marx's view that ownership of land is an abstraction, because land is in one sense tangible. Ownership becomes even more removed from tangible reality, however, when we consider ownership of a business. It is hard to imagine what, apart from legalisms, it could possibly mean to say that someone owns a business. Surely a business is not equivalent to its physical property. Some businesses do not own any physical facilities. All one can point to is some kind of documentation, but that documentation is meaningless apart from the willingness of the state to acknowledge it as a claim to something.

Return to our cotton sweater and consider it by contrast. Suppose that a man grows cotton on his land (or even, with proper permission, on state-owned land) and works the cotton so that it becomes cotton thread and then cotton yarn. Finally he knits it into a sweater. When he says that he owns the sweater, he means that there is a tangible physical object which he owns and which is reasonably said to be his. The state might back up his right to use the sweater as he sees fit as long as he does not violate the law with it. The role of the state, then, is merely to uphold what is already real.

What does it mean, however, to say that people, called stockholders, own a corporation? Stockholders do not have a legitimate claim to the corporation's supplies or equipment. The stockholders cannot go to a local facility and demand something tangible in return for their ownership. Their ownership of the company is a pure abstraction. It is a claim created by the state. It is not a claim merely supported by the state. Presumably, the stockholders have a claim to a portion of a future stream of earnings. Marx would say they have a claim to the surplus value which will be gained because the corporation, which the stockholders own, will not pay the workers full value for their labor. While Marx did not anticipate the development of corporations, the example is used to drive home to modern readers what Marx meant when he found private property to be a mere abstraction created, supported, and guaranteed by the state.

Furthermore, Marx would have reminded us that this same state, which is politically dominated by the capitalists who benefit from its activities, guarantees the capitalists' hegemony over the workers. Thus, the circulation, to use a Marxian term, is complete.[7] The capitalists control the political and social processes which grant them what they call their economic rights. Those economic rights are then converted into wealth for the capitalists, and they use that wealth to enforce and insure their control over the political process.

Finally, Marx believed that the industrial revolution added another element to the economic, political, and social scene. As the capitalist economy developed, it would be subjected to cycles and swings. The elements of a cyclical theory of economics had already been developed by two capitalist economists who followed Smith and developed capitalism further, Thomas Robert Malthus and David Ricardo. Marx argued that the economic swings would put more capitalists out of business and into the working class. The wealthiest capitalists could survive the downturns and take advantage of their less fortunate capitalist kin by buying them out at low prices.[8]

Revolution

Marx argued that as the production processes became increasingly complex, a well-organized labor force would be necessary. Thus, while the capitalist class would grow smaller and smaller, the working class, supplemented by those forcibly unemployed, would grow larger and more organized. Marx believed that the latter would soon recognize their common, organically related exploited condition, and they would rise up to overthrow the capitalists. Marx believed that the revolution would start in the most advanced capitalist countries of Europe, because that was where the conditions for the proletariat would be worst and where the workers would be most organized. He argued that once the revolution started, it would sweep through Europe like a prairie fire, destroying all capitalist economies in its path. Not only the capitalist economies but also the social and political superstructures necessary for maintaining the capitalist economies would be overthrown. The state would lose its purpose and disappear. Marx believed that the capitalists could do nothing to stop this process. It was inevitable. He argued that in spite of their control of local politics, the capitalists would be unsuccessful in preventing an international revolution.

Thus, the primary criticism by the socialist of capitalism has involved the notion of private property. The socialist sees capitalism committing its most egregious excesses through the state support of private property. The socialist attack was a forceful one, because it claimed that the horrors of the prevailing economic conditions in western Europe (especially) and the United States (less forcefully) were caused by greedy and inhumane people who clung to their property rights without concern for the welfare of other people.

Some Historical and Analytic Observations

The socialists had plenty of grist for their mills. There can be little doubt that laboring conditions in England, France, and Germany in the mid–nineteenth century were awful. Work days averaged sixteen to eighteen hours with no time off. Child labor was common: children less than ten years old were frequently employed in squalid conditions and subjected regularly to whippings, starvation, sexual assaults, unheated factories, and performing the most degrading tasks. Numerous fictional and historical accounts of the time give strong testimony to the deplorable conditions. Robert Heilbroner has described the situation of men and women working together in coal mines most forcefully: they were "Stripped to the waist, and sometimes reduced from pure fatigue to a whimpering state . . . [their] sexual appetites aroused at a glance were gratified down some deserted shaftway; children of seven or ten who never saw daylight during winter months were used and abused and paid a pittance and . . . pregnant women drew coal cars like horses and even gave birth in dark black caverns." [9] Whole cities were constructed so that wealthy ladies and gentlemen would not be repulsed by the sight of what was happening. They wanted to go about their genteel lives ignoring the disgusting conditions, but of course they were fully dependent upon the extraordinarily hard labor of many people under extremely adverse conditions. The socialists would declare: "Under capitalism, those who do the least get the most, and those who do the most get the least." They argued that capitalism was the only alternative to socialism, so they successfully assigned responsibility for the appalling labor conditions to capitalism. In addition, as they developed their argument, private property was specifically to blame for the conditions.

We have, then, an outline of the course of Marx's argument as he condemned the capitalists and capitalism. It is time, now, to draw attention to several points of the argument. First, there is an interesting terminological issue. Adam Smith, the person we acknowledge today as the founding architect of capitalism, did not use that term, nor did he use the term *capitalist*. Marx and the socialists initiated and promoted the use of those terms and their derivatives.[10] Smith did not label his position, but it is clear that he did not see it as a system for promoting the interests of business owners or their associates. We have already seen that Smith could be very severe in his criticism of the business community. Smith's system was designed with the consumer uppermost in his mind, not the group of people Marx called the capitalists.

Second, it is important to draw attention to Marx's argument about private property. As indicated earlier, lawyers and philosophers know that it is wise to construct arguments not on the grounds the opponents would like but on grounds more tangential to the opponents' argument. It may be clear now why I devoted so many paragraphs to the argument about private property in the previous chapter. While Smith and the other ideologists who would support what Marx called capitalism would favor private property, that was not a fundamental premise for Smith's ideology and thus is not fundamental to capitalism. Furthermore, in the rigorous mathematical expression of capitalism, the concept of private property is not needed for the equations, and it is the broader ideological defenses of capitalism which insist on the concept of private property as a central part of capitalism. Marx and the socialists took that condition which is not fundamental for capitalism and reconstructed capitalism so that private property became an essential axiom. They were so successful in this ruse that they even persuaded apologists for capitalism to accept private property as a sine qua non for capitalism. Having succeeded at this clever rhetorical tactic, the socialists then severely criticized capitalists for espousing private property as fundamental to their view of economics!

Third, Marx constructed the argument as a bifurcation. Marx argued that one had to be either a capitalist or a socialist. From his perspective, no other alternatives could exist in an industrialized society. In examining the notion of the bifurcation fallacy at the end of chapter 2, we saw that such bifurcating is also a useful rhetorical tactic. If the proponent can convince the audience that something is wrong with the other side, then the audience must adopt the proponent's side. Thus, Marx left himself with the much easier task of arguing against capitalism rather than the much more difficult task of describing and arguing for socialism. The negative task was easier, because he had only to convince the audience of flaws in capitalism. As could be observed throughout Europe, they were numerous. Through this rhetorical device, Marx did not have to present his socialist alternative with precision or in complete detail. Thus, he evaded defeat of his perspective by evading constructive commitments and by staying primarily with the negative. In the next section we will explore some ramifications of this last point.

The true rhetorical victory for lawyers and philosophers comes not just when they get to present their points of view, but when all parties to the debate agree to use their forms of argumentation and their terms in further discussions. Marx accomplished that victory. What is surprising is not that Marx labeled Smith's economic system as capitalism and its primary actors as capitalists but that the defenders of Smith's ideology have accepted that designation. They call themselves capitalists and the system they support capitalism. Thus, the terminology, which Marx used quite consciously because of its pejorative overtones, has been accepted by both sides in the debate. As a result, it made sense to use the word *capitalism* in the title of the third chapter and, indeed, throughout the book. While we saw that the word *consumer* does not reach as far back as Adam Smith, a more accurate, positive name for the real ideology called capitalism would be consumerism.[11] Admittedly, that term has been taken over by others recently and has achieved an almost anticapitalist overtone, but the opportunity was there for the defenders of capitalism earlier. They accepted Marx's term, however, which meant that many people would be left with the impression that capitalism is an economic ideology designed to support wealthy owners of the major means of production. As Adam Smith himself pointed out, these constitute a small and, typically, an undistinguished group. In addition, many ideological defenders of capitalism simply accepted Marx's notion that private property was a central defining condition for capitalism, if not the only one. Thus, capitalist ideology was left in a position of becoming little more than an apologetics for people who benefited from owning property and from playing the financial markets.

Finally, the defenders of capitalism accepted Marx's clever bifurcation. They then became defensive about many aspects of so-called capitalist economies such as the atrocities already identified, the fact that economies will probably always have some level of (hidden or explicit) structural unemployment, and the fact that points of disequilibrium will always be exploited by clever people. The acquiescence in the bifurcation has led to all sorts of intellectual mischief in so-called capitalist countries, and the self-identified defenders of capitalism have often seen every change which might help alleviate suffering as examples of developing socialism. Social Security, the New Deal, the welfare state, unionization, graduated income taxes, elimination of racial, religious, and gender prejudice, minimum wage policies, old age health policies, environmental protection policies, and affirmative action are all denounced by the self-proclaimed defenders of capitalism as either socialism or creeping socialism. Their argument yields the central case to Marx and concedes to Marxists the view that only two possibilities exist.

At the same time, the rest of the world concludes that since the capitalists themselves declare these developments as socialist, the capitalists must favor racial, religious, and gender prejudice, no help for old people, no commitment to full employment, short-sighted destruction of the environment, and so on. Is it any wonder that it took the so-called Communist countries so long to throw off the shackles of their dictatorial governments? Is it any wonder that they say that whatever ideological system they adopt in the wake of their overthrow, they will be sure it is "not-capitalist"?

In short, Marx essentially wrote the rules of subsequent ideological debate. Those rules were accepted even by his opponents, and they have dominated discussion for almost 150 years. It is fair to say that as a result of his rhetorical success and the acquiescence of the defenders of what he inappropriately called capitalism, he has dominated intellectual thought about ideology, political philosophy, and political theory throughout that time. It is perhaps only a slight exaggeration to say that with the exception of economists, many intellectuals do not even take capitalism very seriously. For example, the eight-volume *Encyclopedia of Philosophy* has an extensive entry for "socialism" but no entry for "capitalism." [12]

Business boosters in the United States often take such discoveries as evidence that intellectuals are all left of center. Senator Joseph McCarthy made something of a career by playing on his presumption of the socialist and Communist tendencies of intellectuals in the United States. His basic argument was quite simple: The intellectuals he resented were critical of something in the United States. The United States is a capitalist country. Only two possibilities, capitalism and communism, exist. [13] Therefore, McCarthy argued, the intellectuals in question must be socialists, Communists, socialist sympathizers, pinkos, fellow travelers. The first proposition results in an empirical question, asking whether the person is now or ever has been critical of anything in the United States. The next two propositions would have been accepted by Marx, and assuming the empirical premise were true, the conclusion would follow. Thus, McCarthy accepted the entire argument of Marx. [14] Part of the explanation McCarthy sought may lie not in the unpatriotic tendencies of intellectuals, but in the fact that both defenders of socialism and defenders of capitalism—even some of the most trenchant—have accepted Marx's terminology and Marx's formulation of the issues.

In addition, it may be that this acceptance of the terms and conditions for ideological debate is what has caused many economists in the so-called capitalist countries to put as much distance as possible between themselves and ideology. Above all, they want to make progress in discovering economic knowledge. If Marx's approach is to dominate all discussion, they may fear progress will be as unlikely among them as it has been among economists in so-called Communist countries.

Marx and Other Socialists

Another important and remarkable example of Marx's ability to set the conditions of a debate deserves our attention, though this time it was to the disadvantage of his opponents within the socialist movement. While he was a university student and later a fledgling journalist, Marx thoroughly analyzed the socialist movement, especially as it was developing in France and England. Members of that movement criticized the horrors they saw practiced in the industrializing countries, and they argued for an alternative to that economic system. They too fixed on private property as the defining characteristic of what would be called capitalism. They were not without good reason in doing so. In spite of Smith's equivocal endorsement of private property and his scepticism about the validity of the labor theory of value as applicable to anything more than hunting and agrarian economies, both Malthus and Ricardo renewed strong arguments in favor of private property and the labor theory of value. Ricardo's labor theory was more complicated and sophisticated than Marx acknowledged in constructing his own, but the label was the same. In addition, Ricardo had constructed a tight and sophisticated deductive scheme which came to the same kind of pessimistic conclusions that Malthus had found in examining the directions of what would be called capitalism.

Ricardo employed reasoning which is more similar to modern mainstream economics, especially as practiced in the United States and Great Britain, than to the approach of Adam Smith. If the desire among mainstream economists to venerate him were not so strong today, Smith would probably be included among what are derisively called the institutionalists among economists, and Ricardo would be identified as their adam and smith.[15] Smith, a close observer of economic activity and institutions, almost always preceded or immediately followed his theoretical points with specific examples drawn from direct experience and observation.

Curiously, Ricardo was a successful stockbroker before he decided to devote himself to the study of economics, but his economic writings are almost devoid of specific references to actual conditions. They primarily develop deductive conclusions based upon a set of assumptions. The pessimism which comes from his system is exacting, and there is no room for maneuvering. Socialists like Babeuf, Cadet, Godwin, Saint-Simon, Fourier, Owen, and Greely, as well as those involved in the socialist experiments in communities in the United States, disagreed with each other on many accounts, but they all believed that there must be a better way to arrange human affairs. They thought that the pessimism of Malthus and Ricardo, which appeared to be indigenous to what would be called capitalism, should not be accepted without challenge. They imagined other possibilities, and they argued for implementing them. Many of them went ahead and created communities based on their views of alternative possibilities. They had ideals and hopes. They wanted a community or a society worthy of the name. That is why they chose terms like *socialism* and *communism* to describe what they wanted. They saw society as something larger than the selfish striving of individuals who were all trying to get more property than the others and all ready to act to strengthen their positions. They believed that if only people could understand that there was something greater than themselves and could commit themselves to advancing that greatness, the conditions outlined by Malthus and Ricardo would not have to occur. They believed that what stood in the way of the achievement of their goal, more than anything else, was the institution of private property. They argued that the existence of private property in capitalism causes everyone to compete with everyone else.

Suppose, for example, that a man was injured at work. The characteristic reaction of the employer in the 1800s was simply to fire him because he could no longer earn his wages. In those circumstances, the former employee would have only his accumulated savings to fall back on for support until he recovered and found another job. Thus, while healthy and on the job, each person competed with every other person in an attempt to accumulate wealth for protection from disaster. Of course, theory says that such accumulations would be minimal, because workers were paid at minimum wage levels. The socialists argued that if there were no private property—if the community owned everything—then the community could provide for the injured man until he was able to go back to work. The community, they suggested, is larger than any individual and is able to help individuals in difficult times. The community would reasonably expect individuals to contribute to it whenever times were more favorable to them. These socialists went on at great length to describe the operations of the community. In a sense, they were forced to do so, because the deductive powers of Ricardo were so strong that they had to show that an alternative could exist.

Like Brahe and Kepler in a different context, these socialists determined to show on the basis of brute observation that Ricardo was wrong. Thus, their writings are elaborate, and experimentation proved important for them. The perceived need for specification led to numerous disagreements and bickering among the socialists and Communists. While they agreed that private property should be abolished and that the community or the state was more than the accumulated desires of individuals, they agreed on little else. Some insisted on absolute equality in income and jobs. Some argued that payment should be proportional to contribution. Some thought that over time a 100-percent inheritance tax would address the worst aspects. Their proposed structures for governance ranged all the way from strong central control by a single individual through rule by especially qualified people to majoritarian rule. In short, they tended to argue more with each other than they did with the Ricardian economists. Marx saw the dangers in becoming bogged down in the internal fights among the socialists. They were not only dangers to him but also dangers which might prevent socialism from succeeding. Thus, he refused to engage in such irresolvable debates. He would say in his *Theses on Feuerbach* in 1845: "The philosophers have only *interpreted* the world in various ways; the point, however, is to *change* it." [16]

There is, thus, an interesting asymmetry in the history of socialist thought. The democratic and utopian socialists were usually quite thorough and complete with their descriptions of how the socialist state would work, but they did not spend much effort describing how the state was going to move from its present position (whatever that might be) to the socialist one. By contrast, Marx and Engels wrote a great deal about how the breakdown of capitalist society would occur, but they had much less to say about the precise details of a socialist society after the revolution. The asymmetry is understandable, because many of the other socialists were willing to work within prevailing political structures in order to bring about reform, so they concerned themselves less with the transition and more with the ideal society. Marx and Engels saw themselves leading a revolutionary movement, however, and they undoubtedly realized that if they or others in the movement were to be drawn into protracted arguments about the details of its destiny, those debates could confuse and divide the revolutionaries. They would weaken the revolutionary spirit and delay the victory of socialism. Furthermore, Marx and Engels believed that the prevailing political structures could not be used as conduits for the new society, because they believed that the base of all activity, whether religious or political or artistic or social or moral, was economic reality. For them, the political structure and the decision-making process were just an elaborate superstructure created on an economic base. They believed that political decisions were disguised economic decisions.

Marxist thought about future states describes a period known as the dictatorship of the proletariat. From that what is called a classless society would arise. During the dictatorship of the proletariat, the political processes employed (whether democratic or not) would be those useful for continuing the Communist revolution. The overarching goal to which all would be called to contribute was the goal of the eventual revolution. Thus, it is clear that the organic aspects are retained in Marxism. Marx and Engels branded the socialists as utopian, intending both the descriptive and the derogatory connotation of that term. In a sense, non-Marxist socialism has never recovered from Marx's label, and from left and right utopian socialism is still patronized as at best amiable but impotent. Once again, the considerable rhetorical skills of Marx proved successful.

The Marxist bifurcation between communism and capitalism also proved rhetorically successful. Marx had rendered utopian socialism as a nonoption. That left only capitalism and communism. His decision to evade a precise description of socialism in action left a vacuum which would be filled to the advantage of totalitarians like Lenin, Stalin, Mao, and Castro. Marx's gambit was a clever rhetorical maneuver, however, because it enabled him to spend his energies criticizing capitalism and arguing for its overthrow.

Toward the end of his life, Marx increasingly turned to using *socialism* to describe his views. An apocryphal story tells that Marx declared he was not a Marxist. It is difficult to understand all the complexities of that development. From reading the work of one of Marx and Engels' favorite disciples, Eduard Bernstein, some people have concluded that Marx and Engels changed their views and came to believe that the revolution as such was not necessary.[17] It may also be that by the end of his life Marx believed he had so completely dominated and won the debate that he could adopt the broader term, perhaps, again, as a rhetorical maneuver. A multitude of explanations may obtain, and Marx was such a complex thinker that the explanation is likely to be complex. In any event, the more generic *socialism* has come to be the accepted term for the alternative to capitalism.

Marx set the terms of the debate. He defined the terms of the debate, and the debate has gone on through the twentieth century within the rules he set. It should not be surprising, then, that many intellectuals are drawn more to the socialist side than to the capitalist side. After all, a socialist defined *socialism* and *capitalism*.[18]

A Workers' Ideology

Marx accepted the labor theory of value as revived by Malthus and Ricardo. However, he did not accept their support of private property for a functioning economy. Marx stayed closely with the socialists on that score, and in *The Communist Manifesto,* he says: "In this sense the theory of the Communists may be summed up in the single sentence: Abolition of private property."[19]

Again, as a direct result of Marx's rhetorical success, the socialists have been on the rhetorical offensive: always attacking the capitalists for their unseemly greed in possessing property and for their unwillingness to give any more than absolutely necessary in concessions to the improvement of labor conditions.

In addition, the socialists sought the support of the poor and working people. Except for those who through inheritance partake of the wealth of the owners, most people are workers. The business owners, who knew little about and cared even less about the theories of capitalism, were willing to be aligned with capitalism and willing to declare that every social change which is to the advantage of workers is ipso facto anticapitalist (and, remembering the bifurcation, therefore prosocialist).[20] The capitalist economists may have known better, but it is not surprising that with both owners and their hated enemies, the socialists, agreeing that private property was the important issue, the timid economists did not have the power to tell the new emperors about their clothes.

Thus, the socialists established two themes which continue to be central to socialism: the elimination of the social power of private property and the identification of socialism with working people. The elimination of the social effectiveness of private property is important because, in the socialist view, the striving for gain in personal property causes the capitalist society to remain divided and unable to act as an organic unit. If each person in the society is to be encouraged to look out for number one, no one will be looking out for the whole. The socialists thought that if self-aggrandizement did not result in gains in property, then selfish behavior would be minimized. Thus, we find in socialist thought the consistent theme that the state should own the major means of production. The socialists argued that under capitalism, each business owner, striving to maximize profits, must ignore any other issues which would detract from that goal.

We can draw a set of contrasting conclusions at this point: whereas capitalism is an ideology with the interests of the consumers uppermost, socialism is an ideology with the interests of the Workers uppermost.[21] Effectively, however, everyone is both a consumer and a worker. The socialists believed that before they could achieve their ends, substantial structural changes in society would have to occur. Some utopian socialists believed that so-called democratic political structures could be preserved but that their economic structures had to be overhauled entirely. As a consequence, these socialists continued the curious tradition born with capitalism of assuming that economics, politics, and other social issues could be addressed and analyzed in separate categories. The revolutionary socialists, such as Marx and Engels, argued that capitalists would rather fight than switch and that only revolution could engender the necessary changes.

The Communists would never compromise with those currently in power.

They believed that those with power would never yield in any event. The revolution was said to be inevitable. *The Communist Manifesto* is unequivocal:

> In short, the Communists everywhere support every revolutionary movement against the existing social and political order. . . .
>
> The Communists disdain to conceal their views and aims. They openly declare that their ends can be attained only by the forcible overthrow of all existing social relations. Let the ruling classes tremble at a Communist revolution. The proletarians have nothing to lose but their chains. They have a world to win. Working men of all countries, unite![22]

Thus, we have described an ideology which is to be entirely focused on the needs of Workers. Its moral warrant comes from the fact that the People are Workers in an organic sense. They are connected in a unity through time. The socialists believed that if revolutionary efforts meant people had to suffer for future individual workers, that suffering would be acceptable in light of the need to promote a social condition which frees Workers to find meaning and value in their lives. Workers are not just universal over the globe today. They are universal throughout time.[23] One of the persistent failures of capitalism is its inability to deal across a time horizon. Organic ideology, however, can take into account the needs of future generations. The socialists believe that if we can abandon our selfish desire for personal gratification, then we can see ourselves as part of a much larger whole, and we can see the importance of contributing to that whole. The whole to which the socialists refer is the totality of Workers.

Determinism

The revolutionary spirit of communism is undeniable. There is to be no compromising with the ruling classes; there is to be an overthrow of all existing social relations. The Communist revolution is seen as an organic development bigger than any individual or any collection of individuals, and Marx argued that it was inevitable. The inevitability arose from the fact that, as Marx saw it, capitalism was in the last throes of its existence.

Curiously, Marx was not as critical of the owners of businesses as many of the utopian socialists were. Marx had read his Smith, Malthus, and Ricardo, and he understood capitalism. He knew that under capitalism the owners had no discretion over what they were doing, and he recognized that it was inappropriate to blame them for working conditions and foolish to expect them to act differently. He saw that the capitalists were forced to treat workers in increasingly harsh ways in the face of inevitable competition. He believed that those capitalists who wanted to act on humanitarian impulses would soon find their products overpriced, and they would be out of business. Marx argued that the fault lay in the system and that people were locked into the system whether they liked it or not. He believed that there might be some ways to delay the inevitable, but there would be no way to avoid its outcome.

In 1859 Marx summarized the insight which originally led him to his outlook: "In the social production of their life, men enter into definite relations that are indispensable and independent of their will, relations of production which correspond to a definite stage of development of their material productive forces. . . . The mode of production of material life conditions the social, political and intellectual life process in general. It is not the consciousness of men that determines their being, but, on the contrary, their social being that determines their consciousness." [24] Socialist and Marxist determinism is what might be called macrodeterminism, to be contrasted with Smith's microdeterminism. In socialism, the development of society overwhelms any individual differences. Personal discretion does not have much effect on the course of events.

In a startling passage, the great historian of economic thought, Overton Taylor, speculates that it is almost impossible for Americans to understand this view of historical inevitability. He says that for Americans "the future is conceived *not as* a continuing outgrowth from the past, inevitably determined or conditioned by it, but as something to be shaped at will by the collaborative efforts of living, free men all unwedded to and uncontrolled by any compelling historic past." [25] It is hard to agree that Americans are unable to understand a system of macrodeterminism. After all, the doctrine of predestination, which is held by many popular Protestant denominations in America, is a form of macrodeterminism. It says that forces beyond human control determine the course of events and life for humans. That doctrine anthropomorphizes God at the head of the causal chain and may be easier to understand than Marx's materialist and atheistic approach, but the intellectual problems are of the same order of magnitude. Taylor's statement does give support to the view of Marx as a determinist.

The capitalist microdeterminism, by contrast, says that economic laws cause each unit, each atom, to act as it does and that the larger social whole is nothing more than the agglomeration of the actions of each unit. As the quoted passage may suggest to some, Taylor suspects that the American inability to understand macrodeterminism arises from the effect of the Enlightenment and the American presumption that individuals can be free to make a difference in the course of history. That may be, but it would pose a problem for microdeterminism as well as macrodeterminism, and for predestination. And yet determinism, as it shows up in science and in religion, continues to be a part of the beliefs of people in the United States. The problems involved in deciding whether any sense can be made of saying that humans are free are lengthy and stretch back to the beginning of recorded thought. Capitalism and socialism accepted different forms of a negative response to that question.

Concluding Comments on Socialism

Socialists presume that the society at large is greater than the sum of its parts. That concept returns us to Rousseau's distinction between the will of all and the General Will. The only will that can be expressed by individuals when they are expressing their own self-interests is the will of all. Socialists believe that there is a People, which approximates what Rousseau called the General Will. The socialists believe that it is possible to imagine conditions in which the individuals in a society would express interests which, when added together, would still add up to social policies that would not be in the interest of society as a whole. The interests of the individual need to be suppressed for the interest of the whole.

The socialists would point to numerous circumstances in which everyone recognizes the necessity of sacrificing the interests of individuals to the greater good. They might point, for example, to an athletic team. If the players simply pursue what they think is in their personal interests, the interests of team may not be fulfilled. It is the task of the coach to make the players follow the interests of the team, not just their own interests.[26] Similar comments can be made about an orchestra. The conductor has the difficult task of getting talented (and often arrogant) people to coordinate their efforts in the interest of the whole. The socialists would argue that the advanced state is no different. The coach finds that the team has considerable power in excess of the power of the individual members alone when it pulls together, and the conductor finds that the orchestra can play in ways which surpass the talents of individual players when it is working harmoniously. Thus, the socialists believe, the society can satisfy much more when it is operating as an organic whole than when each member is doing what interests him or her the most.

We found that the fundamental aspect of capitalism was the insistence on the competitive marketplace which would rapidly adapt to the needs and demands of people. The combination of economic atomism and a survival mechanism is what made the capitalist economy respond to consumer needs and desires. Far from calling his scheme capitalism, Smith never used the term, and if we could leave the sense of anachronism aside, it might be best to label capitalism, at least as Smith conceived of it, as consumerism. The institution of private property, while supported by Smith, was not held by him to be an essential defining characteristic of capitalism. Nevertheless, it was private property which was attacked relentlessly by socialists, and had it not been for the fact that the defenders of capitalism mistakenly accepted the terms of that challenge, socialism might have missed the power it came to have.

Since we are all consumers, the theory of capitalism has some reasonable moral base. If it is cut loose from that base, as the socialists tried to do, it loses its moral warrant and becomes at best a narrow economic theory incapable of handling the full reach of ideological issues. That is essentially what has happened in modern American and British economic studies. Economists transform capitalism as they define it into a value-free economic system with neither a need for justification nor a means for rationally discussing justification.

Socialism centrally argues for the abandonment of private property and the establishment of some system by which the society is recognized as something more than the simple agglomeration of its parts. For socialism, the moral warrant comes in its claim to serve the organic totality of Workers. Workers create all value through their labor, and they have a right to the fruits of that labor. Socialists believe that any society which fails to acknowledge the Workers' rights to their labor is morally bankrupt. Recognizing the centrality of work and of value created by work, they argue that society should be oriented around the needs of Workers. Since the only people who are not workers make up a minuscule proportion of society and since those people avoid work only by living off the expropriated labor of others (through inheritance), the interest of all—the General Will—will be served by attending to the needs of Workers as a totality. To paraphrase Lincoln, in socialism, the proper society will be a society of Workers, by Workers, and for Workers.

Joseph Schumpeter made an interesting argument in regard to the rise of socialism from its capitalist heritage.[27] He argued that capitalism was bound to die, not because of its failures, as Marx had argued, but because of its successes. He believed that too many people would come to enjoy the fruits of the capitalist society. They would then attempt to protect themselves from the risks associated with capitalism, thus modifying capitalism piece by piece until they had killed capitalism and constructed a socialist society. While Schumpeter does not give the attention he might have to the privileges of incorporation, his analysis is closely reasoned and brilliant. He recognizes the inevitable dynamic of society. If Schumpeter had only recognized that even though capitalism was already in the final stages of transformation, there might be other alternatives than socialism, he might have shown us the new direction sooner.

In spite of propagandist and intellectual claims to the contrary, there simply is no substantial evidence that the advanced industrialized societies, especially the United States, are becoming socialist. Furthermore, in those societies which have explicitly embraced socialism, the departures from the fundamentals of socialism are more noticeable than the congruity. When successful self-proclaimed socialist societies have any organic unity, they gain it more from a common homogeneous culture or from control of media than from the implementation of socialism. In the United States, no identifiable increase has occurred in public ownership of the means of production, nor is there any substantial movement in the direction of an economic structure oriented toward Workers. The socialist society, which gains its warrant from being of the Workers, by the Workers, and for the Workers, is not being created in the United States or, indeed, anywhere else. If anything, with the mismanagement and consequent diminution of power of the trade unions, the workers in the United States have lost power over the past decades. Employers no longer fear the negative publicity which once accompanied strikes, in part because there is little negative publicity and in part because what negative publicity there is falls at least as much on the unions as on the "management." Contemporary managers see unions as just one among several special interest groups trying to get a piece of the political, economic, and social pie while returning as little as possible. The society of the United States is no more responsive to the workers than it is to bank depositors or gun owners or senior citizens. When a majority of the members of the AFL-CIO voted against the direct wishes of its leadership in the 1984 presidential election, the concept of the power of national unions was dealt a resounding blow. The union simply could not deliver the vote, and all politicians knew then that, in the future, they could treat unions with courteous evasion. If the unions had been more effectively managed, they would not have let their weakness be so dangerously exposed. It is primarily an act of rhetorical bluster which allows some people to perpetuate an impending socialist menace as the problem with government involvement.

In the dominant self-identified socialist societies, the only improvement in the conditions of the workers which can be proclaimed is a relative one. The working conditions for workers and junior managers are miserable and would not survive the scrutiny of a sophomore-level management course in organizational behavior in the United States. The tearing down of the Berlin Wall was not, as widely reported, a refutation of socialism or communism. It was a refutation of repressive governments which had used socialism as an instrument of propaganda. Socialism and communism were refuted long before the Berlin Wall was torn down, because their fundamental principles were simply irrelevant to the advanced industrialized societies.

I would guess that Engels suspected that Marx's predictions about the development of so-called capitalist societies were wrong and that he tried to modify *Das Kapital* to accommodate those differences. Neither Engels nor Schumpeter, however, recognized how radical the changes under way were, and they both accepted Marx's rhetorical commitment to what we have identified as the bifurcation fallacy.

Logic and Rhetoric

Now that we have some additional substance for the progress of the argument of this book, it is time to follow up the discussion in chapter 2 about the bifurcation fallacy. In this chapter we saw that Marx cleverly set the debate so that all participants accepted the notion that a bifurcation of positions exists between capitalism and socialism. Let us return to the nonfallacious statement of a bifurcation. If the bifurcation is between two truly contradictory statements, no fallacy is involved. In logic, when we talk of contradictions, we mean that if two statements are contradictory, they cannot be true at the same time or false at the same time. The truth of one statement directly implies the falsity of the other and vice versa. For example, suppose we are considering these two statements:

1. All living Marxists believe in economic determinism.

2. Some living Marxists do not believe in economic determinism.

Without knowing anything about Marxism and without meeting any Marxists, we know automatically that if 1 is true, 2 must be false, and that if 1 is false, 2 must be true. Note, also, that there are different ways to attempt to determine the truth-value of 1. We might interview all living Marxists. We might also attempt to show that 2 is true. Once we show 2 to be true, we know 1 is false because of the form of the statements. Statements 1 and 2 are said to be contradictories.

Now let us look at two different statements:

3. All Americans believe in predestination.

4. No Americans believe in predestination.

In this case, showing one statement to be false does nothing to establish the truth-value of the other statement. Even if it is false that all Americans believe in predestination, it does not follow that no Americans believe in predestination. Similarly, even if it is false that no Americans believe in predestination, it does not follow that all Americans believe in predestination. However, if 3 is true, 4 must be false, and if 4 is true, 3 must be false. If all Americans believe in predestination, it cannot be true that no Americans believe in predestination. Statements such as 3 and 4 cannot both be true, but they can both be false. Statements 3 and 4 are said to be contraries.

Now let us apply the logic. Marx cleverly argued that capitalism and socialism are contradictory. If so, all arguments against capitalism automatically give support to socialism. Foolishly, the defenders of capitalism accepted Marx's tactic, so they were reduced to parrying his thrusts and arguing against socialism in order to support capitalism. (The self-identified socialist countries made that last task an easy one.) If socialism and capitalism are not contradictories, but contraries, however, then the falsehood of one does not require the truth of the other. All the condition of contraries establishes is that both cannot be true. Both can, however, be false. A central argument of this book is that, with regard to the contemporary setting, capitalism and socialism are contraries, and both are false in the sense that they do not correspond to reality.

5 Process Applied

Democracy

One of the foremost contemporary democratic theoreticians, Giovanni Sartori, has said: "Communism and socialism can be connected to a single major author—Marx—and assessed as deviations from, and implementations or negations of, Marx. Democracy is not amenable to a similar treatment; the towering, single major author on democracy does not exist."[1] The absence of that single towering figure will make our effort to identify fundamental principles of democracy different from the similar effort in regard to capitalism and socialism. It will be more complicated to identify democratic theory and to analyze it carefully. Nevertheless, there do seem to be some core principles, and this chapter will suggest that democratic government should be government of the people, by the people, and for the people, to use Lincoln's felicitous phrase. Since we are all "the people," democracy is a system of governance which takes all of our interests into account insofar as possible. Like capitalism and socialism, democracy does not promise that each of us will (or can) get whatever we want whenever we want it. What it means is that there is a system, called democracy, which accommodates as much of and as many of our interests as possible.

Identifying the exact meaning of the word *democracy* poses another problem.[2] The denotative function of the word is in danger of being lost entirely. The word itself has become almost exclusively positive, irrespective of its precise meaning. Whenever someone refers to a social action as democratic, we know almost automatically that the speaker wishes to enlist our support for that action. As a result, not only are there no systematic theoretical advocates of democracy, but there are also few theoreticians willing to attack it systematically. Except for Fascists and some religious fanatics, virtually all self-appointed implementers of ideological movements declare that what they advocate or what they have created is a democracy.[3] Every now and then in the United States, someone will remember the famous quotation attributed to Benjamin Franklin after the Constitutional Convention: he said that what they had created was a republic, "if you can keep it." To a large extent, however, we have lost the nuances of such distinctions, and even when Franklin is so quoted, the speaker often falls into the habitual cant of identifying the United States as a democracy. Franklin was right. The Constitutional Convention did not create a democracy. We can leave to further analysis whether what we have currently in the United States, or elsewhere, is a democracy.

In the last half of the twentieth century, *democracy* has become almost exclusively a term of approbation. Consequently, all sorts of governmental structures (for example, the recent German Democratic Republic) claim democracy for their own. No doubt the former minister of propaganda for the German Democratic Republic developed some lengthy apologia defending the country as a democratic state. The only way such arguments can be sustained, however, is by such massive equivocation with the term *democracy* that it loses its denotative meaning entirely and ends up only connoting a positive attitude about some political, economic, or social matters. It would be a shame to turn over *democracy* to the propagandists entirely. The word does mean something, and for many people, it means something very important. We should try to reconstruct that meaning.

Thus, the strategy for the next two chapters is different from that of the previous two chapters. This chapter will examine what might be called the process approach to democracy. This approach identifies democracy as a process ideology with no substantive ideological commitments. There are six tasks to be accomplished. First, we will define *democracy* more precisely. Second, we will identify some problems associated with democracy as defined. After that, a strategy for the defense of democracy will be suggested. Next, we shall examine some of the unresolved problems for democracy. Finally, we shall analyze the views of important modern authorities who develop democratic theories different from the one suggested here. In the next chapter we shall examine the views of some theoreticians who have held that democracy involves substantive commitment in regard to economic theories. They argue that democracy cannot be a doctrine related purely to process and that it implies either capitalism or socialism.

Two Central Characteristics of Democracy

As an example of democracy at work, let us consider a classic New England town meeting. Some people object that such an example cannot be made to work in the large and complicated settings which characterize contemporary advanced industrialized societies, but it at least gives us a place to start, and there should be no controversy about it as an example of democracy at work.

All the citizens in the town old enough to vote are eligible to attend the meeting, to participate in the process of framing proposals, and to vote on proposals. In order for a proposal to carry, a majority (over 50 percent) of those present and voting must support it. Debate on various proposals may be long and acrimonious. People may feel passionately about their positions, and they may express their views vigorously. Amendments may be proposed, and alternatives may be suggested. In the end, some proposal will be put to a vote, and a decision will be made. "The people" will have made a decision, and barring some other democratic procedure, the town will live with the decision. The example is kept simple here because in its simplicity it suggests two characteristics of democracy.

First, democracy stands for majoritarian rule. Surely, if someone were to suggest a modification, such as that only certain citizens get to vote or that, having heard the debate, the mayor will make the decision alone, it would be clear that the suggested decision-making process was not democratic. Second, democracy proposes a process (i.e., majoritarian rule) by which political, economic, and social decisions can be made. It eschews any attempt to provide substance for those decisions. Just as democracy means rule by the majority, it also makes no prior substantive commitment to how the community should rule. Decisions are in the hands of the people, and they can make those decisions however they wish as long as the process is followed. In this sense, democracy provides a forum for the consideration of social, political, and economic issues, and it provides a means for making the decisions. I take it that that is the sense of Lincoln's statement.[4]

In a democracy, when an issue is under consideration, it will eventually be put to some kind of vote of "the people," and however "the people" decide will be the decision of the society. The cumbersome phrase *some kind of vote* in the previous sentence was used because we should not eliminate from our investigation some form of representative democracy in which people popularly elect representatives to cast their vote for them. Some significant problems with representative democracy will be discussed later, but these problems do not eliminate the possibility of representation in a democracy.

Democracy has numerous problems associated with it. We shall see in this chapter that many self-proclaimed defenders do not actually defend democracy. Thus, they have not given a coherent picture of the problems with democracy, and those problems remain unresolved. We shall consider some of those problems and then the defenses of democracy which have been presented recently. Before that, however, it may be useful to outline a basic defensive strategy for democracy as it has been defined here.

A Defensive Strategy for Democracy

While we will see that there are no theoretical defenders of democracy as majoritarian rule, it may be helpful to start with what might constitute the elements of such a defense. Something of a logical problem occurs in an effort to defend democracy as a process ideology. It is tempting to attempt to ground democracy in some substantive commitments such as "natural rights." If that is done, however, then the defense of democracy becomes merely a defense of its efficiency in fulfilling those rights. Nevertheless, it may seem that without some substantive commitments, however implicit, one cannot defend democracy, because it is pure process and, as such, can only be voted up or down by the people. It is this latter task of defending democracy as process without substantive commitment which I set for myself in this section.

Democracy as a process ideology should start with the assumption that the focus and purpose of governance is the people of the society. It could then proceed to argue that the best way to have governance for the people is to have governance by the people. With that understanding, governance by the people should constitute governance of the people. Governance by the people can mean nothing other than majoritarian governance. All nonmajoritarian forms of decision making mean that some minority rules. The strength of democracy lies in its assertion that all nonmajoritarians must favor minority rule. Once that is recognized, the argument shifts dramatically. The defender of democracy should simply ask for a justification for minority rule. (As we shall see, many people who call themselves friends of democracy are ready to provide such arguments.) If defenders of democracy accepted this recommendation, they would shift the burden of the argument to the shoulders of those who overtly oppose democracy or those who, by favoring substantial modifications to democracy, covertly undermine it and support, rather, a nondemocratic (perhaps even an antidemocratic) ideological perspective.

True defenders of democracy would be right to assume such a rhetorical point of view. They should argue that once considered, democracy is the most sensible form of governance in the absence of substantial arguments to the contrary. This last statement should not be taken to imply that no arguments to the contrary can ever be made. Even a robust defender of democracy might concede that in an operating room or during a symphonic performance or on a battlefield, there probably are good reasons to adopt nondemocratic procedures. A nation-state may even experience circumstances in which good reasons exist for violating the principles of democracy. Those possibilities should not be ruled out a priori. In addition, the defender of democracy does not have to rule out the possibility that many other organizations such as businesses, schools, and hospitals might make a convincing argument for the inappropriateness of democracy. The defender of democracy should argue, however, that what needs to be defended is the decision to eliminate democracy. In the absence of such arguments, democracy does not need to be defended any more than parents need to defend caring for their children. It is not an issue on which neither side has a presumptive position. Democracy has the presumptive position because it includes all the people. There may be reasons to deny that presumption, but the burden of the argument should be on the shoulders of the antidemocrat, not on the shoulders of the democrat.

This rhetorical point has been missed by people who wanted to defend democracy. The early articulations of democracy at the hands of Plato and Aristotle were made by people who also attacked democracy and, thus, put its prospective supporters on the defensive. Since then, those supporters have unwittingly accepted the burden for defending democracy from its attackers. That may explain why they have also modified the theory of democracy into antidemocratic conclusions. In short, the defenders save the term while losing the concept of government of the people, by the people, and for the people. Having defined democracy and identified the form of argumentation which should be used to defend it, we can turn to some of the problems presented by democratic theory and not (yet) resolved by it.

Some Unresolved Issues in Democratic Theory

Who Makes Up the Base?

If a majority means more than 50 percent, it is important to specify the base of which the majority is constituted. Historically, so-called democracies have often defined the base in such a way that it constituted a minority of the relevant population. As a consequence, any majority of that base was at best a majority of a minority and, thus, itself a minority. For example, it has been estimated that even in supposedly democratic Athens at the time of Socrates, about 90 percent of the population was excluded from participation in the political process. The precise percentage is not at issue here, but if we recognize that women and slaves could not vote, it is easy to see that those who could vote must have constituted a minority of the population.

Even today we raise unresolved issues in facing this problem. Presumably, no society would want to allow just anyone to vote who wished to do so. If that were permitted, then all sorts of individuals who were not really part of "the people" could vote, and the majority would not necessarily reflect the wishes of the people. Thus far, no one has proposed a satisfactory solution to the problem, though most proposals usually suggest restrictions rather than expansion. The history of the women's suffrage movement and the battles over so-called literacy requirements provide examples of efforts by those within to keep the base small.

In order to solve this issue in society at large, it might make sense to accept the kind of rhetorical move suggested for democracy itself. The burden for excluding anyone from being part of the base in a democracy should lie with those who argue for exclusion. On these grounds, for example, it seems to be more difficult to defend excluding sixteen year olds than to defend excluding people serving a sentence for a felony conviction.

How Should the Conscientious Citizen Vote?

One of the more troublesome problems with democracy is that the proper motivation for a conscientious citizen's vote is not clear. Democracy does not tell us whether we should vote for that course of action we believe to be best for society or that course of action we believe to be best for ourselves. Consider an example. Think about a man who is sufficiently wealthy that, given a choice, it is almost always in his personal interest to have taxes raised in an across-the-board manner, such as the imposition of a sales tax, rather than in the form of so-called progressive income taxes. Thus, if he were asked whether he would prefer an increase in sales taxes or an increase in income taxes, he would say the former. Let us assume, however, that the person we are considering believes it is in the best interest of society at large if income taxes are raised instead of sales taxes. Democracy gives our imaginary person no guidance in voting. Should he vote his personal preference and, assuming others vote that way, let the process decide what the social preference is, or should he vote for what is best for the society and, assuming others vote that way, find what the social preference is? Democracy is silent on this important issue.

Should Representatives Represent or Lead?

A variation on the previous question arises in a representative democracy. First, though, it is important to refer to an earlier point and say that a system of representation is not necessarily antidemocratic. People might decide that having representatives carry out their wishes would be more efficient. There does not appear to be anything which would necessarily violate the conditions of democracy in that case. Something might, but it would not have to do so. In order to retain the democratic base, however, it is probably important to have some provisions for rather easy referenda, so that decisions of representatives could be overridden if the majority wished to do so. Some provisions should be made also for easy recall, so that when the majority believed their representative was no longer carrying out their wishes, they could elect a new representative. Such provisions would make the representatives more responsive to a majority of the people and, thus, make them truly more representative.

A question remains, however: Should representatives vote for what they believe to be in the best interests of the people they represent or for what they believe a majority of the people want? Again, the discussions of democracy do not clearly address or answer the question.

How Should Democracy Accommodate Permanent Minorities?

The problem of permanent minorities has bedeviled the United States almost from its founding. Both native Americans and African Americans constitute minorities in the society, and they have essentially no hope of ever belonging to the majority culture unless they essentially annihilate their heritage. While annihilating their heritage might be useful from the point of view of the majority culture, especially to assuage its spasms of guilt, it is by no means clear that such annihilation is in the interest of the members of the minority. Thus, these citizens are effectively doomed to a minority voice except on those few occasions when one of the spasms induces the majority to reach beyond its fringes. Democracy cannot account for that effect.

Is Democracy Practical?

Arguments about the practical impossibility of democracy, especially in modern industrialized societies, are characteristically brought forward as a preface to suggestions for nondemocratic, if not antidemocratic, modifications. The suggestions are justified with two lines of argument. The first line is that the complexities of modern technology, especially, mean that the ordinary person cannot understand many of the technical dimensions of the problems which need to be addressed in a modern democracy. Such arguments are typically followed by assertions that some subset needs to take over and rule. For example, under the guise of letting experts deal with technicality and complexity, we have created a Federal Reserve Board which is essentially accountable to no one and which exists beyond the reach of majorities.

The second line of argument in the attempt to justify the impracticality of democracy states that the modern postindustrial "democracies" have become so large that they simply cannot be run like a New England town meeting. However, in 1970 Robert Paul Wolff suggested that, far from disabling democracy, technology may have given us the opportunity to overcome the problems associated with size and to allow people to participate democratically in decision making.[5] Wolff suggested that, given the ubiquitousness of television sets in the United States, with some technological changes, each home could be wired for interactive television. Each day, issues could be presented on the television, and people could be invited to vote on them. The democratic society would then adopt the decision of the majority. For example, when the president made a recommendation for an appointment to the Supreme Court, instead of asking for the advice and consent of the Senate, the president might be required to ask for the advice and consent of the majority of voters.

Such a proposal would not do away with the utility of representative government. Representatives would concentrate on framing legislation, preparing packages of compromises, and so on. In fact, legislators at present spend much more time preparing legislation and doing what they euphemistically call constituent service than they spend voting. That act would be taken away from them except in their personal capacity as voters, but the rest of their responsibilities might well remain if a majority of the voters—ostensibly, their constituents—wished it.

As each year passes, the technology Wolff envisioned in 1970 becomes ever more possible and inexpensive. Some radio stations pose a political question of the day and accept telephone calls from listeners, who express their views. A call to one number means a positive vote; a call to another number means a negative vote. Such a system could be adopted on a national scale. The voting would be done easily, and the tally would be available quickly. It is possible that the sudden increased interest in voting in referenda in state elections is an implicit expression of a desire on the part of the citizens to take more control over government decision making. Some may think they could hardly do worse than their representatives are doing currently.[6]

Wolff did not pursue his suggestion, perhaps in part because he does not believe in what he calls majoritarian democracy. Thus, he has little interest in making it work. The democratic theoretician Sartori acknowledges Wolff's suggestion but dismisses it contemptuously, saying, "While Wolff's argument is feeble, he deserves credit for his consistency." [7]

Both lines of argument against democracy seem to be little more than red herrings. There may be good reasons for opposing democracy, and impracticality may be among them, but the opponents have not supplied the proof.

Can a Democracy Commit Suicide?

One of the reasons often given for constraining democracy is that if it is not constrained, it may vote itself out of existence. It is important for those who wish to defend democracy also to acknowledge that democracy may, indeed, commit suicide and either vote itself out of existence directly or vote in such modifications that it is no longer a democracy. If democracy is to be seen as a process, then no proposal can be eliminated from consideration. Nothing in democratic theory says that the votes taken will always (or even usually) prove to be wise or moral or in the interest of democracy itself. The majority may make stupid mistakes; they may make moral mistakes; they may even be venal. Of course, such a finding does not distinguish democracy from any other form of government. It may be harder to imagine a dictator so stupid as to create the conditions for his own downfall, but it has happened. In any event, that is hardly a good reason to prefer dictatorship over democracy.

The majority may vote to turn over their power to a minority. A democracy cannot preclude such a decision a priori, though once it is done, the system is no longer democratic. In addition, the majority could also adopt de facto procedures which, while they might not de jure eliminate democracy, would effectively eliminate the possibility of governance of, by, and for the people. In a democracy, the people—a majority—rule. If the society is such that effectively the majority does not rule, that society is not democratic.

Are the Principles of Democratic Procedure Logically Consistent?

We turn now to one of the most vexing problems for democracy. It is a problem deeply imbedded in the heart of democratic theory, and it may extend beyond democratic theory to theories in general which attempt to determine social choices on the basis of individual preferences. In that sense, it is more of a problem for atomistic approaches than organic ones. As was pointed out earlier, organic approaches always have the problem of resolving who should get to speak for the organic whole, which, by the nature of organic theory, is not coextensive with the collection of individual attitudes. This weakness has a corresponding strength. The organic society can speak univocally through the person who reads the organic destiny.

An atomistic society may create a cacophony which shows deep disunity. That issue is especially clear when war is near or when it threatens. Leaders often try to create organic conditions so they can characterize their political opponents as treasonous. Lincoln supported strong antidemocratic methods in order to gain a kind of organic control over the North during the Civil War. In the United States during both world wars, the executive branch, often with the willful acquiescence of the legislative and judicial branches, took many actions to create an illusion of unity and commitment. It is said that when Lyndon Johnson listened to the hearings of Senator William Fulbright's committee during the Vietnam War, he would say, "Hanoi must be sleeping easier knowing Bill Fulbright is on their side." During the preparations for the so-called Gulf War, it was clear that the executive branch in the United States became increasingly irritated with questions which were raised, and it was not long before hints of disloyalty to the country—organically conceived—became part of the rhetoric. Such is the messiness of a system with some atomistic aspects.

The problem for an atomistic social system is determining how to develop policy out of expressions of atomistic individual preferences. The majoritarian procedure is a proposed solution to that problem. Messy as it is, it nevertheless has been a hope for those who would defend democracy. Unfortunately, some analytic work of the economist Kenneth Arrow suggests that for theoretical reasons that hope is misplaced.[8] Arrow shows that no reliable and consistent set of rules exists by which we can go from a recognition of individual preferences to a social decision.

In order to understand Arrow's argument without becoming unnecessarily involved with the logical technicalities, let us set up an imaginary but realistic case. Imagine that you are asked to help in the search for a new superintendent of schools in your community. The School Committee, which is responsible for the final appointment, decided to create a screening committee to review candidates for the position. They created a committee of seven people who represent the community. You agreed to serve. Your committee is charged with narrowing the list of applicants to three and presenting that list to the School Committee. Your committee will rank the three candidates in order of preference, so if the School Committee accepts your committee's ranking and cannot persuade the first candidate to accept the appointment, they will know which person your committee believes should be offered the appointment next. After some conversations involving your committee and the School Committee, everyone agrees that the most important characteristics to be sought in the next superintendent are educational knowledge and managerial skills. At the first meeting of your committee, the members agree that they should operate on democratic principles. All decisions will reflect the choice of the majority.

After reviewing many applications, the members of your committee agree on a list of twelve semifinalists, and the committee members proceed to interview these people. The committee then narrows the list to three finalists. In order to emphasize the pure process nature of this example, let us name the three finalists A, B, and C. Your committee's members largely agree on the strengths and weaknesses of each candidate. A is an intelligent person who is knowledgeable about educational matters on a broad scale. Everyone agrees that A's knowledge of education is A's strength and that A's lack of substantial managerial experience is a weakness. On the other hand, B has very impressive managerial training and experience. B was very successful as the number two person in a school system even more complex than yours. At the same time, B does not have much knowledge about education or much imagination for the educational development of schools. C has a combination of the two attributes sought. C does not seem as strong in either regard as the others, but C is not as weak in either regard as the others, either.

After extended discussion, the chair says it is time to vote, and no one disagrees. The chair says that since the committee agrees that it has its three finalists, the only task left is to rank them, and the best way to do that is to vote on them by first comparing two candidates. The one who gets a majority on that vote will be compared with the third person to find the candidate which a majority of the committee most prefers. After that, the remaining two can be voted on to find which candidate a majority of the committee places second. The person left will be ranked third in order of preference.

The chair then asks for a vote comparing A and B. Four members vote for A, and three vote for B, so A is the winner. The chair then asks for a vote comparing A with C. Four members vote for C, and three vote for A. Thus, C is declared the most preferred. The chair asks that A and B be compared again, and your committee favors A by four to three. Thus, the ranking which will be forwarded to the School Committee is C first, A second, and B third.

Now, assume the individual opinions of the members of your committee are the same as the opinions which led to the decision described in the previous paragraph, but assume the paragraph is rewritten as follows: The chair asks for a vote comparing B and C. Four members vote for B, and three vote for C, so B is the winner. The chair then asks for a vote comparing B with A. Four members vote for A, and three vote for B. Thus, A is declared the most preferred. The chair asks that B and C be compared again, and your committee favors B by four to three. Thus, the ranking which will be forwarded to the School Committee is A first, B second, and C third.

Somehow a perfectly democratic process has led to contradictory conclusions. C is most favored, and C is least favored. The democratic process is supposed to be neutral with regard to what is being decided, but the decision changes merely by changing the order in which the vote is taken. We can complete the story by examining what would have happened if the only remaining order of voting had occurred (assuming the opinions and votes of the committee members remain constant throughout): The chair asks for a vote comparing C and A. Four members vote for C, and three vote for A, so C is the winner. The chair then asks for a vote comparing C with B. Four members vote for B, and three vote for C. Thus, B is declared the most preferred. The chair asks that C and A be compared again, and your committee favors C by four to three. Thus, the ranking which will be forwarded to the School Committee is B first, C second, and A, third.

In order to understand how these results might come about, we can outline one possibility. Suppose two members of your committee believe that the most important thing for the schools is to have someone very strong in education. Barring that, however, those two members would rather have someone strong in management than someone mediocre at both. Each of their personal rankings will be A first, B second, and C third. Suppose two other members believe that the most important thing is excellent managerial skills and that if the person does not have that, they would still favor someone with some management experience over someone weak in that area. Their individual rankings will then be B first, C second, and A third. One member believes educational knowledge is most important, and if the person who is strongest at that does not take the job, the School Committee should go to the person with more modest educational skills next. That person's ranking is *A* first, *C* second, and *B* third. Another person believes that the best candidate is the one who offers a combination of skills and that if that person cannot be retained, the committee should hire the person with managerial skills. That person's ranking will be *C* first, *B* second, and *A* third. You believe that the candidate with a combination of skills is the best, but you think that if the School Committee cannot get that person, it should turn to the person strong in education next. Your ranking is *C* first, *A* second, and *B* third. The table outlines the individual preferences.[9] Returning to the voting procedures and following the table yields the results described. Perfectly straightforward democratic rules have led to contradictory results.

	Ranking of Candidates		
Committee Member	First	Second	Third
1	*A*	*B*	*C*
2	*A*	*B*	*C*
3	*B*	*C*	*A*
4	*B*	*C*	*A*
5	*A*	*C*	*B*
6	*C*	*B*	*A*
7	*C*	*A*	*B*

Actually, the knowledge of such problems was first discovered by Charles Dodgson (Lewis Carroll). Arrow's great contribution was that he showed that the problem was a theoretical one built into democratic procedures. Obviously, one could impose some constraints on the voting (for example, one might declare that no committee member may rank *C* third, because if members cannot have what they want, their only rational choice is to take the modified version), but those constraints cannot be justified democratically. Nondemocratic constraints cannot be used to save democracy.[10]

We must conclude, then, that no matter what our personal proclivities, democracy is not a perfected theory. Significant problems are either unresolved or, perhaps in the case of Arrow's discoveries, unresolvable. For the defender of democracy, much theoretical work remains to be done. The persistent question, however, should be whether proposed solutions subvert democracy itself.

Alternative Democratic Theories

In this section we shall examine some alternative approaches to democratic theory which retain the view that democratic theory provides a process approach to ideology. The arguments addressed here do not address the issues identified above, and the alternatives do not resolve those issues. They focus on other concerns which lead to the proposition of alternative democratic theories.

John Stuart Mill: Tyranny of the Majority

Mill had such a wonderful way of stating his concern with democracy that it is well to begin by quoting him directly.

> In old times . . . The rulers were conceived as in a necessarily antagonistic position to the people whom they ruled. They consisted of a governing One, or a governing tribe or caste, . . . who, at all events, did not hold [their authority] at the pleasure of the governed. . . . The aim, therefore, of patriots was to set limits to the power which the ruler should be suffered to exercise over the community; and this limitation was what they meant by liberty. . . . It appeared to them much better that the various magistrates of the State should be their tenants or delegates, revocable at their pleasure. . . . Let the rulers be effectively responsible to [the people], promptly removable by [the people], and [the people] could afford to trust them with the power of which [the people] could itself dictate the use to be made.[11]

Mill's argument involves a bit of reconstructed history in order to develop the point he will make next. We should notice in passing, however, that Mill does describe democracy as the previous sections of this chapter did, even though he will go on to attack it. The democracy Mill understands is a rule by the people: where it is representative democracy, the representatives are to represent the will of the people and are subject to being recalled at the pleasure of the people. There is no protection for those who are, as Mill indicates, mere delegates of the people, carrying out their business. Thus, in democracy, at least as Mill conceives it here, the fact of representation does not diminish the democratic characteristic that the citizenry is in control and can exercise its will.

The last fact worries Mill the most. Mill recognizes that the majority can vote foolishly, they can vote immorally, and they can vote to prevent the exercise of what Mill believes to be the fundamental rights of citizens who do not happen to adhere to the views of the majority. It is no surprise that Mill turns to religion for his most telling example. He points out that religions characteristically disagree with each other on numerous doctrinal points. When a religion finds itself in the majority position, it does not recall its earlier minority position and conclude from that a need to be tolerant of other religions. Typically, it becomes as oppressive when it gains a majority as the previous victor was. Thus, Mill and his followers worry about the tyranny of the majority: the capacity of the majority if it is in control to hurt the minority.[12]

In a sense, Mill's claim here reveals nothing particularly new. Both Plato and Aristotle had made essentially the same complaints. The mob could not be trusted to respect what Plato and Aristotle believed to be true. The danger with democracy must always be that it can make bad decisions. Indeed, it can even make decisions which are objectively bad for the people it claims to serve— the majority.[13]

Mill's basic argument is as follows:

> But . . . success discloses faults and infirmities which failure might have concealed from observation. . . . It was now perceived that such phrases as "self-government," and "the power of the people over themselves," do not express the true state of the case. . . . The will of the people, moreover, practically means the will of the most numerous . . . *part* of the people . . . the people *may* desire to oppress a part of their number, and precautions are as much needed against this as against any other abuse of power. . . . in political speculations "the tyranny of the majority" is now generally included among the evils against which society requires to be on its guard. . . . Society can and does execute its own mandates; and if it issues wrong mandates instead of right, or any mandates at all in things which it ought not to meddle, it practices a social tyranny more formidable than many kinds of political oppression. . . . there needs protection also against the tyranny of the prevailing opinion and feeling.[14]

Mill, then, like Plato and Aristotle before him, imagined what he thought the excess of democracy might be. He then postulated that if democracy were to come about, that excess would also come about. He suggested remedies for the imagined illness before it took place. That was not a remarkable position for Plato and Aristotle, who did not claim to be friendly toward democracy. However, it is just the kind of nonempirically based a priori reasoning which Mill criticized when he wrote on epistemological and logical topics.[15]

Establishing rules which would prevent a tyranny of the majority automatically means establishing rules which allow for rule of a minority. There may be good reasons for such rules, but that is a topic for another debate. There can be little rational debate, however, about the fact that rule of a minority is not democratic. Thus, Mill's efforts which start so hopefully in defense of democracy and which are so often used as a classical argument for democracy are at their base antidemocratic.

Robert Paul Wolff: Unanimous Direct Democracy

In an effort to avoid Mill's problem, Robert Paul Wolff developed a different approach to democracy.[16] His strategy was to articulate a more general problem than Mill had addressed but of which Mill's was an instance. If Wolff could find a way to resolve that problem, then he would have automatically found a way to avoid tyranny of a majority or even the tyranny of a minority.

The general problem Wolff identifies is one of maintaining legitimate authority for the state and, at the same time, the autonomy of the individual. We should examine carefully the central terms of this problem. For Wolff, legitimate authority for the state means its morally justifiable authority, not merely its power to dominate. Wolff acknowledges that the state usually has the power to force compliance with its rules. He does not question that. He is asking when the state has the moral right to demand compliance. In addition, for Wolff, the autonomy of the individual means that the individual obeys only what his or her own conscience dictates. An individual who obeys someone else thus becomes an extension of that other person and loses his or her own autonomy. One might do what another wants, but the difference between doing something with autonomy and doing it without autonomy is revealed by asking whether one chooses to do it irrespective of what the other desires. The question, then, which Wolff asks is Why should I obey the law? A possible answer is Because it is the law, and if you get caught disobeying it, you will be punished. In short, a reason for obeying the law is that the price you have to pay for disobedience is too high. That is not a moral reason, however, and Wolff wants us to find a moral reason.

Wolff thinks that this conflict between the legitimate authority of the state and the autonomy of the individual poses an irresolvable dilemma for any political theory. He thinks he has found a way out of the dilemma, though, and he calls that way unanimous direct democracy. This solution, by the way, would also resolve the problems posed by Arrow's findings. In spite of the label Wolff gives his solution, however, it is not democratic.

Let us return to the notion that democracy means at least in part majority rule. It would seem that if more than a majority agreed on some measure, that would be even greater than majority rule. Wolff accepted that line of reasoning and moved to the extreme of the position by proposing that in his unanimous direct democracy everyone would have to agree to all legislation. There could be no dissent. In that system, Wolff's problem is solved, because the state would never command anything of which someone disapproved. Since all of us would get to vote on all legislation and changes in legislation and since there would be no legislation or changes in legislation without our approval, whatever constraints were imposed by the state would be constraints to which each of us agreed. We would not have lost any of our autonomy.

Let us take a personal example first to understand the general point Wolff is making and then see how it applies to the political level. If I put myself on a diet and say that for the next two weeks I shall not eat any candy, I may find after a few days that I want to have a piece of candy. I may remind myself of my commitment and refrain. Wolff would say that under such circumstances, I would not have compromised my autonomy. However, suppose some other people decide, after listening to me complain about being overweight, that I should stop eating candy for the next two weeks, and suppose they engage in some successful constraining actions which prevent me from eating candy. They have compromised my autonomy and imposed themselves on me.

Wolff would argue that the analogy between my personal example and one on a state level holds. For example, I might engage in long debates with my fellow citizens, and in the end we might all agree that because of some circumstances, we need to tax ourselves in order to raise money for our government. Let us say that we all also agree how that money is to be raised and how it is to be spent. Now, when it comes time for me to pay my taxes, I may feel all sorts of personal regret, as I did when I decided to forgo the candy. I did agree, though, and I shall pay without losing any of my autonomy. By contrast, suppose a dictator decrees a tax on all citizens. While we might pay because of the dictator's power, we would all recognize that our autonomy as persons had been violated.

Wolff suggests we extend the analogy to a majority. Let us suppose that instead of a dictator, we have an assembly, such as our New England town meeting. Let us say that the assembly votes on a tax proposal. I vote against it, but the majority votes in favor of it. By standard democratic procedures, the tax is passed and imposed on me as well as everyone else. Wolff argues that my autonomy is compromised, just as it is in the case of the dictatorship. He goes on to argue that the only way around this issue is by requiring that nothing can be done unless everyone agrees to the proposal. Wolff alleges that this is the only legitimate form of democracy, and he calls it unanimous direct democracy.

Wolff thinks that the primary criticisms of his suggestion will be practical ones, and he generously concedes that such responses have much persuasive weight and show that his suggestion to solve the philosophical problem may be impractical. At the same time, he argues cogently that his proposal is not as impractical as its critics will claim and that it might work under some especially favorable conditions. However, Wolff ignores the fact that his suggestion has serious theoretical problems. First, Wolff's proposed solution does not solve his problem of maintaining the legitimate authority of the state and the autonomy of the individual. Second, even if it solved the problem, it does not provide a procedure which can properly be called a democracy. Thus, the phrase *unanimous direct democracy* ends up being self-contradictory. The reasons for these twin failures are related, and we should examine them.

Let us imagine our assembly once again. Suppose that the assembly has an open discussion involving the citizens but that when it comes time for a decision, only one-third of the citizens have voting rights. (For the moment, we can ignore how those are selected.) Let us even say that the one-third themselves vote by unanimity procedures. That assembly procedure is interesting and perhaps bears examination, but it is not democratic. Whether we should describe it as an aristocracy, an oligarchy, a republic, a representative system, what Plato called a timocracy, or some other label might depend upon how the one-third is selected. Since the citizens do not have control, however, it is not a democracy. Let us move one step further and say that instead of one-third's making the decision, the decision will be made by one person. The natural response is to say that what has been described is a dictatorship. Certainly, such an assembly would not solve Wolff's problem, and it would not be democratic. Now, suppose instead of knowing beforehand who the single person might be, let us say a person is selected randomly for each vote. Thus, in this case, as the assembly concluded its debate, lots would be drawn to select a person who would decide based on his or her best judgment. The decision might or might not concur with the majority position.

It is difficult to say whether such a procedure would solve Wolff's problem. Wolff flirts with random and lot voting in an effort to deal with permanent minorities, and he seems somewhat sympathetic or at least intrigued by their prospects, so it is difficult to know how he might respond. The procedure does not solve Wolff's problem of maintaining autonomy for the individual, however, and surely it would not make sense to call this system of governance democratic. It is conceivable that every decision could be the opposite of what the majority wants.

We have only one step further to go. This time, suppose we have an assembly which proceeds in accordance with appropriate participatory and deliberative procedures. At the conclusion of its deliberations, it takes a vote which determines what the majority thinks. After that, another procedure is necessary before the legislation can be approved. Again, a single individual is selected by lot. That individual has a yes or no vote: Should the legislation voted be adopted? If he or she says yes, it will be adopted; if he or she says no, it will not be adopted. This is a curious assembly, but it is not democratic. Once again, the will of the citizenry could potentially be frustrated endlessly and indefinitely.

The case just outlined closely approximates what Wolff calls unanimous direct democracy. Wolff's system has only one additional provision which removes it even further from a democracy. Instead of the single person's being selected by lot, the person is self-selected. In what Wolff calls a unanimous direct democracy, any single person gets to frustrate the will of the assembly, irrespective of majoritarian interests. Notice that this person might represent a lone negative vote. The system thus described is nothing more than a self-selected dictatorship of one. That the one might have a rotating membership makes no difference to the point being made: it is still a form of dictatorship, not a form of democracy.

Like the other qualifications of majoritarian provisions for democracy, Wolff's scheme is a conservative one. In effect, it would create a strong procedural bias in favor of the status quo. For example, let us recognize that until recently we thought our waterways could refresh themselves indefinitely, and as a consequence, we put all sorts of harmful things into the water. Some believe otherwise now, and they believe that restrictions should be imposed on what can be put in our waterways. Suppose someone proposed legislation prohibiting the discharge of unprocessed hazardous waste into lakes and streams. Suppose, further, that all but one person favored the proposition. By Wolff's scheme, the legislation could not be enacted. Thus, Wolff's scheme saves the autonomy of the dissenters only to threaten the autonomy of the supporters. Perhaps this seems too imaginary. Turn to a historical example. Thomas Jefferson and his followers tried for years to eliminate property qualifications for voting and, thus, to extend the vote to the poor.[17] Undoubtedly, if unanimity had been required, we would still be debating the issue, and there would still be dissenters. Conservatives *want* to frustrate change. Few things would serve that purpose more effectively than a requirement for unanimity in order to pass legislation.

Beyond the issue of the conservative function of Wolff's suggestion lies the fact that the procedure is not at all democratic. No system which gives veto power to a minority can be properly called democratic, for it may well frustrate the control of the citizens over their own government. In spite of persistent attempts to modify the majoritarian features of democracy, it seems that the proportion has been given correctly: a simple majority. Identifying that proportion does not solve all the difficulties of democracy, but it does identify its heart.

Robert Dahl: Empirical Polyarchy

The issues concerning the tyranny of the majority, which vexed Mill so much, bothered James Madison too. Madison spent a substantial portion of the Federalist Papers brooding over what might happen if the hoi polloi actually got their way. The issue was taken up by Robert Dahl, who resolved to examine it as an empirical issue for democratic theory. Dahl came to a conclusion which varied significantly from the abstract concerns which had plagued the antidemocrats from Plato through Mill and Madison. Dahl concluded that the concern was generated around a myth: that of the potential of a tyranny of a majority. Dahl said that since majority rule is mostly a myth, then majority tyranny is mostly a myth, too. For if the majority cannot rule, surely it cannot be tyrannical.

The real world issue has not turned out to be whether a majority, much less "the" majority, will act in a tyrannical way through democratic procedures to impose its will on a (or the) minority. Instead, the more relevant question is the extent to which various minorities in a society will frustrate the ambitions of one another with the passive acquiescence or indifference of a majority of adults or voters. . . . The distinction comes much closer to being one between government by a minority and government by *minorities*. [18]

A number of points in the passage just cited deserve attention, and addressing them will serve as a helpful backdrop to a further understanding of Dahl's analysis of democracy. The passage underlines the fact that when at last someone decided to examine the long-standing concern about the tyranny of the majority empirically, it turned out that the concern was more in the imaginations of the people agonizing over it than in the actual life of states and governments. It must be equally arresting, however, to realize that Dahl's analysis turns on his conclusion that majority rule is "mostly" a myth. From the point of view of someone who wishes to defend democracy, it may seem that Dahl has saved the bathwater only to lose the baby.

Dahl's conclusions come from the context of his penetrating axiomatic and empirical analysis of democracy. Our efforts will be repaid if we examine his analysis, not only because it is so careful but also because it, or at least references to it, have had such wide influence. Dahl's analysis of democratic theory is, as we should expect, part of a consistent analysis of political life, especially in many so-called democracies, with special reference to the United States.

He begins by trying to discover some assumptions which might have been at the foundation of Madison's views if Madison had taken time from his busy and active life to develop his views in a neatly structured manner. After Dahl completes his analysis of Madison's proposals, especially as they appear in *The Federalist, No. 10,* he says:

The Madisonian system is clearly inadequate. In retrospect, the logical and empirical deficiencies of Madison's own thought seem to have arisen in large part from his inability to reconcile two different goals. On the one hand, Madison substantially accepted the idea that all the adult citizens of a republic must be assigned equal rights, including the right to determine the general direction of government policy. In this sense majority rule is "the republican principle." On the other hand, Madison wished to erect a political system that would guarantee the liberties of certain minorities whose advantages of status, power, and wealth would, he thought, probably not be tolerated indefinitely by a constitutionally untrammeled majority. Hence, majorities had to be constitutionally inhibited. Madisonianism, historically and presently, is a compromise between these two conflicting goals.[19]

Dahl is largely correct in identifying the conflicting goals which Madison sought. While the issue of the possibility of a permanent minority, such as African Americans or native Americans, was raised earlier in this chapter, we should note that Madison's concerns are not for a disenfranchised minority. Like Aristotle and others, Madison thought that if a real majority actually gained control, it might behave in the same narrow self-interested manner as the minorities who had controlled power previously.

Madison's attraction to democracy as majority rule grew out of the Revolution and all it stood for. At the same time, Madison shared Aristotle's fear of a mobocracy. That tension became an inconsistency when Dahl tried to formalize it, and Dahl's conclusion about Madison's failures is on the mark. Dahl lets Madison off the hook, however, in a passage which turns out to be a defensive preface to Dahl's own view: "So far as I am aware, no one has ever advocated, and no one except its enemies has ever defended democracy to mean, that a majority would or should do anything it felt an impulse to do. Every advocate of democracy of whom I am aware, and every friendly definition of it, includes the idea of restraints on majorities." [20] As we might expect, Dahl is correct in his scholarly reference. The point has already been made that democracy as majoritarian rule has not had strong advocacy. From the beginning, democracy has been described by those who could see its logical direction but sought, for one reason or another, to curb it. Dahl, too, saw the logical direction, and he wrote a chapter on what he called populist democracy, in which he described majority rule. Of course, Dahl's own rhetorical trick is played in concert with the flourishes of other critics of democracy. He gives true democracy a qualifying adjective (this time his is *populist*), as if numerous forms of democracy exist and he is considering only three types: the Madisonian one, this populist one, and his own "polyarchal democracy." We will explore these in a moment.

Let us take the time to consider the imagery here. Suppose someone said that there are different kinds of ice cream. We all could agree to that, just as we all could agree to the proposition that there are different kinds of democracy, kinds that might be practiced in different societies. Then, suppose our imaginary person were to put on a counter a bottle of cream, a dish of vanilla ice cream, and a block of ice. Suppose the person were to say that we have before us three different kinds of ice cream, from the purely liquid to the purely solid. Someone else might interrupt and say that the presenter was mistaken and that we have before us one kind of ice cream and two other things, neither of which is ice cream. With one caveat, the analogy is sufficiently apt for our purposes.[21]

Dahl has placed before us Madison's suggestions for government, which Dahl calls Madisonian democracy.[22] Next, Dahl discusses what he calls populist democracy. Then he describes what he calls polyarchal democracy, which he believes is close to what is actually practiced. Suppose, following the ice cream analogy, he had instead presented these topics as republican government, democratic government, and polyarchal government. The impression of the book in regard to democracy would have been entirely different. Presumably, even the title would have been changed. The book would still be an extremely valuable contribution to the literature of political science—we should expect nothing less from Dahl—but it would not be a preface to democracy theory. Thus, what appears to be a defense of democracy is actually a disguised dismissal of it. Populist democracy, as the term is used by Dahl, is democracy. Dahl's other topics address systems of governance which are not democratic. We should, however, pay close attention to Dahl's treatment of populist democracy, since that is the topic of this chapter. In spite of the already stated objections to Dahl's use of *populist* to qualify *democracy,* I shall retain his terminology in examining his view.

With regard to populist democracy, Dahl has the same problem noted earlier: he has no author to examine and criticize. Dahl's attempt to formalize populist democracy is self-generated, and he finds that the system thus developed is deficient. The problems with Dahl's analysis do not begin with his definition of populist democracy, however, which is workable enough.

> Definition 1: An organization is democratic if and only if the process of arriving at governmental policy is compatible with the condition of popular sovereignty and political equality.[23]

He then adds two more definitions in order to better describe *popular sovereignty* and *political equality,* and those lead him to his first proposition:

> Proposition 1: The only rule compatible with decision-making in a populist democracy is the majority principle.[24]

That proposition seems acceptable, though we may wonder why so much effort went into establishing definitions for terms that are not used in the proposition. Indeed, the terms do not appear in the only other proposition:

> Proposition 2: Populist democracy is desirable, at least for governmental decisions, as a final appeal when other specified processes have been exhausted, and among adult citizens (the condition of "the last say").[25]

Here we see democracy already qualified: Exhaust other specified processes. We should recognize that people in power often say that when they argue against the desire of the powerless to gain change: Go through the system (which, of course, those in power have already rigged to frustrate change).

Democracy does not need to build in the conditions established in Proposition 2, nor should it accept the qualifications. Proposition 1 will do, and if definitions are needed, we should define the terms which might be confusing in Proposition 1, not some other terms which are, at most, glosses on Proposition 1. Rather than quarreling with Dahl about the original proposition, which may be sufficient at least for first-order analysis, however, we should examine what he takes to be the deficiencies in populist democracy. He identifies seven essential deficiencies, and we will explore each one.

The first deficiency Dahl finds is the most obvious: no one really believes in or advocates populist democracy. This claim does not provide much ground for a rejection of democracy, but it does seem to haunt Dahl beyond the difficulty of finding an articulated statement of it. We do not need to quarrel with his conclusion that he can find no defense—at least no theoretical one. Many people say they believe in majoritarian rule, however, and they have some presumptive right to expect theoreticians to articulate their views, even if only to defeat them.

The second objection Dahl raises is that of Kenneth Arrow, that no consistent set of rules for democratic procedures exists. This discovery poses substantial problems, perhaps even insurmountable ones, for democracy. Arrow's problems, however, are no less problematic for Madisonian republicanism or Dahl's polyarchism. They are indigenous to all systems which attempt to make social policy from individual preferences through an atomistic process. Logically speaking, this is the only objection Dahl needs, but since it is an objection to democracy in general, it would have to stand as an objection to Dahl's polyarchal system also, which he says is democratic.

Third, Dahl says that populist democracy ignores intensity of preference. He is correct in the sense that in voting we are not able to express directly the intensity of our preferences for some alternative. One person may feel strongly in favor of an alternative, while another may only mildly oppose it. Nevertheless, when they vote, they will cancel each other out. The balloting process does not take note of the difference in intensity of feeling. Without denying the thrust of what Dahl says in this regard, it is useful to make some qualifications. The democratic process leading up to a vote may provide a way to approach the issue of preference. The discussions and compromises which lead up to the actual votes offer the chance for the representation of different interests. That is even more true when the voters vote on substantive issues rather than on representatives who will then broker some resolution. Thus, intensities can be taken into account. The method for doing so is not very efficient, but it could be democratic.

Dahl says that a fourth objection to populist democracy is "that it postulates only two goals to be maximized—political equality and popular sovereignty."[26]

With this statement, we finally discover the purpose of the earlier definitions which were not used in the initial propositions. The definitions were developed so that these issues could be made part of populist democracy and then populist democracy could be defeated. Even under Dahl's two propositions, populist democracy does not postulate either of these goals, much less the maximization of them. Also, populist democracy does not propose the maximization of anything. We have already seen that it is difficult to find an intellectual advocate for democracy described by Proposition 1. It is impossible to find an advocate for this maximization view. The importance of maximization for Dahl is considerable. It borrows from the success of economics, which has followed the mathematics of maximization for decades and has found it to be a powerful tool. If political science could find something to maximize, it could turn to the powerful apparatus of the calculus to derive conclusions not obvious in the premises. The problem with Dahl's approach, however, is that populist democrats do not need to advocate the maximization of anything. They merely advocate that social, political, and economic policies should be of, by, and for a majority of citizens. That advocacy is not entailed by and does not entail maximization of popular sovereignty. To put the point in formalist mathematical terms, establishing majoritarian standing is a threshold issue, not a continuous issue.

Next, Dahl turns to some additional objections and says: "The theory of populist democracy is not an empirical system. . . . It tells us nothing about the real world. From it we can predict no behavior whatsoever." [27] It is difficult to know how to respond to such a claim. It is as though I said that I believe faculty members should not become romantically involved with their students, and then someone replied that my statement does not lead to any scientific proof. True, but so what? It doesn't lead to a musical score either. Populist democrats do not say what will happen if a society adopts majority rule, nor do they say that any society has done so. They merely say that they believe majority rule is the only justifiable process they can think of for resolving disputes in the particular society for which they are advocating its use. In expanding on his objection, Dahl goes on to say: "No doubt some advocates of populist democracy would like to see every human being living in such a system; but so far as I know, no political theorist has ever advocated a single, world-wide system of populist democracy." [28] We are back at a particular problem in Dahl's work. Finding advocates for a position but no political theorists advocating it seems to provide a sufficient condition for Dahl to dismiss the position. It is not difficult to know how advocates might proceed. They would probably say that populist democracy is the best form of worldwide government and that any person who proposes any other must be prepared to show, empirically and theoretically, why the alternative system is superior. In expanding on his objection to populist democracy, Dahl also raises the issue of the definition of citizenship, which, as we noted earlier, remains an unresolved problem of democracy. His points are well taken, but once again, they do not distinguish problems of populist democracy from what he calls Madisonian democracy or polyarchal democracy.

Dahl's sixth objection to populist democracy follows an argument of Gaetano Mosca: since every society develops a ruling class, popular control is impossible. The first thing to be said is that Mosca's claim is simply not true. Societies exist which have no ruling classes, though admittedly the examples are not nations, but smaller social units. Second, this assertion is ultimately irrelevant to the theory of democracy. All past and present societies have oppressed women, but that is hardly reason to say that we should sanction the oppression of women. If men are incapable of treating women as human beings, the problem lies with men and the theories which they construct to justify their behavior, not with women or those who advocate treating women as human beings.

We come, then, to Dahl's final objection to populist democracy. It has two parts, which are expressed in the same sentence: "A majority might well take actions that would destroy the system; hence some method of minority veto may be necessary to prevent this." [29] We examined the first concern earlier in this chapter. Certainly, the person who believes in majoritarian rule is concerned that the majority might decide to commit political suicide and might vote to abandon majority rule. In that regard, the majoritarian can say little except that such an eventuality would be both unfortunate and shortsighted. There is nothing about democracy or any other form of government which prevents stupid or immoral decisions. No sensible person should favor democracy because it guarantees goodness, truth, and beauty. One advocates it for the same reason one advocates not being prejudiced: absent powerful arguments to the contrary, there is no justification for prejudice. Dahl's view really comes down to something which looks very much like the Madisonian view that he worked so hard to dismiss. The minority veto is designed to protect the society against the tyranny of the majority.

Dahl also raises a related, empirical objection: populist democracy fails to take into account time periods. It seems that he thinks that a parallel exists between that issue and the issue of the failure to take into account intensity of preference. He falls back on his standard criticism that no one really advocates the obvious solution: "No advocate of populist democracy, so far as I am aware, has ever demanded an instantaneous translation of majority preferences into governmental policies; that is, some time lag is assumed to exist between the first occurrence of majority preference and the government action carrying it out." [30] Here again, Dahl is trying to save the majority from itself.

Of course, nothing would prevent a majority from specifying the time of implementation for some actions. In fact, on nonstate levels, majorities do that with some regularity when they have the responsibility. Sometimes one might be inclined to suggest that if the majority became impatient and demanded immediate rectification, it would not be entirely unreasonable. For example, how much longer should we wait in the United States before African Americans and native Americans are given the same opportunities for education and employment that others are given? It would not be entirely irrational to favor instantaneous translation of preference into action. Dahl would presumably want some provision for a time lag, no matter what arguments could be put forward. In general, it is difficult to escape the judgment that Dahl, like Madison, basically does not trust the majority. Like parents who are reluctant to let go of their children when they reach maturity, Dahl wants to continue some kind of control—for their own good, of course.

Having explored Dahl's rejections of populist democracy, we will now turn to his positive suggestion for democracy. He calls it polyarchal democracy. The -archal echoes the element present in *monarchical* and *oligarchical*. It comes from the Greek element *archía*, which means rule or ruling. Dahl seems to want to convey the notion of a rule by many—not many people directly, but many entities—the minorities mentioned earlier: "The more relevant question is the extent to which various minorities in a society will frustrate the ambitions of one another with the passive acquiescence or indifference of a majority of adults or voters. . . . The distinction comes much closer to being one between government by a minority and government by *minorities*." [31] This view is consistent with Dahl's general pluralism and that of other contemporary empirical political scientists. Dahl wants to make this a form of democracy, and since he has rejected the nonempirical base of populist democracy, he wants to be sure this approach to democracy has an empirical flavor. To this end, he uses what he calls the descriptive method: "Consider as a single class of phenomena all those nation states and social organizations that are commonly called democratic by political scientists." Then, having identified the examples of democracy, he wants to apply Mill's system for inductive logic, the method of agreement and difference, by examining the examples, "to discover, first, the distinguishing characteristics they have in common, and, second, the necessary and sufficient conditions for social organizations possessing these characteristics." [32]

The identification of the members of the class poses the greatest problem, and it seems insurmountable. We need to recall that Dahl first proposed this approach in 1956, perhaps at the height of the cold war. It was clear to him what countries belonged in the class of democratic states. Later he qualifies the phrase *political scientists* with the word *Western,* so we can be clear that the Communist countries will not be included in spite of the fact that they and their political scientists call themselves democratic. He even gives us something of a denotative definition: for Dahl, democracies include "certain aspects of the governments of nation states such as the United States, Great Britain, the Dominions (South Africa possibly excepted), the Scandinavian countries, Mexico, Italy, France; states and provinces such as states of this country and the provinces of Canada; numerous cities and towns; some trade unions; numerous associations such as Parent-Teacher's Associations, chapters of the League of Women Voters, and some religious groups; and some primitive societies." [33]

Dahl's parenthetical treatment of South Africa should have given him and his followers away. How could any possibility exist of South Africa of 1956 being a democratic society? Admittedly, he seems to think it should be rejected, but even so, considering it seems like considering including Hitler's Germany in the class of democratic states. Surely, it would not have been hard to argue that Yugoslavia under Marshal Tito paid more attention to the citizenry at large than the South African government did. The giveaway shows the problem with Dahl's proposal: it is circular. He defines all these societies as democratic, and so it follows that his examination of their commonality will reveal them to be democratic. The definition of a term should not include the term, but that is what has happened. Dahl's concern is that we must save the existence of democracy:

> How then shall we distinguish the vote of the Soviet peasant or the bribed stumble-bum from the farmer who supports a candidate committed to high support prices, the businessman who supports an advocate of low corporate taxes or the consumer who votes for candidates opposed to a sales tax? I assume that we wish to exclude expressions of preference of the first kind but to include the second. For if we do not exclude the first, then any distinction between totalitarian and democratic systems is fatuous; but if we exclude the second, then surely no examples of even the most proximate democracies can be found to exist anywhere. We can hardly afford to read the human race out of democratic politics.[34]

We learn two things in this important passage. First, we are back, once again, at the reasoning by bifurcation which has haunted us throughout this book. The hidden assumption is that only two forms of governance are possible: totalitarianism and democracy. Having concluded (sensibly) that the societies listed above (with the possible exception of South Africa) are not totalitarian, Dahl concludes they must be democratic. But of course, there is another possibility: some or all of those systems may be neither totalitarian nor democratic. The second thing we learn is that Dahl is committed to saving at least the rhetorical presence of democracy. Other than expressing some kind of emotional commitment to democracy, it is difficult to know why he takes this view, but he does.

We should be cautious about the logical points which have just been made. Dahl's discoveries of how society actually operates are very important, and in chapter 7 we will see that the analysis suggested follows from some of the important insights he has taught us. The disagreement in this chapter is with calling what Dahl has discovered democracy. It is simply a misuse of the word, and such semantic confusion actually leads to other confusions. In the next chapter we will pursue these thoughts further.

Giovanni Sartori: Normative Polyarchal Democracy

Sartori is respected as one of the leading modern democratic theoreticians. His recent survey of the theory of democracy is nothing short of a tour de force.[35] While Sartori approaches democratic theory from a substantially different perspective from that of Dahl, the two reach quite similar conclusions. In the end, Sartori accepts Dahl's polyarchy terminology, though Sartori develops it as a normative theory rather than a descriptive one. By doing so, Sartori evades some of the logical pitfalls which proved to be a problem for Dahl's theory.

Sartori's Critique of Etymological Democracy

Early in his analysis, Sartori joins those who argue that democracy is not committed to majoritarianism. In place of Dahl's populist democracy, Sartori establishes what he calls etymological democracy. Thus, he recognizes that etymologically *democracy* means rule by the people, and initially he seems to agree that such a formulation must mean majoritarian rule. He quickly goes on to say, however, that democracy does not really mean all that and that we must adopt some constraints on the majority. Sartori's first concern with a majoritarian democracy is that it will commit suicide: "Establishing the absolute right of the majority to impose its will on the minority, or minorities, amounts to establishing a working rule that works, in the longer run, against the very principle it extols. If the first winner of a democratic contest acquires unfettered (absolute) power, then the first winner can establish itself as a permanent winner. If so, a democracy has no democratic future and ceases to be a democracy at its inception."[36] Sartori, we notice, is even more pessimistic than Plato and Dahl about democratic suicide. Sartori believes that it would be all but inevitable. The suicide of democracy is no longer something merely to be feared, but something to be feared and expected at the conclusion of the first election. Of course, *impose its will* is loaded language, and Sartori's description is, no doubt, designed to make our blood run cold. However, it has its obverse. If the majority is not going to impose its will on the minority, then the other choice must be that the minority will impose its will on the majority.[37] Once again, we are back to the question of what good reasons Sartori or anyone else could bring forward for suggesting that the minority should impose its will on the majority. The antidemocrats, parading all the time as defenders of democracy, have put the advocates of democracy on the defensive by cleverly shifting the burden to their shoulders. Since the democrats (majoritarians) have no defenders, there is no answer.

One answer to Sartori is that the suicide he fears is not inevitable. His progression depends not only on elected governance but also on the notion that once in office, officials would elect an absolute dictatorship. Once again, democracy cannot prevent a democratic society from adopting such procedures and legislation. At the same time, nothing forces it to do so, either.

A democracy may establish rules which constrain rulers: the democracy may have easy recall provisions. A democracy may create a system of checks and balances, which prevents the centralization of power. There is almost no end to the ways in which a democracy can constrain its rulers, representatives, administrators, or managers. Almost no end, but there is an end: democracy cannot lodge in anyone power which cannot be withdrawn or redirected or restrained by the majority. It can do so, but then it does commit suicide as a democracy. There is nothing inevitable in that eventuality. Its probability is something that empirical political scientists can try to assess. Sartori's a priori view is not sustained.

Sartori's second argument against etymological democracy is that majorities may engage in truly treacherous acts and, in that context, cannot adjudicate messy and emotional issues:

> Throughout the history of humankind, majorities—ethnic, religious, or sheer numerical majorities—have persecuted minorities, at times to the point of exterminating them. . . . As Nordlinger puts it, "the democratic model in its orthodox majoritarian form is unsuitable for the regulation of severe conflicts." I have no quarrel with Nordlinger's conclusion, but I am struck by his premise, that is, by his reference to an "orthodox majoritarian" model of democracy. What model is that? I am not sure. But I am sure it *is not* unqualified (and thereby limitless) majority rule.[38]

I have no quarrel with Sartori's claim that majorities have done some truly outrageous things in the past. That does not distinguish them from minorities, for whom the record is at least as bad, if not worse. What is striking, however, is his claim that he does not understand Edward A. Nordlinger's reference to an " 'orthodox majoritarian' model of democracy." Perhaps Sartori's ignorance of Nordlinger's reference is feigned, since this assertion comes at the end of a chapter in which Sartori has been at some pains to dispense with that view. One might guess that Sartori's unhappiness is primarily directed at Nordlinger's use of the word *orthodox,* because that leaves the impression that the limited democracy Sartori and others advocate is unorthodox. Nordlinger seems to be right on this issue, and a straightforward reading of the language would support him. One need not doubt that Sartori's concerns with orthodox democracy are well founded, and the alternative system he and Dahl propose is not necessarily inferior to orthodox democracy. The point to be made, rather, is that at some point it is time to say that we are no longer dealing with different flavors of ice cream because we are no longer dealing with ice cream. To some, a chocolate bar may taste better than chocolate ice cream. However, it is semantic foolishness to call a chocolate bar a form of chocolate ice cream or to call chocolate ice cream a form of chocolate bar.

Later in his book, Sartori returns to these points and deals with what he calls direct democracy, participatory democracy, and then referendum democracy. Important lessons can be learned from an examination of those issues.

Sartori's Critique of Direct Democracy

Sartori makes the historical point that if direct democracy means a democracy in which people can deal with each other directly and through extended conversations and debates arrive at governmental decisions, then that is probably a romantic relic of a past era and has little relevance to the nation-states we consider today. Sartori is largely correct on this score. To follow my metaphor, there can be different flavors of democracy.

The literature of political theory since the industrial revolution has given far too little attention to the issue of size. Many theories constructed before then assumed small units which could be brought together in assembly-size meetings. They did not debate the topic of size because it was basically a given. Aristotle turns his attention to size only briefly in the *Politics* and concludes that the best limit of the size of population of the state is the largest number which can be observed in a single view. We should give Aristotle credit for recognizing that size is a topic to be considered. Some gauge of how little importance he attached to it, however, can be taken from the fact that the entire treatment is contained in two paragraphs and concludes with the impatient statement "Enough concerning the size of a state." [39]

Sartori's Critique of Participatory Democracy

One suspects that Sartori decided to analyze what he called participatory democracy because the term was one of approbation for some faculty and some students at the expensive colleges and universities in the United States in the late 1960s and early 1970s. Sartori's own university, Columbia, was one of the central players. What intellectual merit participatory democracy had came from a yearning for a return to direct democracy, and Sartori's analysis subjects it to the same criticism he launched against that. The other direction of participatory democracy which might be discerned is what Sartori calls referendum democracy, and he devotes considerable energy to dismissing that approach.

Sartori's Critique of Referendum Democracy

Sartori picks up Wolff's suggestion that we could have direct democracy again, at least through referenda and new technology, and he discusses the possibility of referendum democracy as a means to etymological democracy. He dismisses Wolff's interesting suggestion with a side comment in a footnote. If Sartori had taken it seriously, he would have found that it posed a significant challenge to his point of view. Let us turn directly to Sartori's criticism, not of the technology (he seems to accept its feasibility), but of referendum democracy. His first counterargument is that it would result in "an outright *zero-sum mechanism* of decision making, . . . no tradeoffs, no compensations, could occur among issues either." [40] We have seen this critique before in different words from Dahl. Here we need only repeat the obvious: it is possible that the majoritarian system might frame issues in a zero-sum fashion, but it would not necessarily do that. Absent some compelling arguments and evidence to the contrary, it seems not even likely. If the disputing sides could find a "win-win" solution, why would they not choose it and guarantee passage by the voters? The a priori case is not proven; it is merely asserted.

Sartori offers a second argument against referendum democracy: "I submit that the untold truth is that even the most extreme participationist realizes that he demands more than he actually desires, and indeed far more than is desirable. Why should he not demand referendum democracy unless he too senses it would be an overkill?" [41] Here we are back to Dahl's argument that since no one really advocates the position, we do not have to take it seriously. After we have said Sartori's argument is a non sequitur, what is left to be said? We need not delay long, because Sartori's real argument is his third one. If we look at it closely, it will help introduce his positive position about democracy.

Sartori's third reason for rejecting majoritarian referendum democracy is not only that people may make stupid decisions but also, and of greatest concern, that their decisions will make a difference. His argument is based on a fundamental assumption which identifies an important difference between having opinions and having knowledge. He does not doubt that in a majoritarian democracy people will have opinions. He also recognizes that they will not necessarily have knowledge. He argues, however, that knowledge is most important in the governing process. Sartori cannot be faulted on this score. No doubt, if most people were asked to describe the likely impact of an increase in the discount rate, they would be stymied. Yet a majoritarian democracy which worked on a referendum basis would be open to such decisions by referendum. From Sartori's perspective, it will do no good to plead for more education. That is delusive. He argues that the range of decisions which have to be made is so enormous that no single person could understand even the first-order ramifications of all of them, no matter how much education she or he had.

Thus, the first half of Sartori's proposition is warranted: the knowledge necessary for the decisions cannot be had by the electorate. The second half is that such knowledge is important, and that argument must be sustained also. Deciding what kind of program to fund for discovering a cure for AIDS, deciding what electronic systems are most effective at jamming enemy radar, deciding the impact of an increase in Pell Grants to college students as distinct from an increase in Stafford Loans, deciding how to respond to a proposal from the EEC at the GATT talks, and deciding how many air traffic controllers are needed are all decisions which must be made at some level of government, and decision makers must have considerable knowledge to make them sensibly. If the choices are made out of ignorance and if that ignorance leads to wrong answers, innocent people may suffer disastrous consequences. Here we find a difference between majoritarian democracy and other kinds of governance. As Sartori says:

> Given an equal amount of information, a person may either be competent or remain incompetent, depending on whether he perceives correctly which means are appropriate to what ends, and thereby which consequences derive from which decision or action.
>
> When the chips are down, it is above all the problem of *knowledge,* of competent understanding, that must be squarely confronted. We can circumvent it, or fudge it as long as electors simply elect; but not if voters are issue deciders. . . . in an electoral democracy the question as to whether we learn how to vote . . . can be left undecided or to wishful thinking; it is not crucial. In referendum democracy, instead, everything hinges on whether people learn how to participate (in decision making) by participating (in pressing buttons on the video). . . . The question is: Does participation (as described) teach knowledge (as defined)? To this question, the answer is surely no.[42]

Sartori is undoubtedly correct that the citizen does not have the requisite knowledge to make reasonable decisions either by participating in voting on referenda or by any other imaginable means. It is not just the tyranny of the majority we need to fear: it is the tyranny of an ignorant but opinionated majority.

Sartori's Contribution: Electoral Polyarchal Democracy

Sartori's proposed form of democracy saves us from the problem just identified because it has representatives to make decisions, and the electoral process is so confused and confusing that no conclusions can be drawn from it. He refers to Dahl on this point: "As Dahl neatly puts it, strictly speaking 'all an election reveals is the first preferences of some citizens among candidates standing for office,' for 'we can rarely interpret a majority of first choices among candidates in a national election as being equivalent to a majority of first choices for a specific policy.' If anything, elections may reveal even less than Dahl suggests, for often enough they do not even express 'first preferences' or first choices." [43] We have come down to it, then. Dahl tells us, and Sartori agrees, that voting really does not mean much, because it cannot be read as indicating preferences for policy decisions. In addition, as long as electors (the citizens) simply elect (representatives), it does not matter whether they elect on the basis of knowledge or merely on the basis of opinion, since their votes do not do much to influence government, legislation, policy, or action. We have a description of a democracy in which voting is merely an empty gesture that has minimal or no impact on governance.

A brief autobiographical digression may help clarify a point about what we have discovered. Some years ago I had the honor to take a course in systematic theology with one of the great theologians of our lifetime, Paul Tillich. At the time he was completing the third volume of his *Systematic Theology* and teaching his last year at Harvard Divinity School. During the course, I began to wonder how his teaching might be useful to preparing clergy in a divinity school. More specifically, I wondered how it made sense to pray on the basis of Tillich's theology, since God, the Ground of Being, was not a personality, would not in any normal sense hear prayers, and was not the kind of being who would respond to prayers by intervening on behalf of the supplicant. The closest I came to gaining some clarity on the question was when one of Professor Tillich's followers said that the purpose of prayer in Tillich's theology was not to communicate with God but to communicate with oneself. The follower argued that for Tillich prayer was a kind of self-therapy designed to make the person who prayed feel better.

We can close the analogical loop now. The purpose of voting in the Sartori-Dahl system is not to influence government legislation, policies, or actions. The purpose is self-therapy. Citizens feel better if they go to the polls occasionally and express their opinions, even though their action actually makes no difference. It is difficult to know how to refrain from calling such a view cynical in the extreme.

In a search for an understanding of democracy, we began with the straightforward notion that it meant that the majority rules. After a careful analysis of some of the great democratic theoreticians, we come to the end and find that, far from the majority's ruling by vote, voting itself is an empty gesture designed largely to make voters feel good even though their votes make no difference. We may have reached reality in understanding ideology in the postindustrial world. However, surely we now have good reason to stop calling this approach a form of democracy.

We can now turn directly to Sartori's normative proposal for society. In developing it, he acknowledges his indebtedness to Dahl, but he wants to move beyond Dahl's restrictive empiricism: "Descriptively, I have said, democracy *is* an elective polyarchy. But what *ought* it to be? Since polyarchy is a *state of fact,* what is its corresponding deontology, its corresponding *state of norms?*" Sartori soon answers his own question: "Let my first axiological definition be: Democracy should be a *selective system* of competing elected minorities. Let it equally be, still more briefly and in symmetry with descriptive definition: Democracy should be a *selective polyarchy.*" He continues, "It can now be implemented by the following definition: democracy should be a *polyarchy* of merit." Finally, he asserts, "With democracy defined as an elective poly-archy . . . democracy ought to be (a) a selective polyarchy, and (b) a polyarchy of merit. As John Stuart Mill put it, 'when we desire to have a good school, we do not eliminate the teacher.' "[44]

We have, then, made the final transition from Dahl's labored attempts merely to describe the system to Sartori's willingness to endorse and advocate it. The question remains: On what possible grounds does it make sense to call this system democracy? The word *elitism* may have such negative connotations, especially in the United States, where we like to pretend we do not have elites, that we might unfairly doom the Sartori-Dahl system by suggesting that it be called elitism. However, it is no more a democracy than it is a dictatorship. Why not just call it polyarchism and stop pretending?

Conclusion

Our conclusion, then, must be twofold. First, democracy does have a defi-nition. It is something like what Mill had in mind originally, what Wolff called majoritarian democracy, what Dahl called populist democracy, what Sar-tori called etymological democracy, and what Nordlinger, to Sartori's dismay, called orthodox democracy. The definition identifies democracy with a pure process approach and with majoritarian rule. Second, appearances to the con-trary notwithstanding, the great democratic theoreticians are not prepared to defend democracy. They all find some modified version to defend, until finally Sartori, following Dahl, dismisses even the efficaciousness of voting while still pretending to present a theory of democracy.

One problem with discussing democratic theory involves the use of the adjectives. Certainly the noun *democracy* can be legitimately qualified with adjectives. In doing so, however, the theoreticians treat the noun as if it needs a qualifying adjective. They need to recognize that *democracy* has a perfectly acceptable definition and that if someone wishes to develop another ideological system, it is that system which needs the adjectival qualification, not *democracy* itself. Democracy as such has neither been attacked and shown wanting, nor has it been defended. In this chapter, I have suggested a strategy of defense, but no one has developed that either. Its further development is beyond the purview of this book and will have to be left to another occasion. We shall turn, next, to those who challenge the notion that democracy can be a purely process-oriented ideology and who believe that democracy is intimately connected with either capitalism or socialism.

6 Democratic Socialism and Democratic Capitalism

We have seen, then, that even at the hands of its friends, democracy is in danger of being defined out of existence. The self-identified democratic theoreticians are apparently quite prepared to name a wide range of principles democratic. As we noted earlier, the word *democracy* may have lost its denotative meaning and now only connotes something the speaker likes. It should not be surprising, then, that in order to establish the superiority of their views, socialists and capitalists would attempt to link them with democracy. The rhetorical strategy is to assume that everyone agrees that democracy is good. Then one argues that democracy logically requires socialism (or capitalism). If that can be shown, then those who were reluctant to accept socialism (or capitalism) on other grounds may endorse it because of its necessary connection to democracy and the virtual universal veneration of democracy.

One may be inclined to guess that the two cases would neutralize each other and that we could ignore the controversy. However appealing such a perfunctory dismissal might be, we cannot afford to ignore claims which are important to understanding ideology. Furthermore, arguments between democratic socialists and democratic capitalists will reveal more about all three ideologies and will provide us with insight for further analysis.

Democratic Socialism: Does Democracy Imply Socialism?

While historically the case for capitalism precedes the case for socialism, the arguments for democratic socialism predate those for democratic capitalism. Capitalism was firmly rooted in the individualism of the British liberal thinkers.[1] It was easily coordinated with the utilitarianism so popular among the British, and it was a comfortable position for those who placed considerable faith in the individual as an element separable from society at large. On the surface, at least, democracy is most compatible with this kind of individualism. The majoritarian view can be achieved by a simple device—voting. The distinction Rousseau made between the will of all and the General Will could be either denied or ignored.

The capitalists had already conceded much of the rhetorical debate to the socialists. They accepted the definition of capitalism as laid down by the socialists; they accepted the terms of the debate; they even accepted the socialist word for their view, *capitalism*. That failure put the socialists argumentatively in the driver's seat in the debates which would follow. The socialists, however, had their own problems. Even though joining socialism and the apparent individualism of democracy would prove troublesome, many socialists shared with others who were not socialists a general esteem for democracy.

The voice of Eduard Bernstein, a close disciple of both Marx and Engels, became an important one in the development of democratic socialism. In his 1899 book, *Evolutionary Socialism,* Bernstein presented a strong case for democratic socialism.[2] He had to face issues connected with the early Marxist commitment to revolutionary change, with Marx's more mature support for a "dictatorship of the proletariat," and, especially, with Marx's impatience with describing what socialism might be like once it achieved victory. Bernstein's approach still retained his indebtedness to Marx, and he was the first to acknowledge some differences between Marx and Engels.[3] Bernstein recognized that the revolution, which had seemed imminent in 1848, was not going to occur even though the underlying exploitive conditions remained in full force. He saw that democracy had a hold on people. He saw that somehow the capitalist economists had convinced many that economics could be distinguished from other forms of social analysis and that their economic theories should be retained irrespective of what was actually happening to people.

Bernstein was no less committed to improving the condition of the working class than Marx had been. He believed, however, that as long as democracy held the persuasive power it did among common folk, they would not revolt in order to get rid of capitalism. Thus, his task, and that of other democratic socialists who have followed him, was to show not only how socialism and democracy could be held together but also how only socialism could be made compatible with democracy.

In understanding the fundamental argument of the democratic socialist, we should recall the bifurcation fallacy: both socialists and capitalists assume that only two possibilities exist and that defeat of one automatically means victory for the other. Democratic socialists returned to the basic anticapitalist argument against private property. They argued that the excesses of capitalism arose as a result of the doctrine of private property. Following Marx, they claimed that it is because capitalists are driven to accumulate as much control over property as possible that they withdraw property from that owned by everyone and hold it to themselves. Thus, the argument for democratic socialism turns on eliminating private property.

The argument then proceeds in two further steps. The first denies the divorce created by capitalist economists between economics and other social analyses.[4] A sophisticated form of that argument was discussed in the third chapter of this book. There we saw that capitalist economists want to isolate economics and remove it from all the difficult social issues, which are, as Milton Friedman said, "differences about which men can only fight." [5]

The next step in the argument of the democratic socialist is an ingenious one, because it introduces the concept of economic democracy, which means something like equality of economic resources, at least in regard to fundamental economic needs. Even to the present, the phrase *economic democracy* remains ambiguous. The intention is reasonably clear, at least when stated in the extreme. Consider, for example, people who have had poor health care all their lives, who have had little or no education, and who have been discriminated against from birth. To assume that they can participate fully and meaningfully in life in a democratic society—even an honestly democratic one—is simply to perpetuate a cruel hoax and to blind others to the consequences of their actions. Thus, at some minimal level at least, some equality is required. That level is, then, defined as a level of fundamental "needs," and the democratic socialist argues that all citizens have a right to have their needs met before others can expect to fulfill unnecessary desires. The problem, however, is distinguishing needs from desires. Presumably no one needs a fur coat, though some may desire one. At the same time, presumably everyone needs basic nutritional provisions. At the extreme, the differences are clear enough: it is in between, where most allocations occur, where it is difficult to establish needs as distinct from mere desires.[6] The democratic socialists argue that without economic democracy, political democracy cannot exist. That is a view which must be vigorously opposed by the capitalist economists, not only because of the threat to link economics and politics but also because of problems involved in the inequality of economic resources.

The capitalists have a ready argument for the empirically unavoidable fact of unequal distribution of economic goods. They argue that the goods are distributed in accordance with the contributions of the recipients to economic improvement. Thus, each year when *Business Week* publishes its issue on the most well-paid executives, a spate of editorials in the financial press argues that the executives are paid handsomely because they have such broad responsibilities and because they make such substantial contributions to the economy at large. The Pennwalt Corporation used to publish an editorial advertisement called "The Goose that Laid the Golden Egg," attempting to persuade people that the compensation of highly paid executives of Pennwalt and other corporations actually redounded to the benefit of all because it encouraged executives to work extra hard. Similarly, when *Forbes* publishes its list of the richest people, activity in the financial media is designed to convince those who would listen that such disparities in wealth are earned and necessary. The argument is brought forward dutifully, and on occasion some economists are recruited to validate the claims. It makes no difference that as often as not, one can demonstrate that the most important decision many of the executives made was to select the right parents.

Such arguments, and their speciousness, play directly into the hands of the democratic socialists. They reinforce the view that capitalism is an ideology that supports business executives at the expense of other people. The democratic socialists argue, in addition, that the business executives use their command of economic resources to gain political power, thus demonstrating that the supposed distinction between economics and politics is fraudulent. As a result, even though each person supposedly has the same voting power, the democratic socialists argue that with the resources at the disposal of the wealthy, they dominate the political process as well as the economic process.

In the face of the logical legerdemain of the capitalists, it is difficult to convince many people that such tremendous disparities result from temporary disequilibria and that in a well-functioning capitalist economy they would not take place. People hear from both socialists and capitalists that the disparities are an integral part of the capitalist system, and they accept that conclusion, since the capitalists and socialists apparently agree on so little else.

The democratic socialist argues, then, that the first step to a better society is to give up capitalism. That means eliminating private property, abandoning the myth of the ability to isolate economics from other aspects of society, and adopting some form of economic democracy. With the establishment of economic democracy, no one will be able to command control over economic resources through the accumulation of extraordinary wealth. Consequently, there will be no group of people who can use such wealth to establish effective control over the political process. Democratic socialists believe that, given those fundamental changes, democracy—true democracy, they would say—can flourish. People will be equal and free to consider the issues facing society. They can influence the social, political, and economic processes through democratic means. Installing economic democracy, of course, means eliminating private ownership of the major means of production and distribution.

We should analyze the three fundamental arguments. We have discussed arguments about private property at length in this book already, and nothing in the democratic socialists' acceptance of them would change any portion of the analysis. With regard to the argument for a distinction between economics and other areas of social analysis, it seems clear that the socialist arguments win the day. The arguments of the post-Smithian capitalist economists cannot be sustained. In the so-called hard sciences, only one serious counterexample will throw a theory into question. Perhaps in the softer sciences, where theory is so meager, it may make sense to suggest that we should continue with a fruitful theory until we accumulate counterexamples. In the case of the argument for the divorce of economics and the rest of social analysis, however, the question comes down to how many counterexamples would be enough. Clearly, we could identify counterexamples for as long as anyone had the patience to listen. The notion may be a useful heuristic for economists in the development of economic predictions. However, the successful predictive base of economics is not so strong that we should recommend accepting its theoretical assumptions as statements about the real world. In fact, Friedman goes so far as to say that in order for an economic hypothesis to be predictively important, it must be descriptively false.[7] Let us leave aside recommendations for the advancement of economics as a science and concentrate on ideology, where we would want our assertions to be descriptively true. In that context, society at large is a complicated, complex, and interrelated phenomenon.

Medical people have, after decades of denial, finally conceded that as medical phenomena, human beings are very complex. Health professionals have largely abandoned the outdated belief in the isolability of the physical aspect of their patients. The inspiration for the medical isolation was the same as the inspiration for economic isolation: gaining proximity to the hard sciences. Let us not debate here whether the desire was useful in the development of medicine or economics. We are interested in reality, not mere local predictability. If individual human reality is complex, it is even more likely that collective human reality will be complex. That may be unfortunate from the perspective of creating a science modeled on physics, but it is hard to see how it can be sensibly denied from a realistic perspective.

We should remember, however, that just because the socialists may have won this round of the debate, socialism is not thereby established. It is established only if we still assert the bifurcation fallacy. It may be that economics and other forms of social analysis should be linked but that the fundamentals of the economy are not socialist. Thus, if we avoid the bifurcation fallacy, we should say that the case for the victory of socialism has not been established.

The third fundamental argument of the democratic socialist, calling for the establishment of economic democracy, has considerable appeal to the casual observer. It has its own internal logic: the wealthy *can* use their power to attempt to exercise control. In addition, people who argue for economic democracy will propose a number of what they think are confirmatory cases for their position. They might point to someone such as John F. Kennedy or George Bush in high office, and they might argue that political success flowed directly from the inherited ability to call upon substantial resources.

The mode of argument is so common among socialists that it is important at this point to deal briefly with the scientific notion of confirmation. After some level of assurance of the repeatability of an experiment is established, physical scientists are not much interested in further confirmations of the theories, except where those occur under changed and presumptively challenging circumstances. The social scientist, by contrast, can easily find disconfirmation of prized theories. In that situation, confirmation is seen as a source of support, but it is a thin reed. Consider an easy, albeit humorous, case.

A man rides the same commuter train to work each day, and he always reads the newspaper while he is on the train. As he finishes each page of the paper, he tears it off, wads it up, and places it under his seat. When the trip is over, he gathers all the torn paper and leaves the train, depositing the paper in a wastebasket in the station. One of the other passengers becomes fascinated with this man's habit and observes it carefully, though it does not vary at all. Finally, the other passenger cannot restrain her curiosity any longer, and she arranges to take the seat next to the paper-tearing man. Toward the end of the trip, the curious passenger politely asks the paper-tearing man if he would explain why he tears up the newspaper in that way. The paper-tearing man explains that he is deathly afraid of snakes, and he tears paper off, wads it up, and puts it under his seat in order to keep snakes away. The curious passenger cannot contain herself and blurts out, "But there are no snakes on the train!" Whereupon the paper-tearing passenger says, "See, it works." Each time the paper-tearing passenger puts the wadded paper under his seat and finds no snakes, he confirms his theory that his activity prevents snakes from bothering him.

The general problem with confirmation is that it is too easy to get false positives. Herein lies the problem of the democratic socialists. They convince themselves and their listeners by citing incidences which confirm their views. Of course, it is easy to cite cases in which wealth and political power coincide. Unfortunately for the thesis, it is also easy to cite cases in which politically powerful people have not been particularly wealthy and vice versa. There just is neither sufficient empirical evidence nor a theoretical base to support the view that in order to have a political democracy, there must be no private ownership of major means of production and distribution.

George Bernard Shaw argued in *The Intelligent Woman's Guide to Socialism and Capitalism* that there should also be equality of income. Shaw's views are interesting because they try to combine the individualism of the British with the socialism which endorses an organic approach. Shaw retains the individualism not only in his commitment to democracy but also in his ingenious revision of socialism. Shaw invents a kind of individualist socialism. He is much more concerned with equality of compensation than with state ownership of the major means of production, on the theory that equal compensation and a 100-percent inheritance tax will render the ownership of means of production uninteresting. Shaw goes so far as to suggest that socialism should be renamed.

He acknowledges that the word *socialism* conveys some attachment to an over-arching society. Shaw suggests, rather, calling the approach *proletarianism,* since that would identify it more closely with individual people. In order to sustain their case, the democratic socialists, whether of the organic variety or the individualist variety, have had to argue that if a democratic community elects to adopt some economic arrangement which deviates from socialism, it will automatically be committing democratic suicide. In the end, the strongest case for democratic socialism forces it to commit the bifurcation fallacy and assume that the only alternative to capitalism must be socialism. Given that premise, the democratic socialists attempt to show that capitalism cannot be democratic.

By the time the democratic socialists had the courage to question the views of Marx, the development of corporations and the divergence from capitalism were already well under way. If they had recognized that and if they had realized that their arguments were not with capitalism but with something else, they might have recognized that their arguments would have to be restructured considerably before the case could be said to have been established that socialism and democracy are indissolubly linked. Absent such arguments, it seems at least conceivable that the majority in some society might choose democratically to adopt an economic system in which the major means of production and distribution were not owned by the state and that the society would not necessarily commit democratic suicide. Thus, the case for the deduction of socialism from democracy has not been made and likely cannot be made.

Democratic Capitalism: Does Democracy Imply Capitalism?

The socialists' attempt to assert hegemony over democracy was bound to provoke a response from the defenders of capitalism. Three important economists, in particular, took up the challenge: Milton Friedman, Friedrich Hayek, and Ludwig von Mises. While the three do not agree on other issues, they are united on this one. Once again, the capitalists followed the rhetorical lead of the socialists and, as a consequence, put capitalism in a defensive posture. They accepted their designation as capitalists, and they accepted the centrality of the proposition that major means of production and distribution should be privately held. However, they had some rhetorical moves up their sleeves when they turned to discussing democratic capitalism. One of those was to try to recapture the term *liberal,* which the socialists and others were shifting to the left.

The history of the word *liberal* is an interesting one. It is not at all clear what it means in journalistic parlance, especially in the United States today. However, it probably means something strongly at variance from its historical meaning. Hayek, for example, says: "It has been part of the camouflage of leftish movements in [the United States], helped by the muddleheadedness of many who really believe in liberty, that 'liberal' has come to mean the advocacy of almost every kind of government control. I am still puzzled why those in the United States who truly believe in liberty should not only have allowed the left to appropriate this almost indispensable term but should have assisted by beginning to use it themselves as a term of opprobrium." [8] Hayek wrote these words in 1944, when he was still teaching in Great Britain. He had remarkable foresight. Surely we can say in the United States as the twentieth century draws to a close that Hayek's concerns have been borne out. The self-identified conservatives have so completely abandoned the term *liberal* that they use it with a practiced sneer.[9] Perhaps Hayek knew even better than we might think, however, for he goes on to tell us about conservatives: "A conservative movement, by its very nature, is bound to be a powerful defender of establishment privilege and to lean on the power of government for the protection of privilege." [10] That is not a bad description of modern conservatives in the United States. In spite of their protestations to the contrary, it is probably a better description of their ideological views than *democratic capitalism* or even *capitalism* alone would be.

Von Mises also lays claim to the term liberal: "I employ the term 'liberal' in the sense attached to it everywhere in the nineteenth century and still today in the countries of continental Europe. This usage is imperative because there is simply no other term available to signify the great political and intellectual movement that substituted free enterprise and the market economy for the precapitalistic methods of production." [11] The term *liberal* is important to democratic capitalists because freedom is important to them. They emphasize freedom more than democracy. They believe that socialism leads directly to a loss of freedom, and they are understandably insistent that *liberal,* with its root meaning in freedom, be retained for their view. They want to appropriate freedom for their view because it is on the topic of freedom that they believe their adversaries, the socialists, are weakest.

At long last, we see the defenders of capitalism beginning to recognize the substantial harm the socialists have done to their position merely by deft rhetorical maneuvers. It may be that they have finally seen that their predecessors gave up too much terminology to their adversaries and, thus, that they are at a substantial disadvantage in debates. Some seem to have decided to take a stand on the word *liberal* and not allow it to become another in the anticapitalist vocabulary. Friedman, who is more aware of the nuances of the language as spoken by Americans than Hayek or von Mises, weighs in mightily on the side of retaining *liberal* for the view of democratic capitalists:

> Because of the corruption of the term liberalism, the views that formerly went under that name are now often labeled conservatism. But this is not

a satisfactory alternative. The nineteenth-century liberal was radical, both in the etymological sense of going to the root of the matter, and in the political sense of favoring major changes in social institutions. . . . Partly because of my reluctance to surrender the term to proponents of measures that would destroy liberty, partly because I cannot find a better alternative, I shall resolve these difficulties by using the word liberalism in its original sense—as the doctrine pertaining to the free man.[12]

We are led, then, to the question of the linkage between democracy and capitalism.

The democratic capitalists not only want to retain *liberalism* as an appropriate term for their views: as if to confirm their dedication to freedom, Hayek and von Mises also get *democracy* right.[13] Hayek devotes a chapter to democracy and its relation to planning. Von Mises understands explicitly what democracy is: "Democracy . . . provides a method for the peaceful adjustment of government to the will of the majority." Later, he writes, "Democracy guarantees a system of government in accordance with the wishes and plans of the majority." [14] It is remarkable how simple it is to state what democracy is when one is not trying to avoid the topic by subsuming some antidemocratic scheme under its rubric.

Furthermore, von Mises understands an important implication of democracy, and unlike those who fret about the tyranny of the majority, he accepts the consequence without suggesting that we should abandon democracy: "But [democracy] cannot prevent majorities from falling victim to erroneous ideas and from adopting inappropriate policies which not only fail to realize the ends aimed at but result in disaster. Majorities too may err and destroy our civilization." Concerning representative democracy, he says: "Democratic elections do not provide the guarantee that the man elected is free from faults, but merely that the majority of the voters prefer him to other candidates." [15] One reason that Hayek and von Mises may be able to see democracy without the qualifications is that they actually have no fundamental interest in democracy itself. One supposes that for the political scientist, political theory may be an end in itself, but for Hayek, von Mises, and Friedman, democracy is merely a means to an end.

Thus, von Mises clearly defines *democracy*. Hayek is equally clear about what he takes to be the proper role of democracy:

> We have no intention, however, of making a fetish of democracy. It may well be true that our generation talks and thinks too much of democracy and too little of the values which it serves. It cannot be said of democracy, as Lord Acton truly said of liberty, that it "is not a means to a higher political end. It is itself the highest political end. It is not for the sake of a

> good public administration that it is required, but for the security in pursuit
> of the highest objects of civil society, and of private life." Democracy is
> essentially a means, a utilitarian device, for safeguarding internal peace
> and individual freedom.[16]

This quotation not only helps us understand Hayek's view of the role of democracy but also helps us move a step further toward a direct answer to the question of this section: Does democracy imply capitalism? Hayek answers in the affirmative: "It is now often said that democracy will not tolerate 'capitalism.' If 'capitalism' means here a competitive system based on free disposal over private property, it is far more important to realize that only within this system is democracy possible." Friedman, in his clear-eyed style, leaves no doubt in the reader's mind, at least with regard to freedom: "History suggests only that capitalism is a necessary condition for political freedom." Thus, for the democratic capitalists, freedom is the end. As a result, they are able to embrace a concept of democracy which allows maximum freedom, at least in the voting booth. By 1962, when Friedman's important book was published, the topic of democracy had almost disappeared, and the near-exclusive emphasis was on freedom: "We are, thus, led to accept majority rule in one form or another as an expedient. That majority rule is an expedient rather than itself a basic principle is clearly shown by the fact that our willingness to resort to majority rule, and the size of the majority we require, themselves depend on the seriousness of the issue involved." [17] Obviously, if democracy is merely an expedient, then the nature of the majority which will rule is also an expedient. Thus, we finally find people who understand democracy. At the same time, we are forced to conclude that they are also fundamentally antidemocratic and, at least insofar as Friedman is concerned, quite willing to manipulate the alleged democracy to some other end.

What is the end? It is freedom, as the title to Friedman's book indicates. The person who wishes to uphold democracy might be inclined to retort: "Professors Hayek, von Mises, and Friedman, let me accept for the sake of our discussion your contention that capitalism is a necessary condition for democracy. Let me, then, suggest a second thesis: democracy is a necessary condition for freedom. Since capitalism is a necessary condition for democracy and democracy is a necessary condition for freedom, through the logical property of transitivity, we can conclude that capitalism is a necessary condition for freedom, as Professor Friedman explicitly argues. However, if the central premise is left out, then we have a very different understanding of the relation between capitalism and freedom. Democracy is the necessary linkage. Whatever can be said about your thesis of the relation between capitalism and democracy, there is greater assurance that my thesis is the stronger of the two. It would be easier to argue that an economic system is an expedient for freedom than that democracy is the expedient." The defender of democracy might mount such an argument, but as far as I know, no one ever has done so. That is not my concern in this book, but I am concerned that we continue to be intellectually honest about the true nature of democracy.

As we might expect, the democratic capitalists reserve some of their most trenchant arguments for criticizing the defenders of democratic socialism. Of course, they define *socialism* as state ownership of the means of production.[18] The basic thrust of their argument, however, concerns the planning which they believe will be necessary in a socialist society, rather than the mere fact of property ownership. They argue that while such planning may be conceivable in a socialist society which is totalitarian, it is virtually impossible in a democratic state, especially with democracy defined as they do. Hayek's arguments are largely normative:

> It is not difficult to see what must be the consequences when democracy embarks upon a course of planning which in its execution requires more agreement than in fact exists. . . .
>
> Nor can a coherent plan be achieved by breaking it up into parts and voting on particular issues. A democratic assembly voting and amending a comprehensive economic plan clause by clause, as it deliberates on an ordinary bill, makes nonsense. . . .
>
> . . . Even if . . . a democracy should succeed in planning every sector of economic activity, it would still have to face the problem of integrating these separate plans into a unitary whole. Many separate plans do not make a planned whole.[19]

Thus, even when Hayek grants the hypothesis that a democratic society might be able to construct comprehensive plans, his fundamental fear is that inevitably the structure will break down and democratic rule will fall: "Yet agreement that planning is necessary, together with the inability of democratic assemblies to produce a plan, will evoke stronger and stronger demands that government or some single individual should be given powers to act on their own responsibility. The belief is becoming more and more widespread that, if things are to get done, the responsible authorities must be freed from the fetters of democratic procedure." [20] Ironically, if we accept the view that democracy is a mere expedient, then the outcome Hayek fears is even more likely. It might be that another eventuality would occur if the nature of the economy rather than the nature of the polity was taken as the expedient element. The truly democratic society, upon seeing that socialist planning simply could not be made to work in a democratic setting, might elect to become a nonsocialist society rather than a nondemocratic society.

Von Mises, however, focuses more on the simple practicality of trying to accomplish the planning to which the democratic socialists would be committed. First, he argues that the requisite knowledge would never be available. For example, in 1970 very few could have predicted the enormous impact personal computers would have on the society and economy of the United States. A few visionaries speculated about that possibility, but none could present a solidly reasoned analysis. In fact, some of the most important business planners scoffed at the idea for a long time. IBM, perhaps one of the most well-managed and well-planned corporations, initially ignored the development of personal computers. Data General rejected the development entirely, and it may not survive because of that decision. What social planner in 1970 could have made secure plans which included recognition of that development? Thus, one failure von Mises finds for centralized planning is the impracticality of forecasting technological changes.

A second inherent failure of central planning or socialism is the inability to forecast human reactions to opportunities as they may develop. How many telephones are necessary? How much clothing is necessary? Here the classic conundrum of socialism must be faced: How can anyone distinguish between needs and wants? The most one will get from a democratic structure, or even from polling in a nondemocratic structure, is an expression of wants. There can be little doubt that as we approach the end of the twentieth century in the United States, most people would assert that telephone service is a necessity, that television is a necessity, and so on. Obviously, they were not always necessities. Thus, the socialist hope that we might find some inherent natural needs common to all people in all times comes to naught. The competitive system solves all these issues by putting a price on everything and letting individuals decide how they want to spend their money. Some people may wish to forgo some kinds of food in order to afford another remote-control television. Others may find it "necessary" to have a second bathroom in the house or air conditioning or a second car. They make those choices, and the competitive economy (theoretically, at least) responds to those choices by producing what is wanted. The socialist economy would have to plan for all that, and even if we were to put to the side Hayek's concerns that such demands might lead automatically to some form of nondemocratic government, we cannot leave aside von Mises' concern that in any reasonable practical analysis, the calculations simply could not be done.

There is another issue which von Mises did not raise directly but which would prove even more problematic than the issues he did raise. It is the issue of the necessary valuation of human health and life. The infamous Ford Pinto case will illustrate the point. That case is a favorite of professors of business ethics, and they seem commonly to agree that Ford made the wrong decision.[21]

As in any real-life situation, the actual facts are complicated, and we cannot address all of them here. The issue turns to some extent on a cost-benefit analysis which Ford did. The question Ford faced was whether the benefits which would be gained from adding an additional part to increase the probability that a rear-ended Pinto would survive a crash without catching on fire would be justified by the additional cost. Ford sought to use social costs and benefits here, not merely the costs and benefits to Ford.

Ford estimated that about 12,500,000 vehicles would be sold. The additional part cost $11 per vehicle. Thus, the total cost was approximately $138 million over the expected run of the vehicles. Ford calculated the benefits by estimating the extent of additional burn injuries which would result from not having the part and the costs, both medical and personal, of them (estimated at approximately $12 million). To that was added an estimated social cost of deaths which would result from not having the part. In order to arrive at a social cost of death, Ford used an estimate developed by the National Highway Traffic Safety Administration (NHTSA). The total costs of deaths, then, was estimated at approximately $36 million. Finally, added to both those figures was an estimate for the value of the cars which would be burned ($1.5 million). When all the benefits to come from adding the part were added up and compared with the costs of adding the part, it turned out that the costs of adding the part were greater than the benefits. As a result, Ford decided not to add the part.

A common objection to this procedure is that a monetary value is placed on life and on human suffering. The NHTSA needs such an estimate so it can make decisions about the strength of bridges, about the nature of roads, and so on. Unless one puts an infinitely high value on human life (and some do), calculations of some nature must be made. Of course, if a human life is assumed to be of infinite value, no car will be built, because all cars have some probability greater than zero of contributing to death in an accident. Many people simply refuse to enter into the process of putting a monetary value on human life. Not only is it necessary for the NHTSA, however, but it is also necessary for many other agencies. Von Mises might argue that the common reactions to this case give further evidence for his thesis that a political instrumentality, such as a democracy, simply cannot make the necessary economic calculations.

The final argument of von Mises may be his most sophisticated and important in the richness of its implications. In his book *Human Action*, he develops it in his chapter titled "The Impossibility of Economic Calculation under Socialism," which contains the brief section "The Differential Equations of Mathematical Economics." He argues that it is mathematically impossible to make the calculations which would be needed in socialist planning. He concludes: "There is therefore no need to stress the point that the fabulous number of equations which one would have to solve each day anew for a practical utilization of the method would make the whole idea absurd even if it were really a reasonable substitute for the market's calculation." [22] Unfortunately, von Mises mixes mathematics and practicality here. His argument is a powerful one, and it is difficult to imagine any practical rejoinder by the socialist, whether democratic or antidemocratic. Thus, in a sense it may suffice to carry the day, at least with economists. As it stands, however, the argument would prove unconvincing to mathematicians or logicians. They would ask for mathematical proof that the calculation could not be made, perhaps along the lines of Kurt Gödel's proof of the impossibility of showing a sophisticated logical or mathematical system to be both complete and consistent. Von Mises might have been able to provide such a proof. One would want the argument to be general enough so that it did not depend upon differential (or integral) equations alone, since the treatment of time in such equations is questionable as it applies to economic activities.[23]

The basic argument may lie even deeper in algebra and number theory. The most productive track to follow might be one which would show the necessity for more variables than equations, to put the matter in the terms of simple algebra. If that could be established and if it could be established that socialism necessarily involves such planning, then, apart from democracy or nondemocracy, socialism would have a paradox at its base. The democratic capitalists would not have to show that democratic socialism is a contradiction in terms. They would already have evidence of the contradictory nature of socialism itself.

Democratic capitalists, however, do argue that democratic socialism is a contradiction in terms. For example, Hayek says: "It is now even widely recognized that democratic socialism is a very precarious and unstable affair, ridden with internal contradictions and everywhere producing results most distasteful to many of its advocates." Friedman declares bluntly, "A society which is socialist cannot be democratic." Curiously, that leads all democratic capitalists to accept the socialist identification of the centrality of private property with capitalism. For example, von Mises says: "Private ownership of the means of production is the fundamental institution of the market economy. It is the institution the presence of which characterizes the market economy as such. Where it is absent, there is no question of a market economy." Robert Benne, who in 1981 took on the difficult task of reconciling capitalism, democracy, and the Christian morality of Reinhold Niebuhr, joined the assumption by criticizing the tenth edition of Paul Samuelson's famous text, *Economics: An Introductory Analysis:* "Strangely enough, Samuelson does not highlight what for many is the hallmark of a free-enterprise economy—private property." [24] What is most strange is that the defenders of capitalism (von Mises does not count Samuelson among them) have allowed the socialists to put that millstone around their necks. The hallmark of capitalism, as we have seen repeatedly, is responsiveness to consumer wishes, needs, demands, and desires. Whether or not private ownership of the means of production and distribution is an expedient means to that end is another issue.[25]

Friedman, who opposes the expansion of government power beyond that which is necessary, nevertheless argues that an important task of government is protecting private property:

> A government which maintained law and order, defined property rights, served as a means whereby we could modify property rights and other rules of the economic game, adjudicated disputes about the interpretation of the rules, enforced contracts, promoted competition, provided a monetary framework, engaged in activities to counter technical monopolies and to overcome neighborhood effects widely regarded as sufficiently important to justify governmental intervention, and which supplemented private charity and the private family in protecting the irresponsible, whether madman or child—such government would clearly have important functions to perform. The consistent liberal is not an anarchist.[26]

This paragraph offers useful instruction toward understanding the position of democratic capitalists. The government has a role. It certainly is a role one can imagine a democratic society endorsing. Thus, there is nothing inherently contradictory about capitalism (as they now define it) and democracy (as they define it). Without another premise, however, they cannot demonstrate that democracy implies capitalism or that capitalism is a necessary condition for democracy. That missing premise would commit them to the bifurcation fallacy: that only two possibilities for the economic order exist, capitalism and socialism.

Friedman does accept that bifurcation: "Fundamentally, there are only two ways of coordinating the economic activities of millions. One is central direction involving the use of coercion—the technique of the army and of the modern totalitarian state. The other is voluntary co-operation of individuals—the technique of the market place." [27] Obviously, if there are only two possibilities and one way is necessarily totalitarian and the other holds the only hope for democracy, it is easy to support the way with hope. It is the premise which declares that only two possibilities exist which needs examination.

Do Either Socialism or Capitalism Imply Democracy?

While it would be a weaker case for the socialist or capitalist to argue that democracy is a necessary condition for one ideology or the other, nevertheless a logical connection would be made. Showing that a socialist or capitalist society must be a democratic society would be showing something of importance.

If we return to the advocates of democratic socialism and democratic capital-ism, we may answer the question reasonably quickly. Certainly one can imagine a socialist society which is, for example, totalitarian. In essence, that is what Marx described in the dictatorship of the proletariat, though some Marxist apologists want to argue otherwise. Even if we were to grant the case of those apologists, however, the case in regard to Lenin would be resolved quickly against democracy. Lenin said that "democracy is of enormous importance to the working class in its struggle against the capitalists for its emancipation. But democracy is by no means a boundary not to be overstepped; it is only one of the stages on the road from feudalism to capitalism, and from capitalism to communism." [28] For Lenin scholars, it is worth noting that in this passage Lenin is speaking of democracy, not the "bourgeois democracy" upon which he heaps so much scorn. We can leave aside ostensibly empirical claims citing the Stalinist Soviet Union as an example of a totalitarian state. There can be little doubt that it was totalitarian. There can be extended debate, however, about whether it was socialist. As lawyers might say, it would be easier to argue the case that it was demonstrably anti-Marxist than the case that it was Marxist. Beyond statements by advocates and beyond questionable empirical evidence, we can find nothing in socialism per se which would require that it be practiced only in a democratic setting.

The issue in regard to capitalism is not as clear. It would seem clear if we merely turned to the advocates of capitalism, such as Friedman. He states that while he believes capitalism is a necessary condition for freedom, he does not believe freedom is a necessary condition for capitalism:

> History suggests only that capitalism is a necessary condition for politi-cal freedom. Clearly, it is not a sufficient condition. Fascist Italy and Fascist Spain, Germany at various times in the last seventy years, Japan before World Wars I and II, tzarist [sic] Russia in the decades before World War I—are all societies that cannot be described as politically free. Yet in each, private enterprise was the dominant form of economic organization. It is therefore clearly possible to have economic arrangements that are fundamentally capitalist and political arrangements that are not free.[29]

Recalling that our topic is not directly freedom but democracy, one is inclined to review this paragraph substituting *democracy* for *freedom*. That might soften the jarring thrust of the paragraph, but two thoughts suggest that such a sub-stitution would be misguided. In the first place, Friedman is a writer who is careful about the words he uses. He does not write casually, and he has clear deductive powers. Second, freedom is the value that he seeks in the book, which is, after all, titled *Capitalism and Freedom*. Thus, it seems we should take the paragraph as it stands and try to understand it.

The easiest thing to do is to agree with Friedman that Fascist Italy, Spain, Germany, Japan before the world wars, and czarist Russia were all nonfree societies. (They were also all antidemocratic.) The next step is to separate some of these societies. Let us separate Fascist Italy, Spain, and Germany from czarist Russia. The former were struggling with the aftermath of industrialization. Czarist Russia was basically an agrarian society which, in spite of the protestations of Lenin, was not prepared for industrialization, much less the aftermath of it, which Marx had required for the revolution.

Japan is a different case. While industrialization was developing in Japan and while one could even argue for some struggling with the aftermath of industrialization, the context was quite different. Japanese culture was not grounded in the rootless religious revolutions of the Europeans, nor did it have a religious heritage of an impending Armageddon. Thus, the time horizon (to use a modern expression) of the Japanese was much longer than that of the Europeans and Americans. One consequence of industrialization (and, perhaps, of capitalism) is the shrinking of time horizons.

Thus, if we concentrate on the other cases Friedman cites, we can conclude readily that Friedman has made a mistake in categorization. By including czarist Russia, he has introduced a preindustrial society, not an industrial or postindustrial one. We are interested, however, in industrial and postindustrial societies. Thus Friedman's quotation really leaves us with the example of fascism as an antifreedom (and antidemocratic) ideology which is, nevertheless, capitalist.

Once again, the trouble is one of equivocation in regard to the term *capitalism*. If we are to accept the view that the central defining feature of capitalism is private property, then Friedman's case should be granted. However, that view of capitalism which the socialists have aggressively advanced and to which the defenders of capitalism have acquiesced was not the sense of capitalism as originally developed, nor was it the sense of capitalism which gave capitalism its moral base. As long as the defenders of capitalism continue with their argument that private property is the central defining characteristic, the only moral argument they will have for capitalism will be its efficiency: they must claim that it is the best system for improving the economic lot of everyone, a variation on the image provided by John F. Kennedy that a rising tide brings up all vessels. That is a thin reed on which to rest the morality of an economic system, in part because one can identify so many counterexamples. In addition, if efficiency is the primary moral characteristic, then the intellectual and moral environment is set for a totalitarian government such as Fascists offer.

If we return to Smith's sense of capitalism and the assertion that its central purpose is to provide the widest possible choice at the lowest possible price to consumers, and if we can agree that effectively we are all consumers, then not only do we reestablish a moral base to capitalism, but we may also be able to glimpse an argument that asserts that democracy is a necessary condition for capitalism. For the purposes of this book, I cannot construct an argument based on logical grounds alone. I can only conceive of a persuasive argument: Capitalism depends upon numerous producers and suppliers that follow their own guesses about what consumers want. That means that many people will make wrong guesses and will find that what they want to produce in the way they want to produce it is not sufficiently rewarded in the marketplace to command a price which will cover costs. For example, suppose I like a certain kind of bread. Let us say it has caviar in it. I produce my bread and try to find a receptive audience willing to cover the costs, which includes the additional cost of adding caviar to bread. Before offering this bread to the public, I find that it is almost impossible to determine whether it will appeal to a sufficient audience.[30] I may offer my caviar bread to the public at, let us say, four times the cost of a standard loaf of bread. We can only wait and see whether enough people buy it. Stranger things have sold in the past. That kind of individual initiative and testing is required for capitalism to operate and, thus, for the consumer to get the widest range of goods and services at the lowest possible costs. One can imagine such a system surviving in a democratic political system. One can imagine that a majority of the citizens would see the positive and negative aspects of such a system. One can imagine people reasoning to themselves that they appreciate having the greatest possible choice at the lowest possible cost and that at some time they themselves might like to try their luck with producing something, at which point they would not want to be constrained by government regulation. Even though they might do such things, however, they would not necessarily do so.

In addition, under a nondemocratic system, there is less chance that capitalism would be maintained. One can imagine that initially a dictator might grant exploratory privileges to the populace. Following the sceptics about socialism, however, we should suspect that soon enough something would happen which would make the dictator decide to constrain that freedom substantially. Those decisions might be made because of purely selfish motives. They might also be made out of concern for social values. Suppose, for example, prostitution started as a lucrative business. The dictator might decide that prostitutes should be subjected to a health check or that prostitution should be prohibited entirely. After the initial interference in choice, the dictator would have no reason to stop. A dictator or a dictator's advisers could develop many moralistic arguments to justify interfering in almost any area. History and common sense suggest that such interference is likely.

The fixation on the preservation of private property made defenders of capitalism ignore its real erosions. If they had followed Adam Smith and their own reasoning about democracy, they might have argued that private property offers an expedient means to capitalist ends. At that point, their debate with the socialists could have become one about which scheme would be more likely to fulfill the demands of morality. As it was, capitalism became identified by socialists and capitalists alike with the propertied interests, and people concluded that the only moral function of capitalism was to improve the life of those already privileged. That is why capitalism, much to the chagrin of Hayek, von Mises, and Friedman, has become identified with the privileged and with conservatism as Hayek defined it. That is why no one believes capitalism is a liberal doctrine celebrating freedom. Later defenders of capitalism allowed modern so-called capitalism to be cut off from its nineteenth-century roots, and it became primarily a doctrine for the protection of private property. The defenders of capitalism have no one to blame but themselves.

Summary and Prospectus

Democracy is a process whereby a majority of the people have meaningful control of the activities of government and society. As simple and appealing as the idea of democracy is, it has never had a consistent and systematic defender. Historically, people who have developed theories of democracy either have been overtly opposed to democracy or have wanted to transform it into something else so that the majority cannot exercise effective control. Some of its most profound advocates have appeared to defend it but have undermined it in the process. The effort to resolve the debate between capitalism and socialism by arguing for an implicit substantive agenda in democracy has proved a failure. A democratic society is not constrained a priori in the kind of economic system it might adopt, and democracy is not a necessary condition for either capitalism or socialism. Democracy remains a process-oriented ideology.

The bifurcation fallacy continues to haunt us, and the consideration of democracy extends it to another dimension. Not only are capitalism and socialism presented as mutually exclusive and exhaustive ideologies, but democracy and totalitarianism are also presented as mutually exclusive and exhaustive ideologies. The bifurcation in regard to democracy is somewhat more complicated, because many nondemocratic governments cannot be called totalitarian. When attention was constrained to the industrial and postindustrial societies, the belief in a bifurcation between democracy and totalitarianism took hold.

Our approach to ideologies thus far lends itself nicely to a matrix analysis. Suppose that along the horizontal axis of a matrix we place the possibilities of socialism and capitalism, while along the vertical axis we place the possibilities of democracy and totalitarianism.

	Socialism	Capitalism
Democracy	A	B
Totalitarianism	C	D

The matrix may help us understand the conclusions of some of the people we have considered. The democratic socialists argue that the capitalist alternative to democratic socialism is *D* (totalitarian capitalism, or fascism). The democratic capitalists argue that the socialist alternative to democratic capitalism is *C* (totalitarian socialism, or communism). Thus, we can replace the letters in the matrix with labels.

	Socialism	Capitalism
Democracy	Democratic socialism	Democratic capitalism
Totalitarianism	Communism	Fascism

Suppose, however, we change the matrix.

	Capitalism	Noncapitalism
Democracy	E	F
Nondemocracy	G	H

In this matrix, we avoid committing the bifurcation fallacy. Of course, noncapitalism includes socialism, but without some sustaining positive argument, the two would not be equivalent. Thus it is better to refer to noncapitalism using more general terminology. Similarly, nondemocracy might include totalitarianism but not be equivalent to it.

We could also create another matrix which would deal directly with socialism.

	Socialism	Nonsocialism
Democracy	I	J
Nondemocracy	K	L

Comments can be made mutatis mutandis about this matrix.

Let us now combine our matrices, though this time we will add categories that will by definition exclude the terms which we have considered thus far in the book.

	Socialism	Capitalism	Nonsocialism and Noncapitalism
Democracy	*M*	*N*	*O*
Totalitarianism	*P*	*Q*	*R*
Nondemocracy and Nontotalitarianism	*S*	*T*	*U*

The prevailing view is that *O, R, S, T,* and *U* are empty, and if we are to accept that view, we shall be back at the original problems, which are, of course, located in the upper left of the matrix. No one, however, has yet proved those other interesting cells to be empty. It is surely an indication of the paucity of our ideological thinking that we have essentially ignored over half the matrix.

In the next chapter of this book I will discuss the development of an ideology which belongs in cell *U:* it is neither capitalist nor socialist, and it is neither democratic nor totalitarian. I shall try to show not only that the ideology is logically possible but also that it is in fact the ideology of much of the postindustrial world.

7 Managerialism

In the preface to his book *Between Capitalism and Socialism: Essays in Political Economics,* Robert Heilbroner says: "What is needed, then, is a new paradigm that will permit a major enlargement of economics—not one that discards the relationships that economics can often usefully reveal, but one that absorbs them into a much larger and more complex system of social cause and effect. Let me be clear, however, that no such paradigm yet exists. Hence the 'political economics' of my subtitle is very far from announcing a solution to the problems that diminish the scope of contemporary economics." [1] By the end of his book, Heilbroner still leaves the reader choosing between capitalism and socialism, with no perceptible alternative in sight. Thus, the bifurcation fallacy traps even as expansive a thinker as Heilbroner. This chapter attempts to take a step forward by moving us beyond capitalism and socialism. In that way, I hope we can meet the challenge laid down by Heilbroner.

A few comments differentiating the points made in this chapter from some of those made by Heilbroner in the quotation above will prove helpful. First, I eschew the use of the word *paradigm* for what is sought. Even though the word has a history of its own independent of Thomas Kuhn's use of it for his historical analysis of science, the content is sufficiently similar in our cases that I think we would do well to leave *paradigm* for Kuhnian-type use. The social sciences, including economics, do not have a paradigm like the one Kuhn describes for the development of science. At most, they are in what Kuhn calls a prescientific stage. Kuhn says that it was while studying the social sciences and noticing their difference from the physical sciences that he was led to the concept of paradigm, which applies to the latter and not the former. [2] We shall stay with the nonscientific term *ideology,* which will keep us away from pretension, though we will reserve the right to make some comments which might be useful for a science of economics.

Second, we shall be addressing problems which go beyond the bounds of eco-

152

nomics as narrowly conceived. That does not distinguish our efforts here from Heilbroner's. Few economists have been more insistent or persistent in arguing that the mainstream economists' notion that economics can be divorced from polity is spurious. Heilbroner's desire to recover the phrase *political economy* is part of his program in that direction. It is a desire to revitalize the aspirations of people like Smith and Marx. Our use of *ideology,* which is, perhaps, more general than *political economics,* is consistent with his intention.

Third, the effort here will not be directed primarily at expanding or constraining the scope of contemporary economics. In the tradition of Alfred North Whitehead, it is directed at expanding our ideas of ideology. Ideology must include economics, but it is not limited to or dominated by economics.

Finally, while I would agree with Heilbroner that no adequate alternative ideology has been articulated by theoreticians, unlike Heilbroner, I believe that in fact in advanced industrialized societies a new ideology has emerged in the last half of the twentieth century. It has emerged out of the actions of practical people who were forced to make decisions, whether or not articulated principles existed to provide a basis for those decisions. People whose lives are made up of taking action in the face of alternatives soon learn that indecision is a form of decision. There are, of course, times when the best decision is to do nothing, to "buy time." Managers who decide to buy time, though, should know how they are going to spend it. Otherwise, their purchase has been a dangerous waste of a precious management resource. The decision maker cannot avoid making decisions, and implicitly or explicitly, those decisions are made in the context of ideological principles.

We have been distracted from an understanding of reality by thinking the ideological principles which have been guiding those decisions are capitalist or socialist, democratic or totalitarian, or some combination. Part of the reason for our confusion is based in logic and rhetoric. We need to straighten out our logic and our rhetoric in order to understand reality. That is the primary task for this chapter, and it takes its lead from Heilbroner's insight.

Managerialism as an Ideology

At the outset, it is important to say that I am not an advocate of managerialism. Managerialism has had neither serious articulation nor serious advocacy. It will be sufficient to provide the former here. I am not prepared to provide the latter. That may disappoint some who, following a long tradition heightened by Marx, expect the articulation of ideology to include advocacy. Some people may even suggest that the definition of ideology entails advocacy. That commitment, however, was not built into the view of ideology adopted in this book. It is my purpose here to articulate the principles upon which the political, economic, and social order of advanced industrialized societies, such as the United States, is based as we enter the twenty-first century. The person who seeks to criticize this articulation of managerialism needs to show that it does not describe the principles of the ideology. Suggestions that the principles identified are morally offensive are certainly interesting, but they do not challenge the arguments presented here.

As will become clear in time, I cannot find sufficient moral warrant for managerialism which would stand up under scrutiny. Nevertheless, I think managerialism provides a more useful clinical description of what is occurring in advanced industrialized societies than any existing alternative ideologies offer, including capitalism, socialism, and democracy. I do believe that a moral claim could be brought forward as a case in favor of managerialism. I shall attempt to articulate the basis of that case. I cannot at this stage, however, imagine a reasonable way to support that claim. I should also make it clear that in suggesting this ideology, I have abandoned any hope of finding the perfect ideology capable of surviving for an eternal future. Even if eternal verities exist about anything, it would seem, as a result of discoveries such as those of Kurt Gödel, that we shall never be able to know them.[3]

Marx claimed that he turned Hegel on his head, but he emptied only some of Hegel's conclusions. Like Hegel, Marx remained committed to a discovery of the Truth. The early Marx, at least, was firmly convinced that after the revolution, a perfected ideology would take over that would have no need of revision. In short, Marx believed he had discovered eternal Truth. Similar finality cannot be claimed for managerialism. It will be displaced by some other ideology, and we would do well to be alert to such prospective developments. In the meantime, we should try to understand what we have presently.

Perhaps a preliminary description of managerialism would help orient the reader. Managerialism reflects some of the work of Robert Dahl and Giovanni Sartori. Managerialism does not, however, pretend to be a form of democracy. The managerialist society is not one which responds to the needs, desires, and wishes of a majority of its citizens. In the managerialist society, influence is exercised through organizations. The society responds to whatever the managements of various organizations can gain in their transactions with each other. If people belong to an organization which effectively represents their interests, they may get some response. If they do not, they probably will not. Managerialism is both a process and a substantive ideology. Substantively, managerialism says that the fundamental social units are not individuals, as capitalism would declare. Managerialism, like socialism, finds the individual qua individual to be an empty abstraction. However, managerialism also finds the organic existence of the state to be an abstraction without any correspondence to reality. For managerialism, the fundamental social unit is neither individuals nor the state, but organizations. Social decisions arise out of the transactions in which the managements of the organizations are engaged. The movement from individual values to social choice, to use Kenneth Arrow's phrase, is through organizations, and it is arranged in the transactions of the managers of the organizations.

While to the best of my knowledge no author has self-consciously described managerialism, there have been two recent uses of the term, both of which are tantalizing and deserve some attention. First, in a recent and exciting book, *The New Unionism*, Charles Heckscher uses *managerialism* to describe a situation he regards as arising out of a new condition for union-management relationships.[4] There are intriguing similarities between his use of the term and its use here. Heckscher's use is considerably more restricted than mine, however, and he does not seek to challenge basic ideological concepts. For example, he continues to view corporations as profit-maximizing organizations. His primary concern seems to be that corporate managers have become considerably more sophisticated in their management of employees and unions and that if unions do not change their means of operating, they will continue to become an increasingly anachronistic and ineffective force, at least in the United States. He argues that union leaders must be prepared to be more flexible and adaptable in their relations with business managers, because the rigidity of union leadership, combined with the flexibility of business managers, is making the unions irrelevant.

Second, in a recent anthology discussing important developments in political thought since the end of World War II, one of the editors has written a comprehensive and important introduction in which he introduces the term *managerialism* as an ideological description. Leonard Tivey does not systematically develop the reference, and he seems to think that everyone will know what *managerialism* means. His citations associate it most closely with James Burnham's work.[5] While Burnham's book *The Managerial Revolution* has been important for me in my own consideration of managerialism, it has never received much careful consideration from political scientists, economists, or other social theoreticians, and until Tivey, it had not been declared as a precursor of a new ideology. In addition, to the best of my knowledge, Burnham did not use the term *managerialism*. Tantalizing as Tivey's reference is, he provides us with no sustained discussion or understanding of an ideology which might be labeled managerialism.

This book, however, argues that something much deeper and more extensive than changes in terminology or in union-management relations is under way. The deeper issue is an ideological one. The capitalist assumptions which gave rise to unionism may not be wrong in the abstract, but they are irrelevant to the advanced industrialized societies of the late twentieth century and the early twenty-first. In passing, it is instructive to note that many so-called socialist societies have resisted strong and effective trade unions even more than so-called capitalist ones have. Unionism is theoretically inconsistent with that also-irrelevant ideology.

The description of managerialism here lays the theoretical foundation for much of Heckscher's and Tivey's findings. *Managerialism,* as developed here, is a label for a deep social change, not a name for attitudinal shifts. If Heckscher had dropped his assumption of profit maximization and if Tivey had dropped his effort to save democracy, both might have seen how deep the changes were. The attitudinal shifts I suggest are not perturbations in an otherwise stable situation; they are manifestations of a radically changed society. I use the term *managerialism* as a name for the basic principles of the social, political, and economic system which has been constructed in the United States as well as other advanced industrialized societies.

Managerialism presents neither an atomistic nor an organic view of society. It shares elements of both, but it moves beyond them and finds both of them and their lengthy debates in need of transcendence. Previously, it seemed that all ideologies relevant to advanced industrialized societies should fall into one or the other of those two categories. Managerialism falls into neither. At the same time, it is not simply a compromise. Managerialism is, of course, part of history, and it could not avoid being tied to history, but it makes a break from the past and does not merely carry it forward into the present.

Managerialism as Organic

Managerialism recognizes the insight of the organic view. It recognizes that social organizations can take on organic characteristics which cause people in them to rise above their own individualism. It recognizes that in the well-developed organization, power arises from situations in which people act out of interest for the organization, not just for themselves. A characteristic of organic views is that their adherents not only describe but also celebrate the organic capacities and the supraindividual directions they assume societies will take as a result. In that regard, the organic views have taken on their own deterministic aspects, and they have left the individual with no effective discretion. Managerialism recognizes the insight of the supraindividual organic view without committing itself either to an endorsement of any organic direction which might be taken or to determinism.

In addition, the managerialist perspective sheds doubt on the capacity of a country such as the United States to become organic. In the first place, modern postindustrial nations are too divided and diverse to permit overriding social directions to be accepted except in crises.[6] The diversity of the United States in particular is reflected in the frequent description of it as a pluralistic society. In the second place, managerialism is sceptical about politicians and others who claim to be the repositories of the real interests of society. By their nature, organic views are unclear about how one could determine the organic direction of society. In some religions, it is often left to some self-proclaimed advocate to describe what the "Word of God" really is. Anyone who dares to question the position articulated is then branded a heretic. Similarly, the self-proclaimed organic representatives will describe the organic direction of, for example, the General Will, and any who ask sceptical questions about the evidence for that description or who challenge it as an inaccurate description will be called traitors. It is hard to escape the sense of conflict of interest which surrounds this perspective. Of course, the self-proclaimed organic representatives, like the religious gurus, will respond that concerns with conflict of interest are sufficient evidence that the concerned individual is a heretic or a traitor. Managerialism may be the first ideological perspective to recognize the potential for truth in the organic view and yet maintain a strong scepticism about it.

One considerable strength of the atomistic view is that discovering overall social choices is reasonably easy and noncontroversial. In a democratic atomistic approach, one simply counts the votes and determines what the majority has said (i.e., Rousseau's will of all).[7] In a capitalist atomistic approach, one need only see what has been called out of the market. If one doubts whether what is in the market actually represents the society's desires, one need only introduce alternative products into the market and see whether they arouse sufficient interest.

Managerialism does not argue for an overarching organic view of society (or a country). The managerialist society is recognized as being composed of a multitude of social, economic, and political units which may be more or less organic. Managerialism declares that real social decision-making power lies in those units, not in the individual citizens in the society or in the society at large. Individuals express their preferences through the multitude of units to which they may belong and which claim to represent their interests. The interactions of those units create social choices. Arrow tried to resolve the problem of determining how the society could consistently move from an expression of individual values to a social choice. Managerialism evades that problem, because individual preferences are expressed through organizational units and larger social choices are made as those units interact with each other.

Managerialism as Atomistic

Managerialism, then, views the larger society (e.g., the country) in an atomistic fashion. In spite of its sympathy for the insights of the organic view, managerialism does not accept the notion of a national General Will. Managerialism accepts the view that there is only a will of all, as the atomists had insisted. Its will of all, however, is not grounded in the preferences of individuals. It is, rather, the result of the interactions among the social subunits. Capitalism was grounded in the assertion that economic activity results from the purchase and sale decisions of individual consumers. Managerialism does not recognize much effective power in individual decisions. It finds, rather, that social decisions (even economic ones) arise out of the transactions among units which encompass individuals.[8]

Some of the social units are managed in such a way that they become organic and cause their members to rise above their own personal interests to a concern with the totality of the unit. Presumably, that is what is behind the favored management metaphor of a managerial team. The notion of a managerial team is cultivated sometimes by explicit analogy to an athletic team, so that individual participants are willing to sacrifice their own personal interests for the benefit of the team.

Managerialism as Polyorganic

If we were asked to create jargon related to atomism and organicism for the managerialist view, we might say that from an institutional perspective, managerialism can be defined as a polyorganic view. It may be clear, now, why we spent time analyzing the views of Dahl and Sartori. A great deal of insight has been taken from Dahl's empirical polyarchy. Even though his view does not describe democracy and even though other differences exist between Dahl's understanding of society and that put forward here, there are also similarities. Managerialism says that many organic units interact to create overall social decisions.

It is important to point out that the managerialist view does not reach the conclusion that all units develop an organic structure. Some of the units may be internally quite atomistic, with members refusing to subscribe to any overall view or position which does not suit their own personal interests. While the metaphor of a management team is popular currently, not all managements are operated as a team, and those which operate as a team are by no means universally successful. It is possible to develop a management structure in which each of the participants acts only out of self-interest, with no concern for the overall direction of the organization.[9]

Managers, not Organizations

An additional aspect in the perspective just described needs to be added in order to bring it into more complete compliance with managerialism. The groups or units themselves do not interact to create a social decision. Rather, the managements of those units do the interacting. Managers from one unit engage in transactions with managers from other units to arrive at solutions to common issues. Sometimes those transactions are face-to-face. Sometimes the transactions are conducted over a long distance, and the parties may not even know one another.

Social choice, to use Arrow's terminology, results from the numerous transactions among managements. Managerialism, then, borrows from atomism in declaring that the society (nation) is nothing more than the summation of the decisions and transactions which have been made by the managements of the organizations. That is the foundation of the term *managerialism*.

In speaking of management, we include not only business management but also the management of numerous nonbusiness organizations. Managers of all organizations engage in transactions (negotiations) with one another, and out of those transactions the real social decisions arise. In the process of negotiation, the managers remain largely uninterested in the overall social consequences of their transactions. They are attempting to advance their own goals and objectives. Those goals and objectives may be in the interest of the organization, but they are not primarily developed to advance overall national or social goals and objectives.

Sometimes the transactions do not involve the government (for example, when labor and management settle a contract). Sometimes they do involve government instrumentalities (for example, when a television station negotiates with the Federal Communications Commission to secure a license). Sometimes the decisions may involve transactions between government agencies (for example, when a municipality negotiates with the Environmental Protection Agency about effluent from the city's sewage treatment plant). Transactions and negotiations are being conducted all the time in our society. Most of the transactions do not come to public attention. The managerialist perspective declares that the social direction at large is the consequence of these numerous large and small transactions which are taken individually, largely in ignorance of the overall social direction.

Managerialism and Democracy

Managerialism presents a lethal challenge to democracy, because it discounts the importance of the individual in general and, more specifically, discounts the importance of voting in regard to the social choice. Managerialism recognizes that elected officials achieve their positions because of the support they receive and seek from numerous organizations (actually, from the managements of those organizations). The manipulation of this situation is revealed most clearly by the organizations which contribute to political candidates of both parties in order to influence the successful candidate's actions after the election. When a vote on legislation is imminent, the politician may feel as if she or he is making an independent judgment, but by and large, the prevailing forces have already selected (in the Darwinian sense) her or him in order to assure the desired voting pattern. It should be recalled that managerialism is not deterministic. The efforts at control are not always predictable or successful.

Perhaps the effects of the process can be made most clear by looking at presidential politics. By the time the final two candidates have been nominated and have modified their views in order to appeal to the managements of a broad group of organizations and still not antagonize managements of other powerful organizations accidentally or unnecessarily, they have to struggle mightily to establish a significant difference between themselves. The recent rise of advertising in political campaigns is instructive. Advertising is most useful and effective when little differentiates one brand from another. For example, one brand of gasoline is very much the same as another, so factors other than the inherent nature of the product must influence consumer choice. That is the function of advertising whether the product is aspirin, gasoline, or political candidates. Since candidates have been homogenized, prepared, and packaged so they will both appeal to and not offend critical constituencies, they end up not only looking like each other but also sounding and acting like each other, which is why they seem to invent (largely irrelevant) issues to distinguish themselves from one another.

In this context, we may be tempted to interpret managerialism as a conspiracy theory, arguing that managers are engaged in some complex and hidden conspiracy which enables them to run the country. However, managerialism describes a situation in which individual social units are atomistic with regard to one another. In general, managements of organizations try to make the best possible arrangements for themselves (first) and their organizations (second).[10] In making those arrangements, management finds it necessary to negotiate, bargain, and transact with the management of other organizations. Those transactions are not conspiratorial: they are carried on by people with differing interests. Labor-management negotiations offer an easy example. Company management does not work conspiratorially with labor representatives. The two groups are adversaries. However, they usually will arrive at a transaction acceptable to both sides.

It should be noted that only the interests of those who have representatives at the transactions are addressed. If some interests are not at the table, they will not be represented or addressed. It is likely that the reason the automobile industry in the United States became so indifferent to consumer needs, interests, and demands after World War II was that consumers were not represented when labor contracts were negotiated. As a consequence, the contracts satisfied the interests of company management and union management while essentially ignoring the interests of the consumers. In that process, the automobile industry in the United States almost died. Labor and management made deals and passed the costs of the deals along to the consumers in the form of higher prices and lower quality. Since the automobile business in the United States was essentially oligopolistic at the time (a result which came about in some measure from government intervention), consumers were reduced to buying one of the cars made in the United States or going without automotive transportation. The same consumers lived in a country in which, as a result of intense transactions on the part of the automobile manufacturers, mass transportation was the automobile. All managerialism says is that the results of such transactions constitute the direction for the society. Managerialism makes no commitment to the extent or kind of parties which will be present for particular transactions. Society, then, comprises these organizational units, and social direction is derived from the negotiations among the managements of the organizations.

We can identify some of the factors which put managers in a stronger or weaker position as they enter the transaction process.

Membership Size

The more members an organization has—other things being equal—the more power its management has. In general, organizations like the nationally based American Association of Retired Persons, which includes many members who are not retired, have more power than a local organization. The nationally based corporation is usually more powerful than the small or regional company.

Discretionary Wealth

The more a particular management can call on discretionary resources—other things being equal—the more power it has in its transactions. Discretionary wealth can compensate for lack of membership size and vice versa.

Organic Behavior

The more an organization responds as an organic whole—other things being equal—the more power it has in negotiations. Managerialism does not regard the debate between atomism and organicism as an either/or situation. Managers know that team spirit can be encouraged or discouraged and, to that extent, managed.

Management

Effective management can overcome other deficiencies and can negotiate favorable terms for the organization which another management might not get. Successful management can also help an organization become larger, wealthier, and more organic. In this context, intelligence is a factor which can overcome other deficiencies.

Public Rhetoric

An organization with an effective image and public relations campaign can make strength appear where it is absent and can show weaknesses in adversaries, thereby threatening their effectiveness.

Some of these factors can be traded off against others. Probably none are sufficient by themselves, although discretionary wealth is such a common instrument for making other purchases that it may be the closest to sufficient. (This may also explain why it is so viciously attacked by modern neo-Marxists.) Probably none of the conditions are absolutely necessary, though effective management may be the closest. An organization without any management may lack the ability to participate in transactions. In the transaction process, adversaries will try to undermine each other's strength in accordance with these conditions. For example, if a manager claims to represent a large group of people, the adversary may try to show the presence of dissent in the membership. Finally, the list may need to be extended. It may not be exhaustive.

Management and Organizations

Managerialism describes the relations of management and organizations. First, management is often remote from the actual functioning of the organization (though it will deny that fact, since it would seem to weaken its transactional position). The management of the AFL-CIO is well removed from actual workers. In fact, the management of the AFL-CIO lives and acts more like the management of a successful corporation than like the rank and file. Often, the management of a large public corporation interacts with the stockholders of the corporation in only trivial ways. Management is removed by its position on the hierarchy and its numerous responsibilities. School administrators usually have little to do with educating students; hospital administrators usually have little to do with providing health care; administrators of government agencies usually have little to do with delivery of the agencies' primary services; corporate executives usually do not do much manufacturing or selling. This common remoteness from the territory of operations gives support to the popular notion that there is such a thing as professional management. Presumably professional managers possess a body of knowledge and acquired talent sufficiently removed from specifics that they can transfer it from organization to organization.

Second, part of management's job is to manage all the constituencies of the organization. Union executives have to manage the membership, so that when the management of the union concludes the negotiation of a contract, the members will support it. If the union management cannot do so, its future negotiating strength is threatened, because its adversaries will have a chance to declare that the union management does not represent the workers. The management of a corporation will try to manage, or even manipulate, a board of directors so that it will support management's recommendations. In this sense, management always has a dual task: managing the internal conditions of the organization and managing the external opportunities and constraints for the organization. In large, multifaceted organizations, internal management often takes on managerialist characteristics of its own, with organizational decisions arising out of an internal transactional process involving numerous constituencies within the organization.

Third, management presumes that the organization will exist in perpetuity. In this regard, incorporation has proved crucial. Incorporation enshrined in law the perpetual continuity of the corporation. The presumption of perpetuity supported by incorporation is also important in the transaction process. If in the process of transaction one side were to discover that the organization represented by the other side was about to fold, the position of the second side would be considerably weakened, and the representatives of the first side could be much more relaxed than if they thought the other organization would be around for an indefinite period of time.

Furthermore, it is important for management to be able to make long-term commitments in the name of the corporation. If the organization is presumed to exist in perpetuity, then future managers can expect to be held responsible for the commitments of their predecessors. Contrast this situation with Smith's preferred organizational structure: the unincorporated sole proprietorship or the partnership. When negotiations are conducted with a sole proprietorship, the other side has to make an analysis of the longevity of the owners. That is why, when corporations engage in transactions with incorporated sole proprietorships, they often require the managers of those organizations to sign personally as well as officially on behalf of their companies. In effect, they pierce the corporate shield, though usually they will not let that happen to their own corporations. They can do so because incorporation has brought to them considerably more power than the individual proprietor has.

Thus, the government grant of the privilege of incorporation was especially important for the development of managerialism. Incorporation carries with it the capacity for raising discretionary resources and the presumption of continuity and perpetuity. As business was emerging, the state and the church had considerable power: they were capable of raising unneeded resources, and both were supposed to exist in perpetuity. Before incorporation, businesses would not endure after the life of the owner-manager. In that situation, transactions between firms and the church or the state were asymmetrical, since the latter could afford to wait out the business and hope for more favorable conditions (perhaps when the owner-manager was near death). Under the conditions of incorporation, one management may leave, but another will be there to take its place, and it is probably impossible to know whether the new management will be an easier or a harder one with which to carry on transactions. Nonbusiness as well as business organizations look for the protections of incorporation, with its provisions of limited liability and perpetuity.

It is the job of management, then, to manage the numerous constituencies which have an impact on the organization and to give direction to the organization. In that context, management frequently has some discretion in the direction it gives to the corporation. That is not always true, and sometimes management seems to have little choice if the organization is to survive. However, managerialism recognizes that within limits managements have discretion. Evaluation of management should be made on the basis of how well that discretion has been exercised.[11]

Managerialism does not hold that the corporation is so driven by an organic principle that individual managers have no effective choice in giving it direction. Whether the organization behaves in an organic way is, to an important extent, a result of the management's efforts, and the direction of that organic force is something over which management attempts to exercise control. Thus, managerialism has not accepted the underlying determinism of capitalism and socialism.

Unlimited discretion has never been important to understanding human freedom and the responsibility which may be attached to it. Even the most robust advocates of responsibility do not believe people can do anything they want to do. All any sensible person argues for is responsibility within limits or the discretion to make effective choice about some decisions and some actions. Managerialism endorses that notion and, thus, breaks fundamentally from socialism and capitalism. Some impact of these changes can be seen in the areas of strategic planning and management, morality, and leadership.

The discretion assumed in the managerialist perspective has made strategic planning an important activity. In the capitalist ideology, strategic planning is not important, because the owner-manager either makes the appropriate market decisions or goes out of business. With the appearance of effective discretion comes the need to analyze and make choices. Historically, business planning did not become a subject of much attention or interest until corporations grew to the point that management had some control over the variables and could make alternative decisions. Discretion and the subsequent planning brought an entirely different approach to management and gave management a distinct function and role in the corporation and in society. It also gave "business schools" something more intellectual than mere technique to teach. It intellectualized and professionalized management precisely because choice had become possible and, indeed, unavoidable.

Planning and discretion also brought with them a new approach to morality in business. Managers could no longer be protected from the difficulties of ethical concerns because they lacked effective choice. Responsibility presumes effective choice, and effective choice implies that responsibility exists for the choices made. We will deal with questions of ethics at greater length in the next chapter. The important point here is that managerialism introduces an ethical

dimension which is missing in capitalism. While numerous business executives have recently recognized the importance of the ethical dimension, some
of the economists and management commentators have resisted allowing the
ethical questions to have room for valid discussion. Their resistance is probably
based upon their respect for intellectual consistency, which, when combined
with their assumption that the economy is capitalist, leads them to dismiss the
attempt to drag business executives into the moral swamp of confusion and
debate. Managerialism suggests a new approach to the topic and consequent
changes.

Managerialism does not, however, support a particular ethical approach. In
writing about the interactions among managers on behalf of their organizations, I used the term *transaction* deliberately. In this respect, I follow the lead
of James MacGregor Burns, who makes a distinction between transactional
leadership and transformational leadership. It is tempting to oversimplify the
distinction between the two, and Burns's book *Leadership* offers a truly rich
analysis.[12] One of the distinguishing differences between the two kinds of
leadership, however, is the presence of morality in transformational leadership
and its absence in transactional leadership.

The existence of the moral dimension is not without its disadvantages. In
entering into a transaction, managers often find themselves at a disadvantage if
they have rigid moral positions. In general, negotiations and intermanagement
transactions are much more effective when the parties can negotiate without
limitations. If one side has deep moral convictions, its bargaining ability may
be weakened. If both sides have deep moral convictions, unless they share the
same ones, the managers may be unable to find common ground. Thus, we
discover an irony: managerialism makes room for the moral dimension, but it
finds the rigid pursuit of the moral dimension dysfunctional. However, morality
does not have to be rigid or dogmatic. The task of the manager is to engage in
a transactional process and to come to a resolution at the appropriate time.

The Theory of the Firm versus the Concept of the Corporation

The Theory of the Firm

Now that we have sufficient background to understand the relevance and importance of the corporation, we can address the central task of clarifying its
nature.[13] This topic has a bearing on the examination of alternative ideologies and on an understanding of the role ethical considerations might play in a
managerialist society, or, more specifically, the role of ethics in business.

Economists have developed an approach they call the theory of the firm.
That theory underlies much of microeconomics. The theory is consonant with

capitalism and is meant to be a deductive elaboration of capitalism. Economists recognized the importance of business organizations—firms—in the economy, and they sought to derive explanations for their activities.

Stripped of its elaborate superstructure, the theory of the firm holds that firms must strive to maximize profits. If they fail to do so, they will be out of business. The only firms remaining will be those which are maximizing profits. In a kind of circuitous, if not entirely circular, way, then, this confirms the original hypothesis. The hypothesis of profit maximization has been subjected to considerable debate, but little revision.[14] Changes are resisted because the hypothesis seems so useful for mathematical purposes: the concept of maximization allows the economist to apply the apparatus of calculus to economic theories and gain the intellectual power of that application. That, we recall, is the kind of power Dahl sought in his formalization of democratic theory.

Even from a strictly logical (i.e., mathematical) perspective, a problem has always existed with the hypothesis of profit maximization. In order for the mathematical assumptions of maximization to work, the stream of data (in this case profits) must either have a finite life or produce a smooth curve and a completely predictable future. Any actual profit figure, however, must be drawn at some arbitrarily chosen time. The statement of profit and loss must, by definition, specify some precisely defined period. It will do no good to retreat to considering balance sheets: they also address precise periods.

Those time specifications are necessary. They cannot be evaded, and yet even beginning business school students soon learn that sensible conclusions can be drawn from statements of profit and loss only with considerable care. The corporation which has been using up its inventory may show a better level of profit over some period of time than one which has maintained a higher level of inventory. The corporation which has been effectively training and preparing employees for conditions the corporation is likely to face in a decade or so may show lower profits than the corporation which pays little attention to employee development while its management decides to let the next generation of managers deal with their own problems.

There are numerous cases of trading off short-term profits for long-term profits. For example, in the post–World War II period, the federal government, through depletion allowances, subsidized corporate searches for minerals, such as oil, to replace those being depleted as existing reserves were recovered and consumed. Some corporations took those responsibilities seriously and substantially devoted their depletion allowances to exploration. Other corporations simply used the subsidies to increase their immediate profits, on the popular theory that it is cheaper to find oil on Wall Street than in the ground. Here we will not analyze which set of corporations made the right decisions, in part because all the evidence is not available. One cannot help asking, however, if the corporations which decided to use the depletion allowances to enhance profits had instead used them to find reserves and find technological ways to bring those reserves to market, might we have avoided the repetitive energy crises of the past two decades?

To look at profits for some finite period, which is essentially required by the mathematics of maximization, then, is to miss important developments with regard to profits in some period not included among those over which the maximization is to occur.[15] Investment managers have to learn to read through financial statements in order to make decisions about the continuing strength or weakness of a corporation for investment purposes. Yet if the theory of the firm were correct, investment management would be a reasonably simple task, perhaps best accomplished by a computer, which could complete more calculations more accurately than any human manager.

Actually, similar comments can be made of management in general. If the theory of the firm were correct, managers would only need to know the formulae which drive the profit figures and then to apply them. It would not take much intelligence or talent to manage a business.

An autobiographical story may help illustrate the point here. When I was in graduate business school in 1960, the famous mathematician and computer genius Norbert Weiner was invited to give a lecture and to talk informally with students. Weiner's lecture was, as one would expect, both abstract and brilliant. During the informal seminar, he fell to discussing profit maximization and the developing power of computers. He predicted that within our professional lifetime, computers would be able to eliminate the need for managers as graduates of business schools.[16] His reasoning was quite simple: Economists say the purpose of the firm is to maximize profits. Computers should be able to calculate maximization more efficiently than people. From Weiner's perspective, all that remained to be done was to determine all the factors driving profits and to develop computers with sufficient power to deal with those factors. Faced with a set of alternative decisions, computers would then be able to calculate which alternative maximized profits. Managing would be reduced to pressing the buttons on a computer and reading the output. One would hardly need to go to high school, let alone graduate school, to learn to do this.

Weiner understood the theory of the firm in the rigorous way that we should expect of a mathematician. In the theory of the firm, one manager must easily substitute for another. The operations of the firm cannot depend upon the special insight or wisdom of specific managers. Recall that firms are to respond rapidly to consumer wishes, needs, and desires. If the response depends upon the wisdom or insight of some managers, that will create a short supply, which will create disequilibria. The theory of the firm describes an effort to drive the economy to equilibrium, and the theory assumes that disequilibria will always be temporary. Weiner also understood the determinism embedded in the theory of the firm. In that system, managers have no more discretion than computers do.

The Concept of the Corporation

In order to contrast the perspective of managerialism with the theory of the firm, I have adopted the expression *concept of the corporation* from a book by the management theoretician Peter Drucker.[17] While Drucker may not agree with all that is said either in the criticism of the theory of the firm or in the development of a concept of the corporation, I am indebted to Drucker's total work for its consistent attempt to shed old ways of thinking and to understand the new society we have constructed. For many years Drucker has criticized the assumption of profit maximization.[18] His first book identified the fact that after the dramatic transformations of the 1920s and 1930s "neither capitalism nor socialism can be restored." [19] The origins of the book in your hands lie, in part, in an attempt to come to grips with many of the problems which Drucker outlines.

In introducing the concept of the corporation, we must abandon the notion that the corporation exists to maximize profits. The fundamental logical problem with that concept continues to haunt any work which takes the corporation seriously. It is true that procedures could be adopted which would impose arbitrary limits on the time dimension in order to make the concept functional. Much of that may have happened during the 1980s in the United States, as financial communities put managers under increasing pressure to produce short-term profits irrespective of long-term consequences. Many of the economic problems of the 1990s will involve working out the cost of such shortsightedness.

In all candor, we should say that all of that short-term activity occurred as a dramatic growth in business and management education took place in our colleges and universities. As management education grew, it increasingly divorced itself from its humanist background and pretended to be applied economics. As long as the leading business programs were graduate programs which assumed students had a solid undergraduate liberal education, we could hope that after they graduated from business schools, the students could integrate the technicalities and the humanist dimension into the actual settings for decisions. As business education extended to undergraduate programs, however, it involved more technique and became less an extension of liberal education. In addition, as the graduate business programs competed for status with the other university programs, business professors also became less oriented toward reality and more enamored of their own theories. The time was ripe for the business professors to join the arbitrary concentration on short-term profits and to reinforce the latent greed of their students. If part of the role of the professoriat is to swim against the tide, then business education has largely failed.

Beyond abandoning the notion of profit maximization, or its corruption by arbitrary delimitation, we also abandon the notion that the manager has no effective discretion and is, therefore, merely a cog in a larger mechanism. It seems clear that managers do have some effective discretion, and the presence of that discretion creates a big difference between managerialism and the hypothesis of profit maximization. Having effective discretion means that the manager and his professors can no longer hide behind the notion that they have no moral responsibility for the decisions they make. Determinism releases us from responsibility. It simply makes no sense to hold someone responsible for something if that person had no effective discretion in the matter. The assumption of discretion reinstates the responsibility.

For example, if, while I am walking down the street, a car should careen into me, pushing me into someone else and causing that person to suffer an injury, sensible people would not hold me responsible for injuring that person. They would realize that I had no choice in the matter.[20] Managerialism presumes managers do on some occasions have effective discretion in the decisions they make. It assumes that Weiner was wrong and that managers are not just inexpensive computers holding positions until technology catches up. It assumes that at least on some occasions, it does matter who is the manager. It assumes that managers can—and do—impose their personalities on corporations. It assumes what turns out to be true: that some of the best investment analysis comes from those who understand current and prospective management. It assumes that corporations are, or have become, phenomena which need more careful analysis and attention. It is that analysis to which we turn now.

Atomism and the Corporation: John Ladd and Milton Friedman

In regard to the atomistic perspective, two approaches are important to analyze. The first takes the issue on directly, without prior ideological baggage. The second argues for the atomistic view as part of a broader agenda, namely the agenda of capitalism as defined in mainstream economics. We shall use John Ladd's justifiably well-known article of 1970, "Morality and the Ideal of Rationality in Formal Organizations," as the primary articulation of the first perspective and the writings of Milton Friedman and others for an articulation of the second perspective.

It would be difficult to overemphasize the importance of Ladd's article, which provided the background for much of the debate about the nature of the corporation. Furthermore, if its challenge had been more widely accepted, it might have set more productive conditions for philosophical discussions of business ethics, a topic which would later become widespread. Consistent with a primary thesis of this book, Ladd argues that "many of the older and traditional issues of political philosophy . . . have now turned into issues involving the relationship of individuals to formal organizations and of formal organizations to society." Ladd recognizes that the intellectual stakes are high and that the kind of ideological challenge accepted in this book needs to be fulfilled: "The very conception of a formal organization or bureaucracy presents us with an ideological challenge that desperately needs to be met one way or other."[21] Ladd does not appear to have accepted his own challenge, either in the confines of the article or in his subsequent writings. While this book is an attempt to meet that challenge and while I am much indebted to Ladd for being among those who awakened me from my dogmatic slumbers, I depart from the directions he suggests.

Ladd understands and accepts the traditional atomistic view of organizational life and even its capitalist overtones. He recognizes that such a setting cannot depend upon individual initiative or special individual contributions. Ladd argues that managers, like other commodities, must be easily substitutable:

> Individual office-holders are in principle replaceable by other individuals without affecting the continuity or identity of the organization. . . .
> . . . any individual is dispensable and replaceable by another.[22]

He even explicitly accepts the assumptions of the theory of the firm: "The goal of most business ventures is to maximize profits, etc."[23] His logical and philosophical mind trips on this generalization, however, and he takes back much of its power in the sentences which follow.

Ladd's most telling metaphor is that the formal organization is like a machine. Each part of the machine has a job to do in order to make the machine operate. He argues that formal organizations are goal-directed entities and that each member of the organization is required to attempt to accomplish those goals. Thus, Ladd accepts the determinism already identified. He quotes Herbert Simon approvingly: Simon identifies the "abdication of choice" by individuals when they enter formal organizations. Ladd's view is that if, in Wittgensteinian fashion, we understand the logic of the language game which is part of formal organizations, we can see that all formal organizations must have goals and that the task of the individuals in those organizations is to take actions which promote those goals. Ladd hints at this example: it is simply a misunderstanding of the situation to ask an IRS agent to be "kind" when reviewing your tax return. The agent has rules to follow. He or she might make mistakes about those rules, and you might challenge those items. Assuming the agent has made no mistakes, however, he or she has to tell you what your tax bill is and insist that you pay it. It would be as foolish to expect the agent to do otherwise as it would be to expect a postal clerk to sell you stamps at a cut rate because you are a nice person. Assuming no mistake has been made, it does no good to appeal the decision looking for more "humane" treatment from a superior, because "the authority of the superior official is itself based on his 'abdication of choice' in favor of social decisions of the organization." [24] Ladd concludes that it is simply wrongheaded to think that people with responsibilities within the organization should be expected to conform to the kinds of moral standards we might expect of people in the ordinary conduct of life. Ladd believes that the formal organization has an accepted language which it uses and that moral language is no more appropriate there than it is appropriate for criticizing the parts of a machine. As citizens, we might criticize a machine or an organization for what it does, and we might even develop legislation prohibiting certain kinds of machines or organizations. Ladd argues, however, that it is simply a failure to understand the nature of the formal organization if we criticize the activities of anyone in the organization who is carrying out an assigned task merely because we disapprove of the task.

Using a famous expression coined by Gilbert Ryle in another context, Ladd says that making moral judgments about the actions of people fulfilling their organizational responsibilities is a "category mistake." [25] Ladd's analysis draws on Wittgenstein, and he comes to a conclusion similar to Weiner's. For both Ladd and Weiner, the analogy to a machine is apposite. We should acknowledge its relevance to classical mechanics and its economic beneficiary—capitalism. The notion of mechanism and determinism recurs throughout Ladd's analysis. Of course, as has been argued in this book, if the parts are determined and have no choice in what they do, then it is senseless—precisely in the terms Ladd means: beyond the bounds of accepted language—to apply moral categories to them. Sensible people who disapprove of electrocution as a form of capital punishment do not blame the electrodes for acting inappropriately.

It is curious that while Ladd does mention universities in passing as part of the class of formal organizations, his primary examples are not universities but businesses and government agencies. Should we assume that Ladd means to say that faculty, for example, are exempt from moral analysis? Are the moralistic-sounding debates in universities about South African investments, about commitments to minorities, about reforms for women, about the multicultural curriculum, about political correctness, and so forth, just so many category mistakes? Admittedly, universities are strange creatures, and whatever we can say about them may have only limited application to the rest of the universe. If Ladd had considered the university more explicitly, however, he might have found more complexities in organizational life than he and Simon suspected.

For example, examining universities might have revealed to Ladd that informal organizations and informal organizational activities play a substantial role within universities. That discovery would be transferable to other formal organizations. In the article, Ladd explicitly dismisses the informal aspect from his area of interest.[26] However, the executive who does not understand the informal as well as the formal authority and power within an organization will have a difficult time providing significant leadership.

If Ladd had looked at the informal organizational activities in this sense, he might have come to a different conclusion. It is in the informal structure, at least, that moral language is considered appropriate. There people make decisions about how enthusiastically they will carry forward the instructions of the formal organization. In the informal structure people decide how much they will do above and beyond the job description. Formal managements which try to eliminate the effect of the informal soon find employees taking an inordinate amount of time evading what is not in their job descriptions. If the managers look, they find the terrible price which is paid in inefficiency.

Ladd combines his machine analogy with his understanding of the inappropriateness of moral language in formal organizations: "Organizations are like machines, and it would be a category mistake to expect a machine to comply with the principles of morality. By the same token, an official or agent of a formal organization is simply violating the basic rules of organizational activity if he allows his moral scruples rather than the objectives of the organization to determine his decision."[27] However, that is precisely where the formal-informal distinction breaks down. For example, an executive may be required to deliver bad news (e.g., that someone is going to be laid off). The people who remain will often be as concerned with the moral scruples of the executive in taking that formal action as they will with the action itself. Within the organization, one discovers that there are acceptable ways of carrying out the necessities of organizational life and unacceptable ways. Almost universally, an unacceptable way is to say that the decision is purely objective and no one considered the moral issues involved. The executive will find that pursuing the unacceptable ways will soon undermine the implementation of formal orders.[28] Executives who do not pay attention to the whole spectrum may find themselves unable to operate effectively.

Simon's organizational abstraction was created on purpose—to advance Simon's economic analyses. Ladd accepted the abstraction, and it blinded him from understanding organizations in context. Ladd finds formal organizations without moral standing: "Since, as I have argued in some detail, formal organizations are not moral persons, and have no moral responsibilities, they have no moral rights." His affection for the abstraction and the language game (what he occasionally calls the logic of the situation) is so strong that he is unwilling to entertain the possibility that facts might show him to be wrong: "In terms of the model I suggested earlier, this principle [abdication of choice] is part of the language-game; it is a logical requirement of the game whether or not it actually corresponds to empirical reality." [29] My disputes have been directly concerned with whether or not this view corresponds with reality. It is difficult to understand why Ladd is so uninterested in reality as it occurs. It is also difficult to know why one would maintain the abstraction if it does not correspond with reality.

Like Ladd, Milton Friedman does not think we should worry much about reality. Friedman even suggests that the fundamental assumptions of economics should be false: "In so far as a theory can be said to have 'assumptions' at all, and in so far as their 'realism' can be judged independently of the validity of predictions, the relation between the significance of a theory and the 'realism' of its 'assumptions' is almost the opposite of that suggested by the view under criticism. . . . To be important . . . a hypothesis must be descriptively false in its assumptions." [30] However, Friedman has another agenda: economics in general and his version of capitalism in particular. For Friedman, the issue is whether the assumptions of (capitalist) economics yield useful predictions. If they do, they should be retained. If they do not, they should be abandoned whether or not they describe reality, which, he says, they will not.

From the perspective of ideology, Friedman's view has a problem. If the assumptions of economics are descriptively false, then it is difficult to see how they can be of much help in understanding society. If the science of economics is not going to help us understand society, then ideologists will have to find some other economic theories to fulfill the conditions of constructing an ideology. Friedman was discussing the particular assumption of profit maximization. It is tempting to take Friedman at his word. Since he says that the hypothesis is descriptively false, we might conclude logically that its contradictory is descriptively true. Thus, for purposes of predictive power, economists assume that corporations maximize profits, but since those assumptions are false, it follows (deductively) that in fact it is not the case that corporations maximize profits. As we shall see, however, Friedman does not accept this conclusion.

Unlike Ladd, Friedman takes up the cudgels for an atomistic view of the corporation less in the interest of understanding corporate structures than in the interest of promoting his version of capitalism. Friedman argues that the corporation is a mere associational convenience for the conduct of business and that it is in no regard distinct from the firm. In the firm, the owner's interests coincide with the entrepreneur's interests, because the owner and the entrepreneur are the same person. Friedman goes on to reason that in the corporation, while the managers and the owners might be separate people, "the executive is an agent serving the interests of his principle." The principle is to satisfy the stockholders, and thus, "there is one and only one social responsibility of business—to use its resources and engage in activities designed to increase its profits." [31] He reemphasizes the point by saying: "Few trends could so thoroughly undermine the very foundations of our free society as the acceptance by corporate officials of a social responsibility other than to make as much money for their stockholders as possible." [32] In short, Friedman is consistent with Ladd and Weiner in viewing the executive as a cog in the machinery who has a job to do and a role to play. The role of the executive is to maximize profits for the stockholders. Asking the executive to perform some other role is simply asking for something which is inappropriate and even dangerous.

Friedman's commitment to intellectual honesty drives him to follow arguments where they lead, even when that direction is not in his own personal interest. He notes that his analysis would also preclude corporations from making contributions to charities in general and to universities in particular: "One topic in the area of social responsibility that I feel duty bound to touch on, because it affects my own personal interests, has been the claim that business should contribute to the support of charitable activities and especially to universities. Such giving by corporations is an inappropriate use of corporate funds in a free-enterprise economy." [33]

If we follow Ladd's wise admonition to pay attention to language, we notice a curious inversion in the quotations from Friedman. Capitalism presumes that each business person pursues self-interest and that through a deterministic process governed by the wishes, needs, and desires of consumers, the best for society results. As Smith held, it is not through the benevolence of business persons that we should expect the situation to turn out well. It is through their individual pursuit of their self-interest. In Friedman's own language, however, both the determinism and the self-interest are broken. The latter quotation would seem to imply that at least under some circumstances, business executives do have some discretion: they can decide to give the money to the university, or they can decide to use it to lower prices. In a capitalist structure, executives would not have that choice. In addition, Friedman asks them to forgo fulfilling their own self-interest in the name of the interests of stockholders. Suppose, for example, the university agreed to name a building or a major facility after the president of a corporation in return for a substantial gift from the corporation. It seems reasonable to suppose that the president might find it in his or her personal interest to order the gift to be made. Friedman would argue that the president should not do so because he or she has a social obligation to use the resources of the corporation to maximize profits.

If we follow Friedman in this, we will have gone a long distance from arguing that executives are cogs in machines to arguing that they are people with discretion and responsibility in exercising that discretion. Rhetorically, Friedman would do better to retreat to the linguistic protection Ladd offers, but Friedman knows too much about the facts of organizational life. Probably he also knows that Ladd's view applies to very few organizations.

It would be wrong to conclude that just because Ladd and Friedman agree on the atomism of the corporation, they agree on other critical ideological topics. Friedman's ideological capitalism has him advocate that the government should avoid involvement in the economy except in special circumstances.[34] Nothing in Ladd's work would lead us to a similar conclusion. Actually, Ladd argues that since we cannot hold corporations responsible and since we cannot hold people performing their corporate responsibilities accountable, we need to be sure to develop laws and structures which make the organizations operate as we believe they should.

Organicism and the Corporation: Peter French

Given the tension outlined in chapter 2, it was perhaps inevitable that some defenders of an organic view would emerge. Once again, it is to Ladd's credit that he predicted the language of the debate. We recall that Ladd said: "Since . . . formal organizations are not moral persons, and have no moral responsibilities, they have no moral rights."[35] Peter French has led those who argue for an organic approach to the corporation, which results in French's identifying corporations as persons. French's view has developed in response to the criticisms of others, but his fundamental position has not changed.

It should not be surprising that the organic view of corporations took longer to develop, because it is more closely associated with socialism and, as a result of historical circumstances, corporations were associated with capitalism. Nevertheless, it is important to credit French with having the wisdom to see through prevailing assumptions and to see that something was going on in regard to corporations which was not being described by the standard analyses. French, following organic philosophies of biology and psychology, argues that in the complex activities of corporations, something emerges. That something is sufficiently similar to a person to be given that appellation. In short, French believes that there is such a thing as a corporate person and that that person has both the rights and the responsibilities of any moral agent—any person.

To use French's example, the Gulf Corporation is not merely the aggregation of the employees and stockholders associated with Gulf. It is an entity. Just as the Gulf Corporation believes it makes sense to say to individuals, "You are held responsible for payment in full of the amount recorded on your statement," so it makes sense to say, "The Gulf Oil Corporation should be held responsible for destroying the ecological balance of the bay."[36] French identifies a critical element that he calls the Corporate Internal Decision Structure, which is roughly the informal and formal processes for making and implementing decisions in an organization. French wants a generic phrase for those processes, because their details may vary from one organization to another. Thus, he in essence takes on Ladd's two arguments about formal organizations and language simultaneously.

As indicated in chapter 2, organicists have a persistent difficulty in evading language of mystery in discussing the organic element. Consider the issue of the human person. On that level, the organic theorist argues that there is something more to the human than mere biological matter. Organic theoreticians who are also emergentists argue that in the interaction of the biological properties, something we call a person emerges. Something like that organic view (not necessarily involving emergence) supports much of our insistence on the rights and special treatment of humans. If humans are in fact nothing more than biological entities, it is difficult to imagine how we could consistently insist on special ethical treatment of them. If humans are merely animals and animals are merely a configuration of chemistry, why should we grant humans any more moral respect than other chemical configurations (say, rocks or cockroaches)? The fact that we do grant humans some special moral standing is reason to consider thinking about the issue, but it surely does not resolve the issue. Perhaps our linguistic conventions are without justification. In addition, the most difficult thing to specify is the nature of this extra element which makes one organic and the other not organic.

French suffers from the organic malady, and he does not resolve it for us. French's view, which is common among organic theoreticians, is that something is going on and that whatever that something is, it cannot be eliminated or reduced. To put the matter in an epistemological way: French believes an exhaustive description of the individual properties of a corporation will not be a complete description of the organization itself, because it will leave out some descriptions which are necessary to complete the picture: descriptions of the corporation as an entity. But how do we know all that, and how do we identify that extra element? French is not much help, which means he is consistent with the organic tradition. He basically just says that the extra element exists and that unless we acknowledge its presence, we shall miss important phenomena. In addition, of course, he thinks that those phenomena make all the moral difference.

In order to clarify French's view, let us follow some examples. If we hold the Manville Corporation morally responsible for its role in the harm which came from the use of asbestos, we cannot be said to be holding the current executives of the Manville Corporation responsible. In all probability, the executives who made the critical decisions are no longer there. We do not hold the stockholders responsible. For all we know, no current stockholders may have held Manville stock then, and to whom would we turn if we were to consider institutional investors? If, for example, the Colleges Retirement and

Equity Fund (CREF) invested in Manville from the time of the decision to the time of the identification of moral responsibility, should we conclude that those university employees whose retirement funds are in CREF are responsible (since, following Friedman, CREF is just a pass-through agency representing the faculty participants)? Surely all this can move quickly to absurdity, and, to return to Ladd's suggestion that we pay attention to language, this point would not accurately describe what we mean by holding the Manville Corporation responsible.

And what of nonprofit corporations? Consider universities again. It is well known that in an earlier era, many of our most prestigious colleges and universities had quotas restricting the number of certain so-called ethnic students. Clearly, it is not unreasonable to say that the university is morally responsible for such decisions. However, no one owns the university in any standard sense. Another autobiographical story may help illustrate the point French would want us to understand. I once faced just such a case, in which a person claimed he was rejected because of such quotas by the college for which I was responsible. He said he was still hurt by the offense made by the college in an earlier era. In checking out the situation, it seemed likely that the rejection and pain was inflicted on him as he averred. He made it clear that he believed that an official apology on behalf of the college would help him. I could have responded by giving him a lesson in atomism and explaining that no current member of the boards of the college or of the administration or faculty who was responsible for the offense remained at the college and, thus, no one could be held responsible. Presumably, that is the response Ladd and Friedman would have recommended to me. By way of contrast, I could have recognized that what he meant was that he was harmed by the college as a corporate entity and it was from a representative of that entity that he was requesting an apology. Presumably, French would have recommended that recognition to me.

Let's take another case. Suppose someone informs me that I unjustifiably (and perhaps inadvertently) said or did something which hurt her some years ago and indicates that she wants me to apologize. I might reply that all my cells have been replaced in the meantime, that I am nothing but a group of cells, and that I cannot today sensibly apologize for the actions of some chemical configuration of an earlier time. Or I can recognize the common sense of her request and apologize. French and the organic theoreticians would find no dramatic difference between the two cases. An apology on behalf of the college for an action for which the college is corporately responsible makes sense, just as an apology for an action by me as a person makes sense. The polar positions have been outlined. It is not necessary to continue examining the replies and rejoinders. However, one argument in response to French deserves special mention. In a startling article entitled "Corporate Moral Agency: The Case for Anthropological Bigotry," John Danley suggests that we make biology the necessary condition for moral responsibility. He associates himself with what he calls the traditionalists in the debate and says: "Traditionalists, like myself, maintain that only persons, i.e., entities with particular physical and mental properties, can be morally responsible." [37] We may suspect that Danley means us to take the title of his article with some humor. What is striking about Danley's substantive claim, however, is that it relies on bigotry which has haunted humanity throughout history. The prejudice against women, for example, has been based largely on an assertion of the difference between their physical and mental properties and those of men. Danley might say in response that the claims justifying that bigotry have been, as a matter of fact, wrong. However, some assertions of physical differences are in fact true. Women are different from men. Affirmative action cannot do much to change chromosomes. Perhaps even some assertions about different mental properties are also true. The research of Carol Gilligan and others would seem to indicate that differences exist—to the general credit of women.[38] All this misses the point, however, which is that we should give up bigotry not by arguing about which group has which properties but by saying that such analyses are irrelevant because the issue is persons, not biology. Yet Danley would have us believe they are relevant.

A second response to Danley is that since he has apparently accepted the organic perspective for humans, it is difficult to know why he has so much trouble extending it to corporations. There is some respect to be given to the view that organic thinking is simply wrong—superstitious—at all levels. However, to introduce it at one level and then withhold it at another level puts a heavy burden on the advocate: the burden of showing the grounds for introducing it and the grounds for restraining it. Danley provides us with no such arguments, and we must sadly conclude that he really is attempting to revive bigotry in that older sense. Perhaps that is why he calls himself a traditionalist, but he will need stronger arguments if he is going to defeat French's position.

A Middle Position: Larry May

May's recent book, *The Morality of Groups,* takes the analysis of corporations out of a cul-de-sac into which it seemed to have been driven.[39] In previous discussions, the standard conditions of a bifurcation fallacy were being laid. May stepped into the debate and argued for what he describes as a middle position. May acknowledges that we are dealing with an ontological problem: an attempt to identify what is. That is already refreshing, since he recognizes that the stakes extend beyond language games and useful assumptions for a science of economics. He shows how the thesis of the atomists is related to a broader thesis in the philosophy of science and in science itself.[40] It is the thesis of methodological individualism and of reductionism which argues that eventually the only things which really exist are those things which are studied by physicists: atoms, subatomic particles, and their aggregations.

May does not follow that position slavishly, but he does accept the conservative notion that we should not multiply entities needlessly. Thus, if we do not need to posit the existence of entities called corporations, we should not do so. At the same time, he acknowledges that a description merely of the activities of individuals alone will not suffice for a complete explanation of group activity. He acknowledges that, to use an earlier example, there is a substantial difference between a group gathered around a gate waiting for a plane and a group which is a well-rehearsed string quartet playing at its peak. However, he does not want to grant to the string quartet some mysterious extra nonobservable property such as personhood. He says:

> Perhaps the central philosophical problem with fictitious terms concerns whether there must be anything in nature to which these terms refer. . . .
> My proposal is to posit entities only when there are good philosophical reasons for doing so.[41]

He thinks there are no good philosophical reasons for organic views, and I have said a number of times that the major problem for the organicists is identifying clearly what they are talking about. The standard criticism of the organicists is that they posit more entities than can be justified with good reasons. May's scepticism about organicism does not drive him directly into an atomistic view, however, because in describing a football team, for example, he says: "By the collective efforts of all the members, the capabilities of each member are enhanced. It is no longer possible to explain what each player does: some account must also be given of the cohesiveness of the group, or of its division of labor, of its team spirit. These factors themselves have a reality which is not captured by describing what each of the players does. But the team itself does not have a separate reality from that of the members and their relations to each other."[42] Thus, May believes we cannot reduce descriptions of the activities of the team (corporation) to activities of individuals alone, but still we have no need to posit entities to make our description complete.

May believes we can accomplish the task before us by analyzing social groups as "individuals in relationships." That does not reify the concept of the group, but it does allow us to gain a more complete description of the group. It also allows some (limited) notion of group responsibility. May gives us an example of a case in which he was a consultant, involving a charge of sexual harassment at a university. He was forced to raise the question of group responsibility— university responsibility—in that case. He concludes that it does make sense to hold the university responsible under at least some circumstances. Thus, he does not take what might be the atomist's view: that the university does not exist as such and that the aggrieved's case can only be brought against individual members of the university. At the same time, he does not take an organic view: that there is some undescribable entity called the university and that it is that entity which must be held accountable. May argues that the university is, rather, a collection of individuals in certain relationships. If we ignore those relationships, we might as well decide there is no such thing as the university.

Whether or not we should call May's position a middle position, it seems reasonable to credit May with articulating another viewpoint, and that should give us some clue about proceeding. Toward the end of the chapter in which he develops his own position, May discusses David Copp, who had criticized Peter French. May says of Copp: "What is most attractive about Copp's view is that he posits a continuum, rather than a sharp demarcation, between organized and unorganized groups." [43] In the combined insight of May and Copp, we may have a solution to the problem before us. Toward the end of chapter 4, we returned to the bifurcation fallacy and suggested that with regard to socialism and capitalism, rather than having contradictory positions in which the truth of one implies the falsity of the other, we have constructed what the logicians call contraries, in which both positions cannot be true, but they can both be false. In regard to the atomistic-organic debate about corporations, we still do not have contradictory positions, but we have what the logicians call subcontraries, in which both positions cannot be false, but both could be true. The fact that May has found a third position coupled with Copp's approach suggests that we may have something like a continuum, with limiting cases in the positions of atomism and organicism and other possibilities along the continuum. [44]

It is tempting to evade further issues in regard to atomism and organicism by saying that the limiting cases do not even have to exist in order to uphold the position just described. We could say that they can be treated as logical possibilities while empirical reality lies somewhere between. However, we should not conclude this section with that comfortable way out of serious issues. It would seem that representatives of the extremes do exist in reality. Presumably, one does not have to argue much for the existence of purely atomistic groups. The example of a crowd at an airport gate has been used. One could think of numerous variations: people in a theater, the customers of a store, and so on. Noncontroversial organic examples are perhaps more difficult to identify. Some atomists may want to challenge their logical possibility, and such a challenge would surely pose substantial problems for the view taken here. Thus far, however, no one has demonstrated inherent contradictoriness. [45]

Regarding its empirical probability, one can only point to examples and cases. Remembering that May has said that the issue at base is an ontological one, situations do seem to occur in which people say that the organic account of reality is the only one which will do. May even says that some account must be given of the cohesiveness of the group or of its division of labor or team spirit. Perhaps he could give some account of the cohesiveness and the division of labor, staying within his "individuals-in-relationships" account. It is doubtful, however, that he could capture the richness of all experiences of something like team spirit without moving very far toward reification of the team as an entity. Leaving aside the athletic reference, when the members of an articulate group become organic, they themselves discuss their actions by referring to something like group spirit which drives them all to accomplishments beyond their individual expectations. The aficionado of jazz knows when the group has really come together and when it is just going through the motions. If it is the former, members of the group may acknowledge that they are playing above their abilities. It would seem that those experiences and others like them do exist at least sometimes and that while May is appropriately cautious in not wanting to introduce entities needlessly, he should not be so cautious that he restrains his ontology and epistemology to the point that it cannot account for phenomena which exist.

Can such an organic development occur in a corporation? It is difficult to identify reasons to explain that it cannot, and if we listen to some accounts, we shall find reason to believe it does. Must it occur? By no means. Clearly, some corporations epitomize Friedman's apparent model: a group of self-interested people doing as much or as little as they have to do to get the most out of the corporation in order to satisfy their personal interests. In short, some corporations are definitely atomistic. I suggest that there are, also, a range from that individualistic atomism to a tightly knit organic whole, in which people do things even they cannot explain except by reference to something which extends beyond the members of the corporation.

The ethical implications of my conclusion, which we shall discuss in the next chapter, are that the extent to which a corporation rather than individuals within the corporation should be held responsible is in large measure an empirical issue that cannot be solved by painting all corporations or groups with a single brush.

The Midworld: a Mutation

Historically, political theory has addressed the relation between the individual and the state. A world of organizations has intervened in that relationship. Following May's insights, we should recognize that a number and a variety of organizations have a powerful, indeed definitive, influence on the social, political, and economic life of our times. The term *midworld* is used here because in origin, at least, these organizations have existed as something between individual people and the state.

As corporations grew in importance, they carried their capitalist heritage of suspicion of government involvement. We should recall, however, that the suspicion was not because of some cost to consumers but because of constraints on those who ran the organizations—largely businessmen. The growth of the labor movement carried with it an important lesson: even outside the world of purely commercial transactions, problems among organizations can be solved without the intervention of government (though, of course, both sides do what they can to gain government support for their cause). Unions became a midworld between some workers and the government, just as businesses were a midworld between other workers and the government. These organizations were successful mutations in the social adaptive process, and they grew and duplicated themselves. The United States has become predominantly a society of organizations.

What is not as well understood is that the organizations—of which business is the archetype—have grown in size, power, and influence, so that in many cases they can no longer be seen merely as intermediaries between individuals and their government but must be viewed as forces with which the government must contend. In fact, the government does its contending through its organizations, agencies, bureaus, and departments. In the Middle Ages only two sources of social power existed: the state and the church. Asking which was more powerful makes for an interesting debate. The revival of interest in ideology with the coming of the industrial revolution occurred because of the shrinking influence of the church following the Reformation. Nations achieved hegemony, and churches had influence only where they were given official sanction by the state. The only political role for the church was to mediate between the individual and the state, and even there it had limited influence. Stalin asked how many divisions the pope controlled as an acknowledgment that he did not need to think about the pope. Religious organizations became merely some organizations among others seeking to have power and influence, and the extent of their influence varied from one society to another. In a relative sense, however, their power diminished considerably as other organizations, especially businesses, gained power. As other organizations gained power, they came to recognize that, like the earlier church, they no longer merely mediated between individuals and governments but were rivals for government power.

This development may be most easily seen first on a local level. As municipalities bid to persuade corporations to open facilities in their areas, there is little question about where the power lies: the corporation is larger, controls more resources, is more professionally managed and geographically flexible. The question is not whether the municipality will be forced to grant benefits to the corporation in anticipation of having the facility located there, but how good a deal can be cut for the corporation. A similar story can be told at the state level in the United States. Currently, each state has an economic development office which continually attempts to attract business to the state. In some cases, the businesses are larger and more powerful than the state itself. Those economic development agencies also attempt to make sure businesses do not leave, which the businesses threaten to do regularly. The economic development offices are armed with a bagful of tricks with which to do their negotiating. At the same time, on a national level, there is a similar economic development effort. Almost perpetual trade talks, both bilateral and multilateral, are designed to create good conditions for domestic businesses and to attract others.[46] The largest corporations in the United States, Germany, Japan, and other industrialized economies have become larger than most nations. The corporations in the United States continue to be the wave of the future, and increasingly, those corporations, like the earlier church, are losing a sense of national identity. *Business Week* referred to these organizations as stateless corporations.[47] They are no longer intervening between the individual and the state; they are essentially states in their own right. They have achieved the international position the church once had, and while they are better managed than the church and unencumbered by the need to engage in casuistry, they have a strong presence in the personal lives of their employees. For example, the Japanese corporation leaves little to chance, arranging both the time of marriage and the spouses of those novitiates who wish to rise in the corporate ranks. Violation of "the tap" probably means the end of promotion.

Thus, in the course of the evolution, some of the entities which started as part of a midworld have become bigger, more powerful, and more likely to survive than their ancestors.

Managerialism and Other New Ideologies

Polyarchy: Pluralism

We discussed polyarchal proposals in chapter 5. In a sense, those approaches do not suggest a new ideology, because they attempt to proceed under the banner of democracy. If the arguments against them as democratic have merit, however, then we might consider what would be proposed if we examined polyarchy as a rival nondemocratic ideology. In this context, the most common term used for this view is *pluralism*. That term will be used here, since it is more attractive than *polyarchism*. It is important, however, to recognize that the term *pluralism* has gained some use in the popular press, where it seems to mean something like "a lot of divergent views and backgrounds." The so-called liberal press usually applauds pluralism and actions taken to enhance pluralism (for example, bilingual education); the so-called conservative press usually deplores pluralism and actions taken to enhance pluralism (such as bilingual education). Thus, *pluralism* has taken on some of the characteristics of a code word and, like *liberalism* and *conservatism,* is in danger of losing any stable meaning.[48]

Pluralism shares with managerialism the views that associations make up an important aspect of American society and that they influence its direction considerably. In addition, pluralism shares with managerialism the view that an effective way for an individual to get his or her interests addressed is to work through an organization. Pluralism is more optimistic than managerialism about coverage, since pluralism assumes that all of us can always find a group to represent our interests and that the groups are a reasonably good surrogate for what democracy would yield if it were to have its way.

In the distorted sense of democracy identified earlier, pluralism continues with a rhetorical democratic faith. Managerialism recognizes that if someone's interests are not represented in the transaction process, they will most likely not be fulfilled. Managerialism is not a substitute for democracy; it is antidemocratic. Managerialism acknowledges that the extent to which one's interests are realized depends in large measure on membership size, discretionary wealth, organic behavior, the effectiveness of management, and public rhetoric. Thus, in general, if management has done a poor job of representing someone's interests, those interests will likely be ignored.

Pluralism sees the function of government as creating a level playing field (to use a popular metaphor). Managerialism acknowledges that government managers are players in the transactional process and that the metaphor of the level playing field is a myth perpetuated largely by those who attempt to tilt the playing field in their direction. Pluralism does not explicitly acknowledge the importance of management in the social process. As we saw in reference to Sartori, there is a sort of backing into that recognition, but a continuing insistence that somehow it is all democratic. Pluralism apparently continues to assert that the system acts of the people, by the people, and for the people. Managerialism recognizes that the operative ideology has been constructed by managers and for managers.

Pluralism does not recognize the wide disparity in power and influence which occurs among the groups. Pluralism does not recognize that such disparities are largely independent of what "the people" may or may not want. Pluralism thinks elections are an independent check on the pluralist process, whereas managerialism recognizes that to a large extent, the alternatives placed before the electorate are so limited that the choice is an essentially empty one.[49] Pluralism believes in the ideal purity of the election process; managerialism recognizes that the process can be effectively manipulated and that probably the legal forms of manipulation are more effective than the illegal ones.

Managerialism has a broader reach than pluralism and will go a long distance toward explaining events in so-called socialist and Communist countries as well as in so-called capitalist democracies and the Republic of South Africa. The revolutions we have witnessed in the last half of the twentieth century have been, largely, revolutions of the managers who have become tired of the empty rhetoric of others, whether Communist or capitalist, and have recognized that if anything constructive is to happen it will not be as a result of coffeehouse debates but as a result of the management of more or less organized forces within society.

The formerly Communist countries will embrace what outsiders call capitalism, not because they have suddenly become born-again capitalists, but because they want to get something done, because the bureaucracy stands in the way, and because they have no other vocabulary to describe what they are doing. The Western press has no vocabulary either, so it continues to refer to the development of capitalism in these countries, in spite of the fact that there is not much capitalism invoked. What is actually happening is that these countries are creating a form of managerialism adapted to their own history, background, and culture. The mere existence of a stock market, especially one heavily regulated by the government, does not prove the existence of capitalism, any more than the existence of a large abdomen proves the existence of pregnancy.

Finally, pluralism has failed to understand how dramatically organizations have grown and the subsequent impact on their relation to government. Pluralism is a political theory in origin: it shares with other political theories the assumption that the task is to describe how individuals are related to the state. The pluralists have failed to understand, however, that what started as a mid-world has lost that status and that the rules are changing substantially. The question no longer is how the individual relates to the nation-state but how the managers of organizations are related to each other and how they create social, political, and economic conditions. Insofar as the individual is important, and that is limited, the question is how he or she relates to organizations and especially to the managements of those organizations. The midworld has mutated to a new world of organizations, with managers engaged in constant transactions with each other.

Corporatism

In continental European circles, there has been talk recently of an ideology sometimes called corporatism. It shares the continental European's sympathy for organic conceptualizing, and it asserts that the fundamental conditions of the society are settled by a bargaining process between business and labor, overseen by government.[50] As a political theory, it is still struggling with the relation between individuals and the state. It still assumes the hegemony of the state and does not recognize that even in Europe businesses are gaining substantially more power than the states in which they exist (even when some of those businesses are heavily supported and subsidized by the state). It is surprising that with all the talk of 1992 and the development of the European Economic Community, the political theoreticians would still be thinking of the state as an entity of supreme importance. That can be explained, perhaps, by their continuing attachment to organic theories in which the state continues with a kind of Rousseauean and Hegelian mystical importance. In managerialism, the state has no organic property. Government agencies, departments, and bureaus may individually approach some organic standing, but that is not necessary. The personnel policies of most government organizations typically preclude such development.[51]

Corporatism fails to recognize the importance of organizations which are not labor, government, or business. In a sense, corporatism still clings to its socialist heritage, and while its bias is toward the worker and government control of business, it grudgingly grants some power to business and, as the label implies, recognizes the importance of business incorporation as a social function. However, a multitude of other organizations seek to influence government policy. In the United States, at least, the influence of the union movement has waned politically and economically so that, allowing for some exceptions, unions are almost unimportant. Ironically, the greatest power of labor unions in the United States lies not in the business sector but in the public sector.[52] In the United States, the anachronistic personnel policies of government agencies have more recently yielded for the public sector just what they yielded for the private sector some decades ago: unionization. Thus, in the United States, it is not business and unions that need to come to the table under the watchful eye of government. Rather, unions often bargain with government, which, of course, has no interest in providing a level playing field and which has the capacity business always wanted but lacked: to make striking illegal.[53]

In general, the treatment of women and minorities, the treatment of the environment, consumerism, and the development of higher education, among other areas, are more backward in Europe than in the United States. That is so in part because corporatism, insofar as it is a descriptive ideology, has described the primary forces in European society. The other forces have not been effectively represented yet, though murmurings are apparent.

Managerialism recognizes the potential importance of all organizations. Their importance is not a function of historical precedent or romantic wishing. It is a function of their power, which is in large measure a function of their management. There is no interest which cannot be represented, including illegal and immoral ones. There is only the question of the ability of the organization, through its management, to engage successfully in the transaction process.

Corporatism does have the advantage that it is posited as an ideology. While the proposers are probably sympathetic to corporatism, they are generally careful to attempt to describe the theory rather than to offer it as a utopia. They seem to have recognized that the old ideologies have broken down and that something is happening which those ideologies cannot describe effectively. Corporatism shares with managerialism a commitment to a new ideology.

Corporatism also breaks with the deterministic past of post–industrial revolution ideologies. The corporatists recognize that in the bargaining process, the representatives of each of the sides have some effective discretion. Alan Cawson, for example, emphasizes that the representatives are not bearers "of underlying structures, having no free will of their own." [54] They have some discretion. While Cawson does not recognize explicitly that the discretion itself marks a break with the capitalist and socialist past, his recognition of the discretion is an important step.

Finally, Cawson does acknowledge explicitly that corporatism is not a democratic theory. He somehow overcomes the penchant for wrapping modern political theories in the cloak of democracy, and as a consequence, he enables the conversation about emergent ideologies to move one step further. He says, for example, that "corporatist trends are associated with the diminishing importance of parliamentary/territorial modes of representation. What is enfranchised in a corporatist system is the group rather than the individual." He treats this thesis more completely in chapter 9 of his book *Corporatism and Social Welfare: Social Policy and State Intervention in Britain.* [55] While he continues to describe corporatism as biased toward producers and not consumers, his recognition of how far the society has traveled from adherence to democracy is of great importance.

George Lodge and Communitarianism

George Lodge deserves individual recognition, because for many years he has been laboring in the wilderness, trying to call our attention to the fact that the old ideology has disappeared and that a new ideology has taken its place. It is interesting to note that these assertions are made not by a philosopher (he is often too modest about disclaiming his philosophical abilities), a political scientist, or an economist, but by a professor of business administration. Lodge has produced numerous articles and books arguing his thesis. It would not be appropriate to examine Lodge's suggestion for the new ideology here, for it is readily available. [56] Beyond recommending that the reader read Lodge's works, the purpose here is to compare his account and managerialism.

Lodge accepts the distinction between atomism and organicism we identified in chapter 2. In fact, he commits the bifurcation fallacy. He associates the American ideology with John Locke and gives Locke much of the prominence given Smith in this book. That gives Lodge the advantage of solidifying private property at the center of the ideology, though, as we have seen, that in itself poses problems for understanding capitalism. Locke was by no means the economist Smith was. Locke's justification of private property is directly related to his labor theory of value and his belief in natural law (as, for example, it quite consciously appeared in the Declaration of Independence, penned by Jefferson with Locke uppermost in his mind). In my view, the labor theory of value is a little like the phlogiston theory. It is intriguing, and one can construct a parlor game around its defense, but it cannot be taken seriously anymore. In addition, the assumptions necessary to save natural law are extensive and in the end more questionable than natural law itself.

Lodge's acceptance of the bifurcation is followed with a stringent recognition of the breakdown of the atomistic ideology, especially in regard to corporations:

> Many of our most important institutions—notably the large, publicly held corporations, trade unions, and the federal government—have departed radically from the old ideology, or are in the process of doing so. . . .
>
> Corporate America (but not the corner grocery store) has outgrown the ideology from which it and the community in general have traditionally drawn their legitimacy.[57]

The reader will recognize that those statements could have been made in the articulation of managerialism.

Having recognized the breakdown of the traditional atomistic ideology, Lodge assumes that the only alternative lies in the construction of a new ideology, which is organic. In the first chapter of this book, we saw that in one place Lodge makes the organic property a definitional condition for ideology itself. He calls his ideology communitarianism. We can summarize his approach by identifying five characteristics: Communitarianism is organic, not atomistic. It proceeds on the basis of equality of result or hierarchy, not strict equality before the law, and in that context, it presumes consensus rather than contractual relationships. It depends upon rights and duties of membership rather than property rights. It endorses an active, planning state which defines community needs. It endorses a holistic view of society.[58] Curiously, Lodge does not spend much time trying to keep this ideology out of the clutches of socialism, though he does tell us that one alumnus of Harvard Business School wrote to complain that Lodge was teaching managers "for the great socialist future."[59] Surely the alumnus simply fell into the bifurcation fallacy and did not consider Lodge's arguments carefully, since Lodge does not endorse the abolition of private property. On the other hand, Lodge does advocate an active, planning state, and he does so in spite of his clearheaded recognition that "governments . . . far from merely being referee . . . become coach, manager, even an active player."[60] Lodge reconciles an active planning state with advocacy of a vigorous business community through his support of organic communitarianism.

Under that ideology, Lodge believes that we shall all be working toward common ends and shall give up the tendency to divide the society with our narrow parochial interests. Lodge maintains a strong state as part of his ideology, and he believes the state will command our attention and our loyalty.

It is interesting that Lodge recognizes the growth and impact of the large corporation but does not see its tendency to undermine the state itself and to operate outside the confines of the state. Managerialism emphasizes the management function, not the state or any other single organization, though it recognizes the leadership role business has played in the sophistication of the management function. When Lodge moves close to managerialism, he identifies it with the negative catchphrase *interest groups*. Rhetorically, interest groups have become just those interest groups which represent interests antagonistic to the speaker's. Labor unions refer to the chamber of commerce as an interest group, and businesses refer to labor unions as interest groups. The expression was not used in this book because it has taken on such a negative tone. However, if *interest group* is defined broadly enough so that it includes businesses, churches, universities, government agencies, political parties—indeed, all organizations—then managerialism does recognize the importance of interest groups and can be transformed into an ideology which says that social, political, and economic decisions are made as a result of transactions among managers of interest groups. Lodge places the interest-group approach on the atomistic side of the bifurcation, and there is some wisdom in that, though managerialism challenges the bifurcation itself.

Unlike Lodge, managerialism does not find much evidence of the development of a sense of community in the advanced industrialized nations. To speak of recent events, the centrifugal forces at work in the formerly Communist countries seem much stronger than the centripetal forces. While Europe may be coming together slightly, it seems more like an atomistic union than an organic one, and the United States is the archetype of the society which has a multitude of groups, the managements of which are all competing for their interests. In the United States, there is more *pluribus* than there is *unum*. Managerialism allows an organic understanding of the specific organizations, but it does not expect an overall communitarian organic condition to arise out of the transactions of the managements of the organizational units. In that regard, managerialism parts company with the ideology Lodge identifies.

Summary Statement of Managerialism

In summarizing this chapter, it may be most helpful to state what managerialism holds as an ideology and the ways in which it answers the ideological issues. In chapter 1 I argued that ideology is that set of principles upon which the political, economic, and social order of a society is based. Chapter 2 stated that a deep divide exists between atomism and organicism which has separated different approaches to ideology. In chapters 3, 4, 5, and 6, I argued that the ideologies we currently identify in understanding and justifying advanced industrialized societies no longer correspond to reality. With their loss of applicability came a loss of their justification and, thus, the loss of justification for contemporary society. In chapter 1 we saw that all societies must have some ideology, whether or not we can identify that ideology. People responsible for making decisions must go ahead and make the decisions on the basis of some set of principles, whether those principles have been articulated or not. If the old principles no longer apply and if new principles have not been articulated, then decision makers will make their decisions based upon implicit principles. I have argued that that is what has been happening over the past decades. Thus, the decision makers have been in effect creating an implicit ideology.

In the remainder of this chapter I will summarize the fundamental principles of society according to managerialism by answering some questions which might be directed at managerialism itself. Here I will not attempt to defend the description of managerialism provided earlier in the chapter.

What Is the Fundamental Nature of Society?
Managerialism asserts that society is made up of numerous subunits. They may be variously labeled groups, organizations, corporations, or associations. The different labels carry different connotations, and the designation should be inclusive. Managerialism specifically denies that the fundamental nature of society is an aggregation of individuals. It also denies the notion that society has an overarching essence. If we were to conceive of society as a nation, such as the United States, managerialism concludes that there is no single United States and that individual Americans should not be identified as the fundamental nature of the country. Rather, the country is basically composed of numerous groups which collectively make up the country we call the United States.

How Are Social Decisions Made?
Managerialism asserts that social decisions are made as a result of the interaction of the units identified as constituting the fundamental reality of society. Actually, we need to go a step further. By and large, the units do not interact. The managements of the units interact. It is in the interaction of the units that social decisions are made. That interaction is a transaction process which should be seen inclusively. It does not necessarily mean a face-to-face bargaining process. Transactions can occur over a long distance, through intermediaries, and among managers who do not even know one another.

How Is the Society Related to Its Individual (Human) Members?
How Does Social Choice Arise out of Individual Preferences?
Individuals attempt to have an impact on social choice through their membership in groups. The groups have their impact through management. Individuals qua individuals are basically abstractions. They have essentially no impact on the social decision-making process. If an individual is concerned about some issue, she or he is best advised to work for remedy through some group representation. If a set of concerns or interests is not actively represented in the transaction process, typically it will not be addressed. Social choice arises out of group managerial transactions. Effectively, there is no direct linkage between social choice and individual preferences. At the same time, there is no identifiable overarching social personality.

What Is the Role of Government in Managerialism?
The government is a part of the managerial process. The management of different groups will attempt to influence the direction of government action. Their success or failure will depend upon their ability to pursue their case and upon their ability to blunt the case of competitors. Government qua government is as much an abstraction as the individual qua individual and the state qua state. Such entities do not exist independently: they exist, rather, as abstractions, highlighting, by way of contrast, the reality of groups. For example, in the United States, government is composed of the typical breakdown among legislative, executive, and judicial. Each of those is broken down further into subunits, and each of those subunits is itself part of the transaction process. The success of the subunits depends upon the ability of their managements and other factors such as size, cohesiveness, managerial discretion, and control of resources. Government itself is a collection of governmental units. The government is not the state.

What Are the Legal and Moral Limits on the Range of Decisions
Which Can Be Made by the Managerial Process?
There are no inherent legal limits. What legal limits there are exist as a result of the transaction process and, thus, are susceptible to change by that process. There are two exceptions which should be mentioned. In the United States, some legal limits appear in the Constitution and the Bill of Rights, remaining from an earlier, nonmanagerialist period. The question of interpretation of the Constitution is most relevant, however, and the managerialist process has its impact through the interpretation of the Constitution rather than through a direct transaction process. From the managerialist perspective, the doctrine of strict constructionism is as much a charade as the doctrine of the living

document. Both are introduced as part of the transaction process and are susceptible to transactional manipulation. Also, some government actions are so fundamental to managerialism that if they were rescinded and not replaced with equivalencies, managerialism would commit suicide just as democracy might. Consider, again, the granting of incorporation privileges. Without such privileges, it is unlikely that managerialism could survive.

The transaction process itself has no moral limits. Individual managements may make self-imposed limits, as when Polaroid decided to stop doing business with the South African government. Managements may also adopt positive moral goals, such as an attempt to aid in environmental efforts. In addition, individual groups, such as pro-life and pro-choice groups, may exist for moral purposes. However, the process itself places no moral limit on what is or is not a fit topic for transaction.

What Is the Nature of These Units and the Limitations on Them?

The social units come in a variety of shapes, forms, and conditions. They may be large or small, rich or poor, well managed or poorly managed, atomistic or organic. They may range anywhere along these spectra. They may be local and very limited in scope; they may also be national, international, or supranational. They may be more or less powerful than a nation. There are no a priori limits on them, though some conditions will aid or detract from the success of their managers in the transaction process. There are no constraints on what they might represent. They may represent interests which are moral or immoral; they may represent interests which are legal or illegal. The Mafia is an example of such a unit, just as the American Philosophical Association is.

What Role Does the Management Fulfill?

Management has a dual task. It manages the organization internally, and it also manages the organization's external relations. Management may have its own goals and objectives. Typically, management has some effective discretion in regard to the decisions it can take. That discretion may include moral objectives. Beyond the definition of the organization itself, insofar as morality plays a role in managerialism, it will do so only through the exercise of discretionary decision making by managements.

What Is the Justification for Managerialism?

There is no ready justification such as those we found in the cases of capitalism, socialism, and democracy. It evolved in the face of the breakdown of those other ideologies and in the vacuum created by the fact that intellectuals have not constructed an alternative ideology which might have some moral justification. Managerialism is an ideology created by managers. It should come as no surprise that it is also an ideology for managers. That is not justification. It is explanation.

Is Managerialism Atomistic or Organic?

The flippant answer is yes. Managerialism concurs with atomism in the sense that it assumes society is merely a collectivity. It also concurs with organicism in the sense of accepting the view that organic social phenomena can exist. It disagrees with organicism in that it asserts that neither nations nor society at large can be organic. It disagrees with atomism in that it asserts that society at large is not a collectivity of individuals. The less flippant answer is no.

8 Ethics, Economics, and Business

As we conclude this long and sometimes circuitous adventure, it is difficult to avoid expressing some disappointment. Most ideological tracts have an optimistic and uplifting character about them on the assumption that their descriptions are accurate, their predictions will come true, and their recommendations will be accepted. That cannot be said for this analysis of managerialism. Given the diversity of humans, the responses to managerialism will likely run the gamut. The description of managerialism which has been supplied, however, is clinical rather than spirited. We might choose an analogy to understand this approach. Pediatricians believe that sometime around a child's second birthday, they can do a reasonably accurate job of predicting the child's height at maturity. For some parents the news will be heartening, and for others it will be disappointing. The physician's task is not to change the analysis in order to make parents feel better; it is to provide the best clinical diagnosis possible. I have not accepted the role of making readers feel good or bad about managerialism in arguing that it is the ideology on which our social, political, and economic order is based. My own response to managerialism is ambiguous. We can leave an evaluation of the virtues and vices of managerialism for another occasion. At this point, it is sufficient to identify and understand it, because it marks a substantial break from our past and from the assumptions which we hold about our society.

While fundamentally managerialism as an ideology is of, by, and for managers, that does not carry with it the moral legitimacy that capitalism, socialism, and democracy have. Admittedly, many people can be managers, but that does not deny the fact that, as James MacGregor Burns has warned us, we need principles of followership as well as principles of leadership. Managerialism does not contemplate a society in which everyone is a manager. The transaction process would probably collapse under its own weight under such conditions.

In addition, another aspect often associated with ideologies has not been

194

fulfilled. Managerialism does not claim to be the last word in ideologies. Even if what has been said in this book is true at this time, at some future time new ideologies will take the place of managerialism. The tendency to claim eternal truth for an ideology (or any other theory) is pernicious. After all, it is the supposed eternality of capitalism and socialism which has kept us from considering new principles informing social, political, and economic life for more than a century. When we stop to think about the situation, the startling fact is not that these theories might have to give way in the face of new realities and theories, but that they have held on so long in the face of dramatic changes in science, technology, art, and even religion, not to mention the substantial changes in societies and institutional life. The world of the late twentieth century does not much resemble the world of the early and mid–nineteenth century, and the wonder is that such an obvious observation has not been taken as grounds for questioning capitalism and socialism sooner.

We should remain alert to the identification of ideologies other than managerialism which might do a better job of explaining our current situation, and we should remain alert to future conditions which demand new explanations as well as future ideologies used to explain and guide the social, political, and economic order. Readers should feel free to criticize what is said here and to look further. If this book helps break an intellectual logjam, it will have done its job.

Let us return, now, to some topics which have been left unresolved at various places in the book. Perhaps some closure can be achieved for them, and in addition, we can glimpse some of the work which needs to be done in the future. Returning to Whitehead's metaphor with which the book began, we have been on an adventure into ideas. The value of the adventure lies in part in what has been seen and learned, but it also lies in what it suggests for further adventures. Some paths have not been traveled, and we shall be able to travel only the shortest of them here. Other paths have not been taken, and we can only glimpse their direction and set the conditions for following them later.

The directions fall into three broad categories. The first is ethics in general. Managers, and through them societies at large, face continuing ethical problems. A lack of clarity about the context for those issues leaves managers confused and grasping at the wrong straws. Neither in this book nor in any other should we pretend we can construct a successful formulaic answer to all ethical problems. We can, however, hope for some conceptual clarity, some realistic understanding of theory, and some structure in which we can decide first whether we should continue to let such issues concern us.

The second category is economics. The discussion of ethics will lead directly into a discussion of issues deep in economic theory. In the early 1960s, on the basis of the success of economic predictions, some hoped that we could declare economics to be a complete social science ready to do for social policy what physics does for engineering. However, in the 1990s the fear increases that the successes of economists are more like the success of the paper-tearing man on the train than the successes of scientists. If physics or astronomy or chemistry or biology were as incapable of solid prediction, there would be a crisis at their foundations. In this chapter I will venture some suggestions for revision. The creation of more viable economic theory is of first importance.

Finally, we shall turn to further observations about business in the context of managerialism. Those comments, too, can only be teasers for work that remains to be done. Much of the received wisdom about business needs to be challenged and revised, as does much of business education. Now that business accounts for a substantial portion of undergraduate and graduate degrees in the United States, there are substantial reasons to examine critically the assumptions at the base of business curricula. A start is made here by suggesting ways to think more clearly about business and the management of business enterprises.

Toward the conclusion of the section on business, I will offer some comments on business ethics. A more complete analysis of business ethics needs be left to another occasion. I hope that this book has put behind us shibboleths which have frustrated the development of business ethics. Business ethics must be tied in some way to the ideology of society, and we need to be clear about the ideology of our society before we can make sense of what we should do within it. Consider, for example, the arguments of the spokesman for GM-Flint whom Michael Moore uses as a foil in the film *Roger and Me*. The spokesman explains the layoffs in Flint as a natural consequence of capitalism and the need for GM to maximize its profits. If we were to keep his argument within capitalism but make it a little more sophisticated, it would be that the CEO of GM, Roger Smith, had no choice but to order those layoffs. Moore's moralisms are, by that argument, simply inappropriate, and Moore's persistent efforts to get Roger Smith to come to Flint to speak with the people laid off are irrelevant and a waste of time. As John Ladd would have it, Roger Smith was just one element in a large machine. He may have been an important element, but he was just an element nevertheless. Change the ideology, and the arguments, if not the decisions, would have to change. Thus, much business ethics has come to the same frustrating end as economics, because it has not recognized the need for deep theoretical change. While the detailed exploration of such implications is beyond the scope of this book, if the appropriate changes are made, they are important both theoretically and practically.

Ethics

In 1912 Harold Prichard began an important essay entitled "Does Moral Philosophy Rest on a Mistake?" as follows:

> Probably to most students of moral philosophy there comes a time when they feel a vague sense of dissatisfaction with the whole subject. And the sense of dissatisfaction tends to grow rather than diminish. It is not so much that the positions, and still more the arguments, of particular thinkers seem unconvincing, though this is true. It is rather that the aim of the subject becomes increasingly obscure. . . . Personally, I have been led by growing dissatisfaction of this kind to wonder whether the reason may not be that the subject, at any rate as usually understood, consists in the attempt to answer an improper question.[1]

We do not need to accept Prichard's suggested solution to the problem—to accept the distinction between facts and values—in order to agree with him that much of moral philosophy rests on a mistaken assumption about the questions it should be asking and answering. This problem became even more acute when philosophers entered into the fields of applied ethics in general and business ethics in particular. Prior to the interest in applied ethics, philosophy professors could assume that the students they faced were there either because they already had some interest in the way philosophers treat ethical issues or that they were there as a result of some curricular requirement. When philosophers delivered papers at philosophy conferences and wrote papers for philosophy journals, they addressed issues which concerned other philosophers. However, the development of applied ethics changed circumstances considerably. Students were taking courses based on different kinds of assumptions, and the practitioners with whom philosophers consulted were concerned with their problems, not the problems of professional philosophers.

People turn to intellectualizing to help resolve dilemmas they think they face. John Dewey sensibly suggested that people do not normally scratch itches they do not believe they have. Intellectualizing is a way of scratching mental itches which might be called dilemmas. In general, people do not turn to moral philosophy unless they think they have some kind of moral dilemma.[2] Thus, the person who is ready for ethical discourse probably experiences some kind of ethical dilemma.

I suggest that the dilemmatic situation fulfills three jointly necessary conditions for people who experience it: they think they face some ethical choice(s), they are committed to doing what is morally right, and they are confused about what is right. We could summarize those conditions as choice, commitment, and confusion. Once those conditions have been fulfilled, people may be ready to consider the kinds of issues raised in moral philosophy. If those conditions are not fulfilled, people do not think they need any discussion with a moral philosopher. To use Dewey's expression, they do not have a mental itch.

The first condition for an ethical dilemma is the belief in choice. People who believe they face no choice or choices will not find any need for or interest in a philosophical discussion about what they should do, except, perhaps, in the most abstract sense. It is possible that someone may want to try to convince them that they are wrong and that in fact they do have choices which they do not acknowledge. As important as such conversations may be, they are not particularly philosophical conversations, and they may in fact be quite technical conversations based upon the particular circumstances of the situation.

Consider, for example, a loan officer in a bank. Suppose that she has limited power to approve loans. A person has come to see her and has requested that she authorize the bank to grant him a loan. She takes all the information and considers the situation carefully. She thinks that he is a good risk, that he deserves the loan, and that what he wants to do with the money is appropriate. She recognizes, however, that authorizing the loan is beyond her level of authority, so she takes the application to her superior, who reviews the information, listens to the story, and concludes that the loan should not be made. In all likelihood, our loan officer would conclude that she has no choice but to refuse the loan, and she would refuse it without experiencing anything like a moral dilemma. She simply does not think she has a choice, so she experiences no dilemma, though she might, of course, regret the decision. Assuming her superior actually had the authority, *she* might have experienced a dilemma, and she might have thought she had a choice. Whether or not someone believes he or she has a choice is largely an empirical matter, and while the methodologists of social science would tell us of numerous problems with depending upon introspective testimony, probably the best prima facie way to determine whether someone thinks he or she has a choice is to ask.

In a more formal way, the matter of choice is sometimes expressed in management with the use of a tree analysis. The alternatives are laid out as different alternatives, and cost-benefit analyses are completed in an effort to systematize and evaluate the different possibilities. Such an analysis is no less useful in dealing with ethical decisions than in dealing with issues of marketing, for example. Ethically speaking, where there is no sense of choice, there is no ethical dilemma, and where there is no ethical dilemma, there is no relevant ethical reasoning.

The second condition for an ethical dilemma is that the person is committed to doing what is right. One cannot have a sensible ethical conversation with someone who is going to do something no matter what ethical reasoning concludes. The philosopher Charles Frankel used to tell a story about a student he discovered in his ethics class at the beginning of a semester when he was teaching at Columbia. By appearance alone, he could tell that the student was not like most Columbia undergraduates, and after the first class he endeavored to have a conversation with the student. In telling the story, Frankel said that as far as he was concerned, the student was welcome to be in the class, but he wanted to be sure that the student understood what to expect so he would not be disappointed. When Frankel asked, the student said that he was required to attend the class. It turned out that the student had been found guilty of some minor offense, and the judge had decided that, as part of the punishment, the student would be required to take a course in ethics. If the judge thought that by taking a course in ethics the student would become ethical, the judge was mistaken.[3] If the student did not have a commitment to be ethical, there was little Frankel could do as a philosopher to address his condition, and the student probably needed police supervision more than philosophical instruction.[4] People with a moral dilemma must want to do what is right.

The third condition for an ethical dilemma is that the person recognizes that he or she is confused about what is right. If there is no confusion, there is no dilemma. Until there is some confusion, there will be no reason for philosophical conversation. Consider the case of a deeply and religiously committed "pro-life" person who discovers that she is pregnant though she does not want to be. She may believe she has a choice either to carry the fetus to term or to have an abortion. Thus, she meets the first condition. She may be committed to doing what is right. Thus, she meets the second condition. However, she may not be at all confused about what is right, and once again, philosophical discussion about whether or not she should continue her pregnancy will seem entirely irrelevant, as well as irritating.

Thus, the experience of an ethical dilemma (or dilemmas) is necessary for philosophical ethical discourse, and there are three jointly necessary conditions for the dilemma. The three conditions are not, however, parallel. The conditions of commitment and confusion are deeply subjective, and the only way to determine that they exist is to ask the subject. There is no parallel for the issue of choice. The fact that someone says she has a choice does not mean she does have a choice. To use an example from John Locke, I may have entered a room, and without my knowing it, someone may have locked the door behind me. Since I do not know the door has been locked, I may think that I have the choice to remain in the room or to leave the room, when in fact I have no such choice.

Some people have argued that we do not have choices at all, or at least we do not have real choices. Locke used the example cited because he believed it was exemplary, not just of a specific imaginary situation, but of the human condition in toto. The person may think he has a choice, but Locke says he is suffering under an illusion. Those who know the truth also know that he does not have a choice. Universalizing the specific, then, Locke and others conclude that even though we often think we have a choice, in fact we never do. This position, called determinism, has appeared intermittently throughout this book. It is fundamental to both capitalism and socialism. We have not addressed it directly, but it would be appropriate to do so at this point, because if the case for determinism is solid enough, both managerialism and ethics are in trouble.

Let us concentrate on the aspect of determinism which applies to humans. There is a more general version, but we do not have to deal with it directly.[5] Determinism states that all human activity (including, if it exists, mental activity) is uniquely determined to occur the way it does or that, given the conditions, nothing else could have happened. Determinism is not necessarily committed to the view that we can predict what human actions will be in a particular case, but only that there is one and only one possible outcome. It is important to stress the issue of uniqueness, because it has been missed by many who debate the topic. Determinism does not say that some one of a number of events might occur. Rather, it says that one and only one event can occur. It should be clear, then, if it is always the case that only one course of events can occur, that even though I may think I can take alternative actions, in fact I cannot.

Suppose, for example, someone is preparing to sell her car as a used car. Suppose the car is not acting right, and the seller suspects a broken head gasket. Suppose the prospective seller finds that if she puts extra heavyweight oil in the engine, the problem can be covered up, at least temporarily. Our imaginary seller now faces a dilemma: Should she put the heavyweight oil in when prospective buyers come to inspect the car? Should she tell unsuspecting buyers about the problem? Our imaginary seller thinks she has some choices to make.

She thinks she has some choices. The determinist would say, however, that she has no real choice and that under whatever conditions prevail at the time she makes the decision, that will be the only decision possible. The question which must be faced is whether the position of determinism makes any difference for ethics. On this topic, William James makes a useful distinction between what he calls hard determinism and soft determinism.[6] The former asserts that it does make a difference; the latter asserts that it does not. Let us outline the arguments briefly.

Hard determinists argue that people are determined in all they do and that, as a consequence, it makes no more sense to hold people responsible for what they do than it does to hold the sun morally responsible for causing a sunburn. All events are the unique result of a set of conditions, and all those conditions are a unique result of some other conditions, and so on. Similarly, the fact that I wrote this book and you are (still!) reading it is the unique result of a set of conditions, and those conditions are unique results of some other conditions. We do not have to resolve the nature-nurture debate which plagues social scientists. We can allow that the conditions are either or both, but the hard determinist would say that under any circumstances my actions are a unique result of those conditions, and it makes no sense to hold either me or those conditions responsible. I inherited a specific—unique—genetic structure from my parents. I was brought up in a specific set of environmental conditions. Let us assume for the moment that those two sets of conditions are what determine my actions. I did not choose my parents, and I did not choose my environment. Thus, it makes no sense to hold me responsible either in a positive or a negative way for what is a direct result of those conditions. Under this reasoning, choices are illusory. The illusion is caused by the fact that I do not know what causes the decisions I make. Hard determinists often point out that when we do come to understand causes, we no longer hold people responsible. For example, until recently we used to think that people who became depressed were just being lazy, selfish, or self-indulgent, and we criticized them, suggesting that they needed to exercise more initiative and change their attitudes. Even depressed people believed that diagnosis. We now know that depression is a biological condition which can be triggered by certain kinds of stimuli. We know how to treat it, and only the most ignorant hold victims of depression responsible for their condition. Thus, the hard determinist argues that moral language based on an assumption of freedom, as most moral language is, is simply anachronistic. With time we shall learn to dispense with it as we learn to dispense with other attitudes based on superstitions.

The people James calls the soft determinists agree with the hard determinists in saying that all human actions are uniquely determined. However, they believe that it still makes sense to hold people responsible for their actions. They argue that the purpose of moral language is not to assume that people are free but to influence their future behavior. Thus, when I say that someone did something wrong, I am actually trying to influence that person and perhaps others who may be listening. If I say that someone was wrong to cheat on his income tax returns, I mean to attempt to influence people to be honest with their taxes. I do not, however, mean that the person freely chose to cheat. Unfortunately, the soft determinists have not been as clear as they might have been with regard to the issue of choice.

Even after James, the notion was popular among soft determinists that there is a useful distinction between actions which are chosen and those which are coerced. Presumably, I have decided to continue writing the material I am working on presently rather than doing something else. No one has coerced me to do so. No one is in the room holding a gun to my head; no one is threatening to take something away if I do not continue. Thus, one might take the view that my reasons for continuing are all my own and, thus, of my choice. It should be recognized, however, that under determinism, I could make no other choice unless the conditions changed. Thus, this version of soft determinism still maintains that in the end choice is an illusion. However, some soft determinists want to make a distinction between causation and coercion.

The distinction finally comes down to an external versus an internal source of causation, and the sense is that internal causation is less threatening to the rational use of moral language than external causation.

More recently, determinists have seen that developments in psychiatry and elsewhere cast considerable doubt on whether such a distinction can be sustained. The drug addict seems as much in the grip of forces over which he has little control as does the person who is threatened by someone else. Thus, soft determinists have fallen back on the first argument: that the function of moral language is not to make subtle commitments to human freedom but to express the speaker's attitude and to influence behavior. The soft determinist then argues that in fact even people who disagree with determinism nevertheless assume determinism. When we criticize our children, we intend that they learn a lesson, and we are trying to become a determining force in their lives. If we assume that the children's actions are not determined, the soft determinist would argue, we should give up using moral language, because we have no idea whether it will do any good.

Other people believe that determinism itself is wrong. Let us call such people indeterminists. Everyone must be either a determinist or an indeterminist. This is not a case of the bifurcation fallacy, because the two positions are contradictory. Indeterminism is simply the position that determinism is false. To put the matter directly, refer to the definition given of determinism. Indeterminism is the position which says it is not the case that all human activity (including, if it exists, mental activity) is uniquely determined to occur the way it does. Some conclusions are important to notice here: since the positions are contradictory, the truth of one implies the falsehood of the other and vice versa; since determinism is a universal theory about all activity, indeterminism only needs to find one genuine counterexample to defeat determinism; and indeterminism does not by itself establish responsibility. It is possible for indeterminism to be true and for there to be no rational grounds for responsibility. Suppose, for example, some human actions are not uniquely caused but are random. It makes no more sense to hold people responsible for random activity than it does to hold them responsible for uniquely determined activity. Holding someone responsible means that the person had some choice and some control.

Endorsement of free will requires more than indeterminism alone. The view of free will must hold that determinism is false and, in addition, that on some occasions humans (at least) have a nonuniquely determined ability to make real choices which actually change the future from what it would have been if they had made other choices. This view says that choice is not an illusion but is, at least sometimes, real. The view does not hold that every time we think we can make real choices, we can. It holds, rather, that at least sometimes some people can make real choices. It holds, further, that when people do make real choices, it makes sense to hold them responsible for those choices.

The point has been made repeatedly in this book that capitalism and socialism are deterministic theories. The first is a microdeterministic theory, in that what determines individual actions are other individual actions. It is deterministic nonetheless. In capitalism, the entrepreneur has no effective discretion, since any exercise of such discretion would mean nonexistence. Socialism is a macrodeterministic theory, in that there is assumed to be an overall direction for the society and the individual is simply a part of that overall plan. Any deviation would, once again, be aberrant and uninteresting, since the direction the society is going to take holds no matter what individuals do. The individuals have only the "choice" to go along with society. As with Spinoza's rock, people think they choose to go along with the direction of the society, but in fact they have no choice. The determinism of both excused them from moral influence.

In that sense, and in view of developments since James's time, it seems that James was right that the real choice is between hard determinism and free will. Soft determinism and indeterminism are curious and interesting as logical possibilities, but they do not save moral language. Determinists and the adherents of free will seem to be correct in that if every activity is uniquely determined, moral language makes no sense. Unlike capitalism and socialism, managerialism asserts that managers do at least on some occasions have some effective discretion. If that is right, it would make sense to hold them morally responsible for their decisions.

Consider an example. The editor of a newspaper has a series of pictures before him. All of them deal with a tragic drowning. The pond where the drowning occurred has been a source of concern in the town for some time. Children like to swim there unsupervised, sometimes playing hooky from school. One photograph shows the dead child's body already in a body bag with the bag opened so the family can have one last look. The photograph also shows a face-on picture of the grieving parents and a sibling consumed in grief over the bag. The photographer believes that he has taken a picture which may well receive professional attention and that if it is printed uncropped, he may be a candidate for a prize. The assistant editor says that whenever the newspaper publishes photographs of dead bodies, they get sacks of mail objecting to their insensitivity. Publishing such photographs apparently violates community standards. The reporter who covered the story argues that something needs to be done to alert the town to the danger in the pond and that the photograph will help do it. The editor considers the following possibilities: print the photograph as is, print it cropped, print it on the front page below the fold, print it on the front of the second section, put the lead of the story on the front page and bury the picture with the remainder of story on an inside page, don't print the photograph at all. It is time to put the paper to bed. People who prepare the layout are waiting for the editor's decision.

Undoubtedly, the editor believes that all those possibilities are real and that he has a real choice to make. The editor believes he has some effective discretion in his decisions. The determinist believes the editor's sense of choice in this case and in all others is an illusion and that the editor will do whatever he will do and could have done nothing else. None of us can prove conclusively that the determinist is wrong. We should continue to examine the question.

The original case for determinism which seemed most attractive to the Greek and Roman philosophers was what might be called a logical case for determinism. Continue with the consideration of our editor. As he is laboring over his decision whether or not to print the photograph, we know that it is either true that it will be printed or false that it is printed. We do not know which, but we know that the picture cannot both be printed and not printed in tomorrow's paper. Let us assume for the moment that it is true that it will be printed. Then, no matter how much the editor labors over the decision, the fact is that there is only one possible outcome: it will be printed. Nothing the editor does while struggling with the decision can change that fact. Let us look at another possibility: that the picture will not be printed. If that is true, then once again, nothing the editor does can possibly change that outcome. It follows, then, that the outcome is already determined. Aristotle used the example of a sea battle: even before the battle begins, we know that one side or the other must win, and since that is so, the outcome of the battle is determined. It often appears to observers that there is something tricky about this argument, and it seems like a bit of linguistic sleight of hand. Logically, however, there is nothing wrong with it. Richard Taylor revived the argument in the 1960s.[7]

It was not a long stretch from the logical form of determinism to a religious form, especially as Christianity began to have an influence. Many Christians believe that God is omniscient. That means simply that God knows everything. Trivial as it may be, surely one of the things God must know is whether or not the photograph will be printed. If God knows it will be printed, then the editor has no choice but to order that it will be printed, for otherwise God would not know something. It will be the same, mutatis mutandis, if God knows the photograph will not be printed. Actually, this doctrine does not depend upon God's knowing things in the sense of being conscious of them (if that expression makes any sense when applied to God). All that is required is that if God were asked whether the photograph would be printed, he could answer the question, and his answer would always be correct. If it is said that God cannot answer the question, then God must not be omniscient. Since the presumption is that God can answer the question, there is really no human choice. John Calvin may have put this most succinctly when he said: "Before the first man was created, God in his eternal counsel had determined what he willed to be done with the whole human race." [8] We usually label this doctrine predestination, but the effect of determinism in the context of religion is still complete. Obviously, in this understanding, there is no effective discretion, for God has determined everything for the whole human race.

As science gained more persuasive power, it too developed a form of determinism. Newtonian physics was a great spur toward a sense of determinism which did not depend on an assumption of God's existence. As humans gained the power to predict astronomical events accurately, to predict the tides accurately, and to predict numerous other events, the sense grew that the expansion of physical determinism throughout the universe was a most reasonable expectation. With the advent of Freud, determinism took another step forward, so it is fair to say that the prevailing psychological and psychiatric opinions today are that people's activities are uniquely determined to occur as they do. Clarence Darrow had a great deal of success with this approach in court, where he would convince juries not that his client was innocent but that his client had no choice but to commit the crime in question. Courts continue to struggle with this issue, and it remains unresolved.

Determinism, then, has a great deal of intellectual weight behind it. It is no wonder that the deterministic ideologies of capitalism and socialism hold such power.[9] It is also no wonder that a competing ideology has not come from social scientists. In an effort to imitate the physical scientists, they have been under the sway of determinism. If they had thought to construct a competing ideology, it probably would have been a deterministic one. Managerialism was created, not by intellectuals, but by people, like our editor, actually involved in making decisions. Those people can be told endlessly that they do not make decisions and that the choices they think they make are but illusions, but they simply do not believe what they are being told (if they pay any attention to it).

Thus arises a most curious phenomenon. Social scientists are supposed to explain what humans do, but when one asks the humans some basic questions, they invariably deny what the scientist assumes. The strength of the soft determinists was to attempt to make sense of this strange phenomenon, and they did so by telling the people that they were right in thinking they made choices but that they were not really right. It would seem that even the most devoted hard determinist still holds students responsible for getting papers in on time, still makes decisions as if there were choices, still acts as if she or he had a free will (while all the time denying it). One suspects that even the most devoted hard determinist would still hold the editor responsible for his decision about printing the picture. However, the problem the adherent of free will has is not unlike that of people who believe in organic theory: they want to assert that something is going on and that the something is not a figment of their imaginations. But unfortunately, the adherents of free will are not very clear about what that is, and they tend to fall back into a kind of mysterious language, which casts further doubt on their views.

One of the ways to consider a theory carefully is to look at its implications with some care. That has been done in regard to capitalism, socialism, and managerialism. We shall return to the topic of free will and some of its implications in the next section. Thus far, there is no irrefutable proof on either side. The reader has to listen to the arguments, the evidence, and the implications and then decide what makes the most sense. We know the assumptions of socialism and capitalism, and we know how they differ from the assumptions of managerialism. The implications of this issue have been with us thus far in the book, and they will remain with us for the remainder of the book.

Economics

Decision making is the defining characteristic of what managers do. The determinism of economics turns all that effort into an illusion. The reference to Norbert Weiner in chapter 7 simply gave a dramatic and anecdotal account of basic assumptions of economics. Managers are probably inefficient substitutes for the ideal computer of the economy. Human managers make mistakes. They can be lazy and more concerned about personal welfare than maximizing profits, and they can get tired. Under current circumstances, managers are a scarce resource, which is why they can command such a premium in compensation. They are a major source of disequilibrium, and thus, they have an opportunity to take advantage of the market in pressing their case for compensation. When Weiner's ideal day comes, managers will be replaced by computers which will be at once accurate, not subject to bouts of laziness or selfishness, and easily substitutable for others of the same kind. In that context, the managerial function will disappear in favor of rapid calculation based upon deterministic formulae.

Such is the ideal of mainstream economics. The problem is that it does not correspond in any significant way to what managers actually experience in their daily lives. They experience an endless need to make decisions, some large, some small. They experience a sense that they have numerous alternatives before them and that making one set of alternative decisions rather than another will actually define the future. While managers are not typically reflective to the extent this book has suggested for its readers, at the same time they do not seem to experience making necessary decisions with little or no effective alternatives.

In addition, managers do not find that the range of decision making has diminished as managerial expertise and technological aids have improved. The manager of an enterprise today probably has more, not fewer, decisions to make than did a manager in the past. Consider, for example, something as simple as the development of the personal computer and the ubiquitous spreadsheet programs. As recently as thirty years ago, if spreadsheets were constructed— and such an activity was by no means as universal as it is today—they were done by hand on large sheets of paper. If there was any technological support beyond the slide rule, it extended no further than the electric calculator. Invariably there were errors and long debates about assumptions and calculations. In those days, if the staff could construct one or two spreadsheets with some variations, they would have done a good job.

That situation has changed radically in the past few years, and we still have not understood the impact of all the changes. Currently, even middling managers can create much more sophisticated spreadsheets than were created thirty years ago, and they can create numerous spreadsheets, varying the analysis with different assumptions as may be necessary or merely interesting. They no longer need to have long debates about the assumptions before they run an iteration. If someone wants to vary an assumption, it is almost a trivial act to run new iterations. Thus, if anything, choice has expanded, not diminished, as a result of this technological innovation. Weiner's prediction seems even more improbable than it did in the early 1960s. Let us concede that with luck the new technology has prevented managers from making inadvertent mistakes. Nevertheless, instead of converging on a single solution, as economic theory would have had it, the technology has expanded the range of viable options and increased the number of decisions to be made. There simply is no evidence that anything like a utopia in which the managerial function will be simplified is about to arrive. Technology and the increased knowledge which comes with it may decrease choices of one form, but at the same time it increases the range of other choices because it makes us aware of other possibilities we could not have considered previously.

Nothing said in this section shows the deterministic position to be false. I have not shown that the choices which managers make regularly and frequently are not illusory. I have just suggested that it is not an illusion which managers experience no matter how much they experience new technology or economic reasoning. They believe they still have to make decisions, and they believe that those decisions change the future. If they make the right decisions, about capital structuring of the corporation, for example, they may have a viable and active corporation in the future; if they make the wrong decisions, they may have a struggling corporation faced with difficulties and compromises.

Consider the life of the manager of a pension fund. The set of available choices before her is enormous. She can use a vast array of financial media.

She has considerably more technological help than her counterpart had as recently as twenty years ago. She can perform analyses and analyses of analyses. If there is any danger in all the mathematical sophistication, it is not that the mathematics will make the decision for her but that it will debilitate her so that she will be unable to make a decision. Successful managers, however, will make decisions. Will they have made choices? Real ones or illusory ones? As far as I can tell, in financial management, there has been no convergence on singular decisions as mathematical sophistication and technology have improved. If anything, divergence has occurred.

Decision making is where the manager touches reality. It is the world of management. Knowledge allows the manager to touch reality at more points. To use an analogy, it is as if the realm of management decisions were the exterior of a balloon. When the balloon (knowledge) is relatively small, it touches on reality in relatively few places, and the range of decisions stays small. As the balloon (knowledge) expands, it touches on reality in more places, and the range of decisions increases. There simply is no evidence that decision making has decreased in the face of the development of more knowledge and its application or in the face of technological developments. If anything, the opposite seems to have taken place.

It is possible to continue to maintain an intellectual apparatus which assumes that all these decisions are merely illusory and that they make no difference to outcome, since the outcome is already contained in and determined by the conditions. After a while, however, as reality corresponds less and less to theory, it makes sense to ask why we continue to cling so desperately to the theory. The current state of economics and its basic theoretical assumptions is reminiscent of the theologians who refused to look through Galileo's telescope. They believed they already knew that the planets did not move as Galileo suggested, and they did not need to listen to Galileo's account of his contradictory experiences. From the theologian's perspective, Galileo was just suffering from illusions.

Another diversion may be instructive in making the point that is important here. The developmental psychologist Carol Gilligan realized that theories about human development, which were created by psychologists such as Freud, Piaget, and Kohlberg, were based on analyses of the development of males. They identified stages of development and assumed that females were simply pale imitations of males, incapable, for example, of the highest developmental levels such as abstract, mathematical, and moral reasoning. The mainstream developmental psychologists presumed that if they could understand male development, then understanding female development would only require a rather simple application of the theories. Gilligan suggested that it was time to look directly at the development of females, and when she did, she found that the least distorted interpretation of what she and her colleagues learned from listening to females was that they did not develop in accordance with the principles laid down for male development, but that female development was different from, not merely a diluted version of, male development.[10] My suggestion for economics parallels Gilligan's for developmental psychology. When too much reported experience and testimony has to be dismissed as mere illusion, when it is more cumbersome to adjust the theoretical apparatus in order to account for the data which will not fit, the time may be approaching when radical revision should be considered. Such may be in the offing for economics.

Unfortunately, even in the physical sciences, it is never clear when one theoretical structure should be overthrown and another adopted. The question is When is it time to begin considering a radical revision of theory? No final resolution of this issue is available. Readers have to consider the alternatives and—dare I say it—make a choice. Managers think they make choices no matter what their economics professors have taught them over the years. The suggestion here is that in the absence of any economic theories which have taken that experience seriously, managers have been quietly creating their own economic theory based on their own experiences. Just as the young girls in Gilligan's studies went on developing in their own ways in spite of the pronouncements of the developmental psychologists, the managers have been going about their business in spite of the pronouncements of economists.

The actions of managers have been based on some economic theories. Those theories, however, are not part of the mainstream of contemporary economics. Could we continue to extend, amend, adapt, and distort both reports of reality and theory so that mainstream economics can be maintained come what may? Yes, just as we could save Ptolemaic astronomy if we wished. The question is whether it is time to acknowledge thinking which has occurred outside the mainstream and to begin to bend to the task of constructing new theories. My speculative answer is that the time has come. That is said in spite of the mathematical grandeur of modern economics and in spite of the fact that scientific theories are not overthrown in the abstract. They are, rather, replaced by other theories. Thus, mainstream economics will maintain its hold until some alternative theories come forward which take the testimony of managers seriously and which explain the operations of the economy in the context of managerialism—in other words, until a genuine managerialist economics emerges. There is reason to hope for some positive development, but there are also much deeper issues which should be encountered.

First, on the scale of positive developments, let us acknowledge at the outset that some mainstream economists, especially Alfred Marshall in an earlier era and Herbert Simon and Kenneth Arrow currently, have given considerable attention to the orientation of the decision makers in the economy. Unfortunately, even their interest turns quickly to economics at large and not to following the lead of the decision makers until their activities are fully understood in theory and practice. We have to turn to someone like G. L. S. Shackle to find an economist who looks carefully at the decision-making process. There are others, such as Ludwig Lachmann and Robin Marris, but Shackle has been perhaps the most rigorous and the most penetrating.[11] Shackle takes the decision-making activity of the manager (and, for that matter, the individual consumer) seriously. In doing so, he reminds us that to decide means to make a "cut" in the universe. The decision cuts the events and makes new events. When managers decide to abandon a product line or establish a new one, they are making a cut in the flow of events, a cut which would not be there if they had not made those decisions. When our investment manager decides to buy or sell some security, she is making such a cut, and when our editor decides to print the photograph, he is making such a decision. The decision, says Shackle, makes a difference in the future of the world. If the editor decides to print the photograph, tomorrow's newspaper will be different than if he had decided not to print it. To the extent that the paper has some influence, the world from then on will be different.

Shackle argues that the decision is not made before the editor makes it. The editor can make any one of a number of decisions with regard to the photograph. There is nothing uniquely determining his decision, which is not to say that there could not be under some circumstances. Shackle says:

> In economics of the accepted, Western maximizing kind, we are confronted with a basic contradiction: men are choosers; they choose the best, each for himself; what is best can always be known to each person, either by merely consulting his own tastes or by applying the techniques of engineering or, where knowledge lacks a *simple* precision, by applying statistical techniques which turn ignorance of the particular into knowledge of the aggregate. Thus, that action which will attain "the best" can always be discovered, its prior discovery is part of that policy of rational action which is attributed by economics to the Economic Man in his modern sophisticated form; and all men in some degree approximate to this situation: what is "the best" for him is known to him uniquely and for certain; how to attain it is dictated by circumstances and can be inferred from them. What, then, is left for him to do in the way of *choosing?* Where is there room for his judgment, for the artist's discernment of beauty, for the inspired creation of what is essentially new?
>
> Conventional economics is not about choice, but about acting according to necessity. Economic man obeys the *dictates* of reason, follows the *logic of choice*. To call this conduct choice is surely a misuse of words,

> when we suppose that to him the ends amongst which he can select, and the criteria of selection, are given, and the means to each are known. The theory which describes conduct under these assumptions is a theory of structure, not of creation of history. Choice in such a theory is empty, and conventional economics should abandon the word.[12]

Shackle, with the hard determinists and the adherents of free will, recognizes that if determinism is really true, choice is an empty illusion, and he recognizes that that assumption is packed into what he calls conventional economic theory. In suggesting that conventional economists abandon the word *choice,* he is only suggesting that choosing is not determined and that it does make a difference for the future.

Presumably, most of us believe that we are free to choose, for example, whether or not to watch the evening news, and we believe that watching it might make a different future for other choices we might make. Curiously, the philosopher C. A. Campbell, in an important article defending a belief in free will, suggested that a belief in determinism is a common person's belief and that the belief in freedom takes theoretical sophistication.[13] It is hard to agree with Campbell on this issue, and it seems likely that Shackle would not agree. It takes a considerable amount of theoretical sophistication for someone to believe in determinism. The common response of most people is that they certainly do make choices and that they could have made other choices.[14]

Suppose, however, we take Shackle's suggestion seriously. Suppose we decide that we need to save the appearance of choice and make it a definitive reality in a new economic system. Suppose we decide to start with the testimony of decision makers, and suppose we decide that their decisions could have been otherwise and that they might make a difference to the future. All apart from the substantial reconstruction of economic theory those suppositions would call for, what are we going to do about the arguments identified earlier as favoring determinism through logic, religion, and science? Shackle's answer is that nothing short of a revised concept of time itself will be called for.

Shackle notes correctly that in the advancement to calculus, economics has allied itself with the classical physics of Newton and his followers. Newton had invented the infinitesimal calculus in order to advance his physics further. Adam Smith knew the astronomy and physics of Newton well. Smith said: "Such is the system of Sir Isaac Newton, a system whose parts are all more strictly connected together than those of any philosophical hypothesis. . . . all the appearances, which he joins together by [his system], necessarily follow." [15] As I have argued, Smith tried to create an economic system which would take Newton's physics as its example. While Smith did not make use of the infinitesimal calculus, it is part of the testimony to his brilliance that subsequent economists could apply calculus without disturbing the basic assumptions of Smith's approach.

We do need to recall, however, that the Newtonian system was thoroughly deterministic. Milič Čapek has shown persuasively that in Newtonian physics, there is what he calls an implicit elimination of time: "Any instantaneous configuration of an isolated system logically implies all future configurations of the system. Its future history is thus virtually contained in the present state, which, in its turn, is logically contained in its past states." [16] Before drawing my final conclusion about time in mainstream economics, let us follow the reasoning of Shackle and Čapek further, because people often find it hard to understand.

Let us return to the discussion of the omniscience of God. The point made there under that assumption was that choice would be illusory, just as it is in determinism without God. For example, I may think that by going on a diet, by exercising, and by eating the right foods, I am going to live longer. However, God knows when I am going to die, and there is nothing I can do which will make that moment come any sooner or any later. Of course, God also knows whether I am going to go on a diet, exercise, and eat the right foods. Suppose, following the quotation from Calvin and standard religious thinking, at least with regard to those religions rooted in Judaism, we imagine that there is a beginning and an end to the universe. We call those times Creation and Armageddon. God, of course, is outside such end points. God exists before Creation and will exist after Armageddon. Sometime between Creation and Armageddon, I have my own beginning and end: I am born, and I die. God knows those times as well as all others. God, who is outside the boundaries of time, must "see" the world at once.

An analogy may help one understand the point here. Imagine opening our morning newspaper and looking at, for example, the comic strip "Peanuts." We see one panel to the right of another. We look across the panels, and we see what "develops." Of course, we know that nothing really develops. We know it is there all at once. The only real change is a spatial one, not a temporal one. Even though we may see, for example, in the leftmost panel that Lucy is trying to persuade Charlie Brown once again that she really will hold the football while he kicks it. In the rightmost panel, Lucy picks the ball up, and Charlie Brown falls.

Move this analogy to one larger level. Consider a movie. A movie represents a double illusion. First, there is the illusion created by a series of frames of still action played in front of a light at the right speed to create the illusion of movement on the screen. Second, there is an illusion that events are really occurring and that they might be different. Directors who are successful persuade us that alternative futures are really possible, that the hero and heroine might get together or that they might not, and we wait anxiously to learn the outcome. If we are rational about the situation, however, we know that no such alternative futures are possible. As they say in Hollywood, it is all in the can long before we enter the theater. The difference between the comic strip and the movie is that we do not usually spread the whole film out in front of us. But we could, and if we did, we would find that the differences are not temporal at all, but spatial. One frame is in a different space than another. Now let us complete the analogy.

God, in his infinite wisdom, can look at the universe from Creation to Armageddon all at once. In a way which is similar to the way we can see the panels of the comic strip or the frames of the movie all at once, God sees the universe in a timeless way. God's reality is, of course, true reality. Anything which disputes his reality is, by definition, false and illusory. Perhaps if one could get into the comic strip or into the film, one would believe time was passing, but we know time does not really pass in the comic strip or the film. God knows time does not really pass in the world. We are locked into this world. We believe that time really passes, but when that belief takes into account God's omniscience, we are forced to recognize that the sense of a passage of time is an illusion which humans suffer because of their finitude. Within the religious context, this is what Čapek meant by the elimination of time: not only has choice become an illusion, but also the passage of time has become an illusion.

What happens if we abandon the religious context? Suppose we say that we want to stay strictly with science and take no notice, positive or negative, of religious claims. That is not a difficult transition to make. I have already pointed out that we do not need to attribute omniscience to God in the sense that he is consciously aware of the answers to prospective questions. The argument about the elimination of time in theology holds even if we put it strictly hypothetically: that God could give an accurate answer to the question if asked. That means that we can eliminate God from the formulation altogether. If an accurate answer could be given (in principle) to the question, then not only is choice an illusion but also the passage of time is an illusion. Čapek quotes the famous passage from Laplace: "An intellect which at any given instant knew all the forces acting in nature, and the position of all things of which the world consists—supposing the said intellect were vast enough to subject these data to analysis—would embrace in the same formula the motions of the greatest bodies in the universe and those of the slightest atoms; nothing would be uncertain for it, and the future, like the past, would be present to its eyes." [17] That intellect is physics for Laplace. The task of the physicist is to learn all that needs to be known and to create the conditions of the sufficiently vast analysis. That is the program of determinism, and its implication is that choice must be an illusion, since if there were real choice, there would be alternative futures. Its further implication is that the sense of the passage of time is an illusion.

The economists' attempt to absorb classical physics has led to these conclusions also, and Shackle recognizes it explicitly: "In the classical dynamics of the physicist, time is merely and purely a mathematical variable. The solution of the differential equation, if it can be found, is complete in an instantaneous timeless sense." [18] The problem, then, lies in the implicit assumptions of the calculus.

That leads us naturally to ask about the logical argument for determinism. To say at the moment of a child's birth that he or she will or will not be married thirty years later seems to be a simple application of logic and to be harmless as such. However, we now know to be on our guard. When this was discussed earlier, it was said that the argument seems to hold unless we change some assumptions. We have already seen that the price we must pay for determinism is to conclude that our sense of choice and our sense of the passage of time are both illusory. The same would also seem to hold in the case of the logical argument. Suppose, however, we were to say that we are not ready to consign persistent experiences of choice and the passage of time to the trash heap of illusion. Suppose we were to say that we want to make the changes in theory which would be sufficient to save those experiences as real. What might we do?

That is the program to which Shackle asks us to address economic theory. He can only see some implications: for example, that we cannot say that future conditions follow necessarily from past and present conditions. I suggest we accept what I think most people are quite prepared to accept: time is not symmetrical. While we cannot change the past, we can in some ways change the future. As a teacher, I cannot change my students' past experiences with education, but I may be able to change their future experiences. As a manager, I cannot change the past history of discrimination, but if I am given the opportunity, I can try to change the future. It is important to point out that neither Shackle nor I is arguing for randomness in the future nor are we arguing that anything is possible. I cannot sleep on Mars in my lifetime, and any ethical theory which required me to do so would be deficient. I cannot run a four-minute mile. That is not in the realm of possibility. Having said that some choices are closed to me, however, does not imply that all choices are closed to me. Similarly for a manager. Some alternatives are simply beyond reasonableness, and no sensible person suggests that it is otherwise. Having recognized the limitations of reality, however, we recognize that sometimes there are real alternatives. The editor may or may not decide to run the photograph. Having decided, the editor should feel responsible for his decision unless it can be shown that in fact he had no choice.

In order to develop the theory of managerialism further, then, we need to develop an economics which assumes the reality of the passage of time and the reality of choice. When Einstein started to develop his general theory of relativity, he found the Newtonian assumptions about time were too confining, and he developed the tensor calculus. Something of that order is needed for the mathematics of managerialist economics.[19] Beyond that, we need to pay close and serious attention to those who make decisions, and we need to be cautious about writing off their claims as illusory or naive.

We should recognize problems which need to be addressed so that we can have an economics which makes sense in application as well as in rigorous theory. I do not know what that will be like, but I am convinced we need to turn our attention to it, and I am convinced that when we do, economics will have its rightful place within ideology and will make ethics meaningful as applied to decisions.

Business

A system for the application of the consequences of managerialism for understanding and practicing business needs to be developed. Many of the assumptions we have had about business, especially as those have been developed in the context of capitalist theories, need to be challenged and changed.

Perhaps the most obvious adjustment is to recognize that the distinction between business and nonbusiness is not as clear as it once was. We should not exaggerate that recognition. There are stockholders of a business, alumni of a university, and parishioners of a church. They are not the same, and they are not even meaningfully analogous. They are, as the jargon says, stakeholders in organizations. That means that some believe they have a stake in the priorities of the management of the organization. It does not mean, as it is often interpreted, that they have or want to have a stake in the organization itself. An environmental group, for example, may want to influence the priorities of the management of a business, but they may have no real stake in the business itself. In fact, their greatest desire might be to see the business close and leave the area, but barring an ability to accomplish that, they want to influence management's priorities. Managers are sometimes confused about this issue. They are so accustomed to dealing with labor unions as stakeholders that they assume all stakeholders care about the organization's survival and health as do management and labor. The managers of so-called nonprofit organizations have different stakeholders, but they have stakeholders nonetheless, and their success or failure will be largely measured by the extent to which they can deal effectively with them.

A second change to notice is that the former notions of external forces in regard to an organization should be revised. Too many managers continue to operate on assumptions learned in their secondary school civics course. The presumptions are sometimes supplemented with some college-level political science courses, and the naïveté about the actual situation continues. There is considerable danger that the manager will make decisions based on unrealistic assumptions. For example, we often learn in school about the fourth estate—the media. The theory is that the media exists as an independent fourth estate and is part of the system of checks and balances, especially of the government. Supposedly the media exists to help maintain a well-informed public ready to exercise the franchise responsibly and realistically. Media advocates would like to convince all of us that if we have nothing to hide, we have nothing to fear from the reporter or interviewer. Nonsense. Managers believe that at their peril.

The media is an organizational structure with a management. At the most advanced level, reporters are very skilled at asking loaded questions and guiding interviews toward the end they wanted the story to take before they began the interview. It may take a lifetime to build a business; it will take less than sixty minutes to destroy it. No serious reporter wants to have a casual conversation when interviewing. The reporter is there because an editor or producer wants a story which will get attention. No decent reporter will do anything illegal or even perhaps unethical, but managers should remind themselves that in many cases they are dealing with professionals who are basically in the "bad news" business. Had Michael Moore been able to get his interview with Roger Smith, he would have subjected him to the same humiliation to which he subjected the GM advocates and Pat Boone and Anita Bryant. The general rule should be to recognize the media as stakeholders. They have goals and objectives just as any other management does. Unless managers can find a way to make their goals consonant with the goals of the media representative, they should do what media people do when other media representatives come after them and they cannot structure the situation: make no comment. Roger Smith retained his job and continued to exercise his values at GM. Michael Moore got his movie, which deserved the considerable praise it received. At the same time, it would be hard to trace any negative impact on GM from the movie.[20] GM makes cars, not movies.

I have shown elsewhere how managerialism changes the concept of stockholders.[21] It is perhaps the final insult to capitalism that stockholders are no longer the only stakeholders, as Friedman would have it, but it is an insult that will have to be suffered in the interest of reality.[22] At the same time, one of the problems faced by management in the 1980s was that it had systematically ignored the stockholders. Since the stockholders were not represented at the bargaining table, so to speak, their interests were not taken into account. Friedman's moral admonition was not enough, and he should have known it would not be, since he is so supportive of the principle of self-interest at the base of capitalism. Until the 1980s stockholders were diffuse and without a voice. Their voice became united and effective when they found people who would represent their interests. Those people were not managers of the corporations of which the stockholders were partial owners. They were people who were branded by corporate managers as raiders. However, the raiders showed that stockholder disaffection with the indifference of corporate management could be mobilized into a powerful force. Stockholders became stakeholders in the classic sense: a group with power and a management to represent it. The situation remains fluid, but few corporate managers are as complacent today about their stockholders.

Employment at will, once a supporting principle of capitalism, which became enshrined in law, has been constantly eroded, not by some creeping socialism as the demagogues would have it, but by the development of managerialism. From labor contracts at the bottom of the hierarchy to employment contracts at the top, the concept is in retreat everywhere. It is probably not an exaggeration to say that with the exception of some workers in small businesses, almost no one is employed at will anymore (which is not to say that no one can be fired).

Our civics courses vacillated between teaching us about limited government and teaching us about government as an insurer of a level playing field. Surely no one believes government is in any regard substantially limited (which is not to say it should not be more limited). Government is involved in most aspects of our lives.[23] Government is not government: it is a mass of agencies, bureaus, departments, and so forth. Each of those has a management with an agenda. That agenda may be to create a level playing field, but probably it is not, and a manager who wants to be successful needs to find out what the agenda is. Government is a stakeholder in much of our lives, and it is critical that managers know what the stakes are a government agency is pursuing and what the values are of the management of the agency.

Assumptions about the environment, too, must undergo substantial change. I have tried to show elsewhere that under capitalism, the environment was a zero-cost alternative and that as long as we profess to cling to a capitalist analysis, the environment can be expected to deteriorate.[24] I also showed that while it has taken time for the environment to acquire a management to represent its voice, that is now happening. Thus, there is nothing which by definition might be eliminated from consideration or representation in managerialism. Any position can be represented in the transaction process. What it takes is an organization and then power of some form or other in the process. In short, from stockholders to employees and from government to the environment, there is nothing left to the conceptual baggage of capitalism. The sooner managers recognize that and get to tending to their work with realistic assumptions, the more successful they will become, if for no other reason than that they will no longer be required to tilt at windmills.

Managers have discretion. There is no benefit to be gained from repeating the arguments for that view. If the reader is not convinced at this stage, there is nothing that can be said that will help secure the argument. Managers make decisions all the time, and the nature of those decisions shapes the future of their organizations. Managers cannot, however, do whatever they want to do. The decisions are made within the context of constraints. Sometimes those constraints are so severe that the managers have no effective discretion. More likely, there is some room within the constraints, and decisions can be made. When management makes decisions in a systematic way, it does so in the planning process.

It is through planning that management can have the greatest long-term impact on the corporation. Planning carries with it discretion. When business was closer to the capitalist model, planning was not of much interest to the business executives. They had to do what they had to do to survive the rigors of the marketplace. There is some managerial discretion today, however, and that is what makes planning important. The conceptual changes suggested are enormous, and they entail substantial changes about a range of issues, from how organizations should go about planning to business education itself. If the argument of this book is correct, then our work has just begun.

Business Ethics

If these changes are persuasive, then a particular area of concentration for the future should be business ethics. In a sense, this whole book is a prolegomenon to business ethics. By and large, the approaches taken thus far to business ethics have not gone deep enough philosophically. The task of the philosopher is to raise questions, especially those questions which are not being raised by others because they share too many unexamined assumptions. We should not avoid that duty. If managers find that discomforting, we should remind ourselves that that is why we ply our trade in colleges and universities, and we should continue plying our trade. While I do not accept argument by aphorism, I am attracted to the rhetorical thrust of John Gardner's expression when he said that a society which does not value its plumbers and its philosophers will find that neither its pipes nor its theories will hold water.

Persistent questioning led to this book, and it is just that kind of persistent and fundamental questioning which should find a more important place in the subject of business ethics. That is why, when introducing John Ladd's notion of organizational life, I said that business ethics might have taken a more productive turn if it had pursued the example set by Ladd of asking the right questions. That is also why we should admire the work of George Lodge. Not because we necessarily agree with it. I have made it clear that I do not. By asking about ideology, however, Lodge has been asking important and fundamental questions which are, in fact, deeply philosophical. That is why I have called attention to Peter Drucker. Among many economists and business professors, it is chic (to use his term) to belittle Drucker's accomplishments. However, Drucker has been trying to call our attention to the fact that something fundamentally important is going on in our society. While his case in his essay "Ethical Chic" against business ethics is facile, his other searches and his scepticism about what John Kenneth Galbraith called conventional wisdom have been most important.[25]

I am not suggesting here that the questions which have been pursued by people who have thought about business ethics are unimportant. I suggest, rather, that by and large they have been questions about superstructure, not about foundations. Examining the foundations should provide a more productive and philosophical approach. Obviously, a detailed analysis of business ethics based on these new foundations has to be left to another time. In that sense, this book provides an introduction to the field. However, we can make a few additional preliminary observations.

One advantage to the ideology we have now is that we can securely locate business ethics as a function in the organization. Its primary location should be in the planning process itself. Even though some stakeholders will dress up their pressures with the rhetoric of ethics if that gains them power in the transaction process, ethics will have no real stakeholder force. If ethical issues are to be given attention, that will occur in the planning process. It is in that process that the definition of the corporation is established. It is in that process that management has an opportunity to create the nature of the corporation and, in that sense, to create the corporation itself. In 1982 Kenneth Goodpaster and John Matthews published an important article which argues persuasively that a corporation, like a person, can have a conscience. On the topic of corporate conscience, it is worthwhile to cite Drucker also: "There is a need in any organization for a 'conscience' . . . and conscience functions are top management work." [26] Matthews and Goodpaster's article is another installment in the debate about the organic versus the atomistic nature of the corporation, and it comes down solidly on the organic side. They say that while a corporation can have a conscience, not all corporations do. They are not very helpful, however, on locating where and how the conscience will be created. I think the answer to that question is in the planning process, more specifically in the process of establishing the "mission" of the corporation. Establishing a corporate mission should not be an empty, nonanalytic activity, akin to having a séance. It should be a rigorous process informed by empirical facts and careful analytic work.

The best organizations will not face a constant barrage of ethical questions. If they do, then the conscience has not been articulated, communicated, accepted, and set. There will always be problems of such a dilemmatic nature that the planning process did not foresee them or solve them. However, few routine ethical issues should arise, because the planning process and its implementation should make the decisions clear. Consider an analogy from the field of medical ethics. We hope that in the normal course of normal events, physicians do not face deeply disturbing ethical issues. The medical problems presented to physicians are complex enough that we hope they spend most of their energy solving those problems without becoming engulfed in ethical debates. We do not want our physician to be torn between caring for us and going out to play golf. Admittedly, that is an ethical issue if it should arise, but in ideal circumstances, it should not even arise, and we have a right to expect that our physicians have decided to be the kind of persons for whom it will not arise. On the other hand, some medical cases cannot be anticipated or are so morally problematic by nature that no physician can have a ready solution. In those cases, it seems that many physicians and hospitals have decided that wide discussion with a variety of people, including moral philosophers, is helpful. Those discussions are rarely univocal, but they have been found to be informative if the participants know what they are talking about or are ready to learn when they do not. Interestingly, journalism seems to have been developing a similar approach, not because it imitates medicine, but because effective newsrooms make excellent places for such discussions to occur. The Poynter Institute for Media Studies has pioneered in the development of this approach and proselytizing for it. It may be because the early and influential faculty at the Poynter Institute came from outside the mainstream of journalism and journalism schools that they could bring a fresh perspective to the questions.

The analogy to business may be complete now. Surely the ideal situation obtains when managers and employees avoid doing something wrong simply because, as they might say, "that is not the way things are done here." No sensible senior manager wants employees to wrestle constantly with moral concerns. The senior manager should want employees to know what is acceptable in that corporation, what is not, and what warrants further discussion. That should be established in the process of defining the nature of the corporation. In the end, the situation revolves around the executives themselves, the kind of organization they choose to lead, and the formal and informal structures they cultivate in providing that leadership. They will become transforming leaders, as distinct from transactional leaders, to use James MacGregor Burns's phraseology, when they introduce values into their leadership and into the nature of their organization.[27]

The rhetoric of top management alone, however, will not do, either in the development of the conscience or in the implementation of it. The temptation to preach to the organization is likely to have about as much impact on the behavior of the people in the organization as most preaching does elsewhere. Planning in regard to numerous aspects of the corporation may involve centrally only those who possess expertise and interest. Such division of labor and interest does not apply equally to ethical issues. Sensitive people in the corporation believe they have something important to say, believe their view should be heard, and believe they have valuable factual information to bring to the process. They need to be involved, or the managerial rhetoric will be wasted. They also need to be involved because if they are not involved, the implementation of the conscience will not be effective. People are not always what they say they are. As Fichte would remind us, they are what they do. The same is true of the corporation. It may say one thing and do something else, and that is more likely to happen if planning which involves establishing the nature of the corporation is disconnected from the people who are the corporation.

I have shown elsewhere in an article how a program can be carried out in a practical way which avoids the issues raised by Arrow's paradox.[28] There is no sense in repeating that suggestion here, for other processes may be more appropriate for specific organizations. The article does, however, answer the frequently expressed frustration of managers that they cannot figure out how to accomplish the requirements of ethics. It can be done. Managers do have the discretion. The question for managers now is whether they want to exercise it.

Beyond Managerialism?

It is to the credit of managers, administrators, and other decision makers in the advanced postindustrial societies that they have created ideological foundations where none had been articulated. The Greek word for truth, *alétheia,* may be translated also as unconcealedness or uncoveredness. It is in that tradition that I have sought to uncover managerialism. Its reach is extensive—from theory to action and from society to individuals. While it has been developed in the world of action, it requires us to reconceptualize the foundations of our social, political, and economic theories. The needed changes in economic theory were emphasized in this chapter because economics, more than political science or the other social sciences, seems to lay claim to a unified methodology and body of theory. While individual political scientists may present their views with an air of scientific presumption, even the casual observer soon comes to recognize deep and healthy disagreements among political scientists. A lesson to be learned from managerialism is that, while the divisions among the academic disciplines may be convenient for the organizational purposes of colleges and universities, they do not correspond to reality. In this regard, managerialism is a recurrence of the concept of political economy, which would have made more sense to Smith and Marx.

Since managerialism is a recurrence in that sense, it is reasonable to ask what lies beyond managerialism, either descriptively or normatively. While it is likely that a new realistic ideology will appear beyond managerialism, I do not know what it is. Descriptively, I simply cannot see what may cause managerialism to break down or what might follow it. At this stage, the resilience of managerialism is more impressive than its brittleness.

If we return to Drucker's image of an age of discontinuity and if we suppose that managerialism is the ideology which has emerged from that discontinuity, then it should not be surprising that we cannot see our way out yet. Managerialism may be in its early stages. While I suggested that the seeds of the downfall of capitalism were planted at about the same time Smith wrote *The Wealth of Nations* and while Smith should be given credit for rejecting incorporation privileges, there is no evidence that Smith imagined the extent of the developments which would follow. As we saw, even Marx, with the advantage of more than a half century, did not see the dramatic impact that corporate organizations would have. Thus, it may take more time to glimpse beyond the next period of discontinuity. That is a task for intellectuals, and while our glimpses will include false starts, it is important that we not miss again. Our faith should be in an open process of criticism which allows intellectual hypotheses to advance the adventure toward truth.

Normatively, managerialism comes to a frustrating conclusion. One of the reasons this book has been so long in coming forward is that I do not enjoy ending a book or a musical performance in a minor key. It would be most pleasurable to say that having uncovered managerialism we can rest content and conclude that all is well in this best of all possible worlds. But that is denied us. While a moral rationalization for managerialism can be articulated (i.e., that it is of, by, and for managers), I cannot imagine how that articulation could stand up to incisive moral criticism.

The aspect of managerialism which concerns me most is the loss of the individual. Social psychologists and sociologists might say that that concern reflects a kind of native bias of a citizen of the United States. Even so, it may be justifiable. From a normative perspective, then, I am inclined to suggest merging managerialism with an aggressive form of democracy as that is defined in chapter 5. That might come through a kind of direct referendum democracy, which, since it would be binary, might evade the problems Arrow discovered. If we return to the final matrix presented in chapter 6, that would mean examining further the cell designated O (democratic, nonsocialist and noncapitalist). Such a normative ideology might be called democratic managerialism. The operations of managerialism would be checked by a direct referendum democracy. However, I continue to insist that reality lies in the cell designated U

(nondemocratic and nontotalitarian, nonsocialist and noncapitalist).[29] Whether democratic managerialism is anything more than a forced marriage, whether it is self-contradictory, whether any sense can be made of it, and whether it can be justified are all topics for further consideration. One of the joys of an adventure of ideas is that it always reveals new vistas.

Notes
Index

Notes

Preface

1. Aristotle, *On Rhetoric: A Theory of Civic Discourse,* trans. George A. Kennedy (New York: Oxford University Press, 1991).

2. I am taking some liberties in describing capitalism and socialism as nineteenth-century ideologies. Since Adam Smith published *The Wealth of Nations* in 1776, we might prefer to refer to capitalism as a late eighteenth-century ideology, but 1776 seems to me close enough to the turn of the century to avoid such a categorization. Marx worked on *Das Kapital* until his death in 1883, and Engels continued the project. Thus, we might refer to Marxism as a late nineteenth-century ideology. The main ideas of *Das Kapital,* however, were worked out by Marx at least by 1848, and as I shall try to show, neither he nor Engels took account of major developments in the economic world which began in earnest in the late nineteenth century. If I were to qualify this description for academic purposes, I would refer to the two ideologies as originating in the first half of the nineteenth century. Their distance from the closing decade of the twentieth century would merely strengthen my point.

3. Unhappily, the debate has also spilled over to the popular world, where it is pursued in the same intensely negative fashion of the more ideological debates. In order to help keep that debate out of the cul-de-sac into which it seems headed, I suggest two fairly simple rules: the disputants should know thoroughly both the works they advocate for inclusion and the works they advocate for exclusion, and the primary thrust of arguments should be in favor of those works and authors they wish to include rather than against those they wish to exclude.

4. For reasons which will become clearer, I resisted most strenuously the argument that there are no democratic countries in advanced industrialized society, but even there I finally capitulated.

5. In January 1992 I heard Alan Murray of the *Wall Street Journal* respond to a question about how the economy of the United States would fare in 1992. Murray said that at the start of each calendar year the *Wall Street Journal* brings a number of the best-known professional economists to New York City for a meeting with its editors and reporters. The economists are asked to discuss their views of the future of the economy over the next year. Murray said that the consensus of the economists was that

the recession would be concluded by the spring of 1992. Murray had a wry smile on his face, and in the silence which followed, he added that these were, of course, the same economists who the previous year had predicted that the recession would be over by the spring of 1991.

Chapter 1. Ideology: Definition, Comparisons, and Defense

1. Alfred North Whitehead, *Adventures of Ideas* (New York: Macmillan, 1933).

2. John Maynard Keynes, *The General Theory of Employment, Interest, and Money* (1936; New York: Harcourt, Brace and World, 1964), 383–84. To late twentieth-century ears, Keynes's specific reference to men is arresting. It is especially surprising when we realize that Keynes was a member of the Bloomsbury group of which Virginia Woolf was a central figure. Here the implication seems to be that either there are no practical women or that those which exist can be safely ignored in a treatise on economics.

3. See, for example, Marx, *The Eighteenth Brumaire* and *The German Ideology;* Daniel Bell, *The End of Ideology,* rev. ed. (New York: Free Press, 1967); David E. Apter, ed., *Ideology and Discontent* (New York: Free Press, 1964); Chaim I. Waxman, ed., *The End of Ideology Debate* (New York: Funk and Wagnalls, 1968); Hubert M. Blalock, J. G. Miller, and Heinz Eulau, *The Behavioral Persuasion* (New York: Random House, 1962); Karl Deutsch, *The Nerves of Government* (New York: Free Press, 1963).

4. Kenneth M. Dolbeare and Patricia Dolbeare, *American Ideologies* (Chicago: Markham, 1971); George C. Lodge, *The New American Ideology* (New York: New York University Press, 1975).

5. A lot of foolishness has been written about this issue, because popularizers have assumed that those who could find no proof believed that no external world existed. Even Berkeley, whose thought influenced Condillac considerably, said that he believed there is an external world which is guaranteed by God. The difficult question is not about what we should believe but about what we can demonstrate.

6. In the present day we have descendants of physiocrats: some people believe that wealth cannot be derived from a service economy and thus fear the decline of the industrial base.

7. One should ignore the obvious inconsistency in that characterization. Such inconsistencies were not hobgoblins for Napoleon's mind.

8. Words abbreviated in the entry have been spelled out.

9. Lodge, *New American Ideology,* 7, 8.

10. For the purposes of this discussion, I have left the term *organic* at an intuitive and nondefined level. Chapter 2 includes a lengthy examination of the concept, especially as it relates to ideology. It will be seen that the use of *organic* there is consistent with Lodge's use of it in his definition.

11. C. Northcote Parkinson, *The Evolution of Political Thought* (New York: Viking Press, 1958), 7–15.

12. See chapter 6 for a more complete treatment of this word.

13. The metaphor of the machine was developed in a sophisticated fashion by Brown University professor John Ladd, who published an article on the subject in 1970. Ladd's treatment is philosophical, and he did not indicate whether it was developed in response

to the campus unrest which was peaking as he was preparing the article. For an extended treatment of Ladd's article, see chapter 7.

14. Robert Paul Wolff, *The Ideal of the University* (Boston: Beacon Press, 1969), 71, 73.

15. Ibid., 74, 75.

16. Dolbeare and Dolbeare, *American Ideologies*, 3.

17. Joseph A. Schumpeter, *Capitalism, Socialism, and Democracy* (New York, Harper and Brothers, 1942).

18. His methodology had one demonstrable consequence which would contribute to the retardation of intellectual thought for the next two thousand years. Aristotle decided that since, in all his observations, women were not active in politics, they were not naturally suited to political life or, indeed, to any life beyond the household. In Athens, for example, women were not allowed to be active in political life. Contrast Aristotle's view on this topic with that of his teacher. Plato held that women should be free to take the same tests men took in order to determine their suitability for political service and that leaders should be selected on the basis of performance on the tests without regard to gender.

19. Thomas S. Kuhn, *The Structure of Scientific Revolution*, 2d ed. (Chicago: University of Chicago Press, 1970).

20. Peter F. Drucker, *The Age of Discontinuity: Guidelines to Our Changing Society* (New York: Harper and Row, 1969).

21. *Lynch v. Donnelly*, 465 U.S. 668 (1984).

22. 1 John 4:9, KJV.

23. This cross was nine feet tall, and a substantial structure. It stood at a well-traveled intersection. One can only imagine the difficulties involved in cutting it down and hiding it.

Chapter 2. Approaches to Ideology and a Logical Point

1. Reference here is to economics as taught and practiced especially in the United States, Great Britain, and other English-speaking countries. Unlike physics, economics as such does not survive unchanged across cultural borders.

2. See I. F. Stone, *The Trial of Socrates* (Boston: Little, Brown and Co., 1988).

3. For a further analysis of some of these issues, see Willard F. Enteman, "Economics, Ethics, and the Environment," in *The Corporation, Ethics, and the Environment*, ed. W. Michael Hoffman, Robert Frederick, and Edward S. Petry, Jr. (New York: Quorum Books, 1990), 217–26.

4. William Galston, "Neutral Dialogue and the Abortion Debate," *Report from the Institute for Philosophy and Public Policy* 10, no. 2 (Spring 1990): 12–14.

5. See Raymond M. Smullyan, *What Is the Name of This Book?* (Englewood Cliffs, N.J.: Prentice-Hall, 1978). This book provides an excellent and entertaining explanation of Gödel's theorem, to which we shall have occasion to refer later. By the way, based on what readers have been told thus far about Smullyan's book, they can answer the question Smullyan poses in his title. See how informative logic is?

6. In the utopia of Houyhnhnmia, no one is required to do anything. Rather, every-

one reasons together about what should be done, and when the reasoning is concluded, everyone is exhorted to carry out the consequences of that reasoning. Gulliver never tells us what happens to those who do not follow the exhortation. We are led to suspect that is because there would be no such individuals, since all Houyhnhnms are rational and would, thus, follow what rationality suggests.

7. For an example of an expanded treatment of rationality, see Mary Field Belenky, Blythe McVicker Clinchy, Nancy Rule Goldberger, and Jill Mattuck Tarule, *Women's Ways of Knowing: The Development of Self, Voice and Mind* (New York: Basic Books, 1986).

Chapter 3. Atomism Applied: Capitalism

1. Milton Friedman, *Essays in Positive Economics* (Chicago: University of Chicago Press, 1953), 3; John Neville Keynes, *The Scope and Method of Political Economy* (London: Macmillan, 1891), 34–35. John Neville Keynes was an economist and the father of John Maynard Keynes.

2. Friedman, *Essays in Positive Economics*, 4, 5.

3. Feminists may be inclined to point out that Friedman refers only to men in that quotation and that perhaps he is right that men can find no way to resolve such disputes except by yielding to their usual temptation to fall into some variation on barroom brawling, whereas women may be able to resolve such issues without descending to incivility. See, for example, Virginia Woolf, *Three Guineas* (New York: Harcourt Brace, 1938), 8ff.: "Here, immediately, are three reasons which lead your sex to fight."

4. Douglas A. Irwin, introduction to *Essays on the Intellectual History of Economics*, by Jacob Viner, ed. Douglas A. Irwin (Princeton, N.J.: Princeton University Press, 1991), 18–19.

5. It is useful to recall that psychology at that time was considered part of philosophy. Psychology would not develop its scientific and antiphilosophical phase for another hundred years or so.

6. For all their allegiance to empirical science, the scientific economists have rarely tested the hypothesis empirically. As we shall see, some of the few times it has been put to a test, the results have been less than resounding in its favor.

7. In the context of the earlier points about moral psychology, it is relevant to note that Hume's subtitle for this treatise was *An Attempt to Introduce the Experimental Method of Reasoning into Moral Subjects*.

8. At this stage of this book, it may be important to refer to a point which will be developed later. All this effort to save scientific economics is not merely pure methodology. It has an ideological basis. The capitalist scientific economists want to establish capitalism as scientific economics and save it from the necessity of answering to moral analysis. Thus, the distinction is important to them. The assertion that their view would not be endorsed by Adam Smith himself could be sidestepped by reconstructing Adam Smith. The lesson would not be lost on later Marxist economists, who, of course, also insisted that *their* view was the only scientific one. Beneath such methodological discussions, which tend to make the normal person's eyes glaze over, lurk serious ideological issues.

9. Of course, some philosophers do change their minds, and when they say that they

have done so, commentators have no prima facie obligation to attempt to see the writings as a whole. When it is clear, as in this case, that the author saw no contradiction, however, it would seem to be a prima facie obligation of the commentator to find an interpretation which makes them coherent.

10. Patricia Werhane, *Adam Smith and His Legacy for Modern Capitalism* (New York: Oxford University Press, 1991).

11. Of course, the word *consumer* is not Smith's word. It is a contemporary one. That shift in language is not merely semantic: it is a shift in concepts. It is examined further in chapter 7. Nevertheless, since this book is written for a late twentieth-century world, for purposes of communication, it seems preferable to use this term here rather than to create a longer digression dealing, again, with definitions.

12. Smith criticized people who lived on inheritances. See Adam Smith, *An Inquiry into the Nature and Causes of the Wealth of Nations,* ed. Edwin Cannan (New York: Random House, Modern Library, 1937), 361–64; hereinafter cited as Smith, *Wealth of Nations.*

13. The word *social* has been put before *freedom* to indicate that the complex question of whether or not humans have free will is not directly at stake here. Social freedom, in this context, means something like freedom from social, especially governmental, constraints external to the actor. The topic of human freedom and free will is discussed later in this chapter and again in chapters 7 and 8. There remains, also, an interesting question about what relationship exists between social freedom and freedom of the will.

14. Smith's actual views on profit are confusing and perhaps even contradictory. I have presented here a commonly articulated view of profits consistent with Smith's intent and with capitalism. See, for example, Frank H. Knight, *Risk, Uncertainty and Profit* (1921; New York: Harper and Row, 1957), which presents a clear and forceful explanation of the view.

15. It is important to note that I said unnecessary, not false. Part of the brilliance of Newton, Smith, and later Darwin was that they could evade troublesome issues rather than facing them directly. Smith admired that intellectual strategy in Newton.

16. Friedman, *Essays in Positive Economics,* 22.

17. The language of the market mechanism is more modern than Smith's, but the image, as taken by the economists, is an appropriate one, following Newton and the antiteleological approach.

18. Hume showed that we could not prove the existence of motivation or, for that matter, cause and effect, though both concepts are used regularly in his *History of Great Britain from the Invasion of Julius Caesar to the Revolution of 1688.* I believe that rather than thinking that Hume or Smith showed that motivation does not occur, it is more reasonable to suppose that what they showed was twofold. First, they showed that such assumptions were unproven and, perhaps, unprovable. Second, they showed that a great deal of scientific discovery could be made without entering into the metaphysical quagmire of the existence of motivations (and, for Hume, causes). If my suggestion is not accepted, the philosophers who admire Hume will have a David Hume Problem analogous to the economists' Adam Smith Problem.

Historically, the substantial attack on the existence of human motivation waited until the twentieth century and the so-called behaviorists in psychology. Following Wilhelm

Wundt and John B. Watson, psychologists veered into the view that such things simply do not exist (though when they are being most careful, even the behaviorists retreat to the position that the supposition is not useful). In the contemporary setting, B. F. Skinner is, perhaps, best known for his unyielding pursuit of this program. See, for example, his *Science and Human Behavior, Walden Two,* and *Beyond Freedom and Dignity.* The behaviorists argue that if we look at the human as a "black box," giving attention only to input and output—thus, observable phenomena—psychology will have a chance of achieving the stature at least of biology if not of physics and chemistry.

Friedman's approach to economic matters is similar to Skinner's approach to psychological matters. Friedman is quite ready to treat the human beings in the economic process, whether they are business executives or labor or consumers, as "black boxes" and to confine his attention to measure of input and output. Friedman believes the economist has no business inquiring into motivations of business executives, and such inquiry would yield economic information on a par with the medical knowledge one might gain by asking octogenarians to what they attribute their longevity. (This is Friedman's graphic example in *Essays in Positive Economics,* 31.)

19. Erwin Esser Nemmers, *Dictionary of Economics and Business* (Totowa, N.J.: Littlefield, Adams and Co., 1968), 57.

20. The labor theory of value is discussed extensively in chapter 4.

21. In a recent ruling (*Two Pesos, Inc.* v. *Taco Cabana, Inc.,* no. 91-971, decided June 26, 1992), the Supreme Court seems to have extended the definition of trademarks to include so-called trade dress. In the specific case, Taco Cabana argued that Two Pesos had imitated Taco Cabana's "festive eating atmosphere" in constructing and equipping its facilities. As I read the decision, the Court held that Taco Cabana had a right to trademark protection for its festive eating atmosphere irrespective of whether the putative imitation by Two Pesos had any demonstrable impact on the business of Taco Cabana.

22. A synopsis of this story appears in the *Wall Street Journal,* Sept. 13, 1990, p. A5.

23. There is an excellent book on the history of incorporation in England: Carleton Hunt, *The Development of the Business Corporation in England, 1800–1867* (Cambridge: Harvard University Press, 1936).

24. Smith, *Wealth of Nations,* 123, 129, 135, 699–700.

25. After 1990 it is difficult to pass over this section without taking note of what has come to be called the S&L situation in the United States. Through the 1980s that became almost a manager's dream come true. Managers could risk enormous amounts of other people's money. The government guaranteed the downside for both depositors and investors. Both owners and managers could take full advantage of any upside potential and abandon the project before the downside had to be faced. In spite of some prosecutions of the most greedy people who allowed themselves to get into allegedly illegal activities, many people legitimately made personal fortunes mismanaging money that belonged to other people, such as innocent depositors and an innocent general public, which faces a charge upward of five hundred billion dollars.

26. Peter L. Berger, *The Capitalist Revolution: Fifty Propositions about Prosperity, Equality and Liberty* (New York: Basic Books, 1986), 56–57.

27. Ibid., 56, 232.

28. Engels, in *Capital*, by Karl Marx (New York: International Publishers Co., 1967), 908.

29. See Alfred D. Chandler, Jr., *The Visible Hand* (Cambridge: Harvard University Press, Belknap Press, 1977).

30. Engels, in *Capital*, by Marx, 438.

31. Ibid., 909.

32. Just to forestall any lingering privatizers: it does no good to blame the banking debacles on government and the usual inefficiencies of bureaucrats. In Maryland, Ohio, and Rhode Island, where banking insurance was private, the comparative losses were even more dramatic. In Rhode Island, some financial institutions were closed for more than a year.

Chapter 4. Organicism Applied: Socialism and Marxism

1. In order to emphasize the persistence of this primary need to reject capitalism, it is instructive to note that a sociologist and a political scientist have recently produced a fascinating and promising book about what they call global capitalism. They declare that they are writing in the Marxist tradition of social analysis. In explaining their "tools of analysis," they carefully develop a notion of capitalism, which, of course, they then spend the bulk of the rest of their book destroying. It is curious to read this book in the wake of the dissolution of virtually all self-proclaimed Communist regimes except those in China and Cuba. The authors argue that capitalism has been elevated to a new stage—the global one. They recognize the importance of the development of global corporations, but they persist in distorting the notion of capitalism so that it bears no resemblance to the capitalism of Smith (or others such as Ricardo and Malthus) but remains a foil for their modern version of Marxism. One gets the impression that socialists believe they must maintain at least the appearance of capitalism in order to sustain their socialism. It is all the more curious in light of the fact that, as we shall see, Marx argued that an imminent international revolution in support of socialism was inevitable. Now, as we enter the twenty-first century, we have self-identified Marxists telling us that it is capitalism which has survived. Obviously, in any practical sense, communism as a social movement is dead. Marx, like Smith, was both intellectually powerful and a close observer of the society around him. Can any serious scholar of Marx believe that if he were alive today, he would still be bitterly denouncing capitalism? It makes the most sense to assume that Marx would declare that he is not a Marxist and that, while there remain many egregious activities committed by those who have control of economic power, it is not capitalism, but something else, which should receive our attention. Contemporary self-identified Marxists, however, have to maintain the semblance of capitalism and have to ignore the fact that, as we enter the twenty-first century, it makes the most sense to say that Marx's predictions of the mid–nineteenth century proved to be false even if we are generous with what *imminence* might mean. The current intellectual situation is all the more regrettable because important analysis of much of what is implied in the creation of global corporations is diminished by the contortions which are necessary to fit it into the debates of the nineteenth century. For example, examining Lodge and Vogel's *Ideology and National Competitiveness* might have pushed Ross and Trachte's analysis out of the cul-de-sac into which the authors

placed it. See Robert J. S. Ross and Kent C. Trachte, *Global Capitalism* (Albany, N.Y.: State University of New York Press, 1990).

2. While it is tempting to develop another digression which would examine at length the various uses of the two terms in an attempt to arrive at a justifiable differentiation, the result would not be worth the effort, at least for the needs of this book. Where a strong difference is intended, it will be noted explicitly.

3. It is interesting to note that in some of the states in the United States, this Marxist distinction is maintained in the tax code in the form of distinguishing "earned income" from "unearned income." Typically, the latter is subjected to a higher tax rate.

4. Marx may have inherited this view directly from Smith, who says in *The Wealth of Nations*, "The acquisition of valuable and extensive property, therefore, necessarily requires the establishment of civil government. Where there is no property, or at least none that exceeds the value of two or three days labour, civil government is not necessary." Adam Smith, *An Inquiry into the Nature and Causes of the Wealth of Nations*, ed. Edwin Cannan (New York: Random House, Modern Library, 1937), 670.

5. The socialist Proudhon declared: "Property is theft!" Of course, he meant private property.

6. The concept of alienation was important to Marx and later became central for people like Adorno and Marcuse, as they tried to assimilate Marx and Freud. In the case chosen, the issue of alienation may be seen dramatically in agricultural issues in the United States. We maintain an almost romantic notion of the "family farm." The notion is easier to maintain in an urban and suburban society which knows little more of the real demands of farming than the requirements of tending superfluous private vegetable gardens. Real farming is risky and dangerous. Almost surely, if OSHA regulations were applied to the family farms of our romances, the remaining few would be shut down. As we enter the twenty-first century, agricultural reality in the United States is agribusiness, which gains the advantage of subsidies provided through the myth of the romance but which is conducted on manufacturing principles much more characteristic of factories than of family farms. In agribusiness, the workers, who are farmers only by extensive equivocation, are almost entirely removed from any identity with the final product or its use. If the family farmer was concerned that his customers appreciated the fruits of his labor, the products of the modern agribusiness worker are turned over to another corporate abstraction, just as the worker on the production line has little or no attachment to the final product. We need to be careful, however, in our concern with alienation. The fact remains that the main problem of agriculture in the United States is not that so little can be produced and marketed, but that so much can be produced and marketed that it would threaten the pricing and profitability of the market itself. That is the foundation of the numerous governmental activities in agriculture. Whereas we seem to debate endlessly whether we should have an industrial policy, we have a clear and expensive government-sponsored agricultural policy.

7. See, for example, volume 2 of *DasKapital*, entitled *The Process of Circulation of Capital*. Karl Marx, *Capital* (New York: International Publishers Co., 1967).

8. Smith argued that in the constant interplay of the atomic units, the fluctuations of the economy would be dampened to insignificance. It was part of Smith's general

faith and insight that out of each element's striving for its own interest, the general good would be served. Ricardo suggested that the system could have permanent swings and that they could become disastrous at some extremes. Marx accepted Ricardo as against Smith on this topic. Newton had created the calculus in developing his natural philosophy. In 1838 Cournot published his *Researches into the Mathematical Principles of the Theory of Wealth,* in which he applied Newton's calculus to economic matters. I know of no evidence that Marx or Engels read Cournot, though if they had, they might have discovered that Smith was mistaken in his assumption that price competition will necessarily lead to a dampened equilibrium but that Ricardo's analysis did not provide a solution. Differentiating the equations shows that they can, under perfectly acceptable assumptions, lead to fluctuations which increase with each iteration. Perhaps we can excuse Marx and credit Cournot by observing that it would take economic thought almost a century to return to this problem and provide solutions for it through what is known as Ezekiel's cobweb theorem.

9. Robert L. Heilbroner, *The Worldly Philosophers* (New York: Simon and Schuster, 1953), 29; also quoted in W. Jack Duncan, *Great Ideas in Management* (San Francisco: Jossey-Bass, 1989), 135.

10. I have tried to establish the earliest use of the terms in the economic sense, and I have been unable to find an authoritative answer. Marx and the socialists may have picked up the term *capitalist* from Ricardo, who uses it occasionally in his *Principles.* It is by no means a preferred term for Ricardo, however. When he refers to people we call capitalists, he typically speaks in much more precise terms, identifying them as bankers, manufacturers, farmers, landlords, hatters, hosiers, shoemakers, and so forth. As far as I can tell, Ricardo does not identify the system he expounds as *capitalism.* Marx and the socialists promoted the use of those terms.

11. It may be interesting to know that I have also tried to determine the origins of the use of the terms *consumer* and *consumerism* in the history of economics. Once again, I find the earliest use of the former in Ricardo. Although it appears more often than *capitalist,* it is not pursued in any depth by him. Marx and the socialists advanced the terms *capitalist* and *capitalism,* but they did not advance the use of the terms *consumer* and *consumerism.*

12. Paul Edwards, ed., *Encyclopedia of Philosophy,* 8 vols. (New York: Macmillan, 1967).

13. Neither McCarthy nor Marx cared much about the differences there except for rhetorical purposes, and both tended to favor *socialism* as the more general term capable of describing a greater range of people. In addition, neither McCarthy nor Marx was much interested in the details of a socialist society or how it might operate.

14. It is tempting to suggest that we should conclude, therefore, that McCarthy was a closet Marxist or at least a fellow traveler.

15. For references to the adam and smith of economics, see "The Adam Smith Problem" in chapter 3. Institutionalism is an economic approach which emphasizes the importance of actual institutions and their role in economic life as distinct from constructing deductive schemes which are not meant to be realistic (see "Economics," in chapter 8). In a sense, this book is in the tradition of institutionalism. The strongest

form of derision with which mainstream economists treat institutionalism is to deny its status as economics (or sometimes, more mildly but equally condescendingly, as "serious" economics). Once again, rhetoric is very important. An autobiographical story may illustrate my point. As a graduate student, I once went to a lecture by the famous institutionalist John Kenneth Galbraith, after his return from his tour as ambassador to India during the Kennedy administration. The title of the lecture was "What an Economist Learned in India." The next day, toward the end of an economics class, one of the students said that he wanted to ask a question about a point made by Galbraith. The professor of the course broke in to ask the student once again the title of the lecture. The student repeated the title, and the professor asked who, besides Galbraith, had lectured at that meeting. When the student replied that no one else lectured, the professor asked the student if he were not angry that he had been subjected to false advertising, since, obviously, no *economist* spoke at that lecture.

16. Robert C. Tucker, ed., *The Marx-Engels Reader* (New York: Norton, 1972), 109.

17. See Eduard Bernstein, *Evolutionary Socialism* (New York: Schocken Books, 1961). This book was originally published in 1899, four years after the death of Engels.

18. There is also a modern capitalistlike explanation for the phenomenon in the United States. Remember that modern capitalists insist that the only motivation for human actions is self-interest. Recognize that most intellectuals are employed in colleges and universities, where they believe they are underpaid and underappreciated, especially by board members, who are often corporate executives. There is not much self-interest on the part of the intellectuals for promoting a system which they feel exploits them. There is an expression wealthy people are fond of: "If you are so smart, why ain't you rich?" It is only partially a joke. That "capitalists" have created conditions under which intellectuals would become alienated from capitalism is almost as remarkable as the fact that the capitalists have given away the terms and conditions of the ideological argument.

19. Tucker, *Marx-Engels Reader*, 346.

20. Theoretical learning is not likely to assist one in maximizing profits.

21. In capitalizing the first letter of *Worker*, I follow a convention for identifying a group organically.

22. Tucker, *Marx-Engels Reader*, 362.

23. Both temporal and geographic senses of universality were used effectively by the Solidarity movement in Poland in the 1980s.

24. Tucker, *Marx-Engels Reader*, 4.

25. Overton H. Taylor, *A History of Economic Thought* (New York: McGraw-Hill, 1960), 282.

26. It is interesting to speculate on why baseball is thought to be the national pastime, so much so that it is the only professional sport which is exempt from the antitrust laws. The answer may lie in the fact that baseball is a sport which requires something like a team (as against tennis and golf, for example) but is an atomistic sport. Whatever team spirit may exist will have little impact on the outcome of a game. By way of contrast, many other sports are changed dramatically as a result of team spirit. To use the terms of this book, baseball is an atomistic sport, even when played well, whereas other sports

are organic and cannot be played well unless that organic characteristic is nurtured. If the past of the United States is rooted in atomism, that may explain our fascination with baseball.

27. See Joseph A. Schumpeter, *Capitalism, Socialism, and Democracy* (New York, Harper and Brothers, 1942). A recent revival of interest in Schumpeter has occurred among intellectuals. A perceptive biography advances that revival: Richard Swedberg, *Schumpeter: A Biography* (Princeton, N.J.: Princeton University Press, 1992).

Chapter 5. Process Applied: Democracy

1. Giovanni Sartori, *The Theory of Democracy Revisited* (Chatham, N.J.: Chatham House, 1987), 3.

2. The word *democracy* is derived from Greek: *demos* means people, and *karos* means rule. Thus, *democracy* means the rule of the people.

3. Some weeks after the so-called Gulf War was concluded, the crown prince of Jordan explained on television that the reason the Jordanian press continued to report the conclusion of the war as a victory for Iraq and Saddam Hussein was that Jordan is a democratic country.

4. I am suggesting that that is the plain meaning of Lincoln's statement. I am not suggesting I know what Lincoln himself meant. For all I know, Lincoln may have been a "modern" president who made statements for their effect without necessarily believing what they meant.

5. Robert Paul Wolff, *In Defense of Anarchism* (New York: Harper and Row, 1970), 34–37.

6. During the 1992 presidential election in the United States, a prospective candidate from neither party, H. Ross Perot, suggested that he would seek referendalike votes from citizens if he were to become president. Ancient arguments about republican government (called "democratic" for purposes of the debate), about the dangers of direct governance by an ignorant and irresponsible majority, and so forth, were dusted off. Perot comes from a "high-tech" background and probably knows, more than most, that his suggestion is technologically feasible.

7. Sartori, *Theory of Democracy Revisited*, 129n64. I shall show later that appearances to the contrary notwithstanding, Sartori is no friend of democracy either, which may also explain his lack of interest in the procedure Wolff suggests.

8. The most important volume in the initiation of what would prove to be an extended debate is Kenneth Arrow, *Social Choice and Individual Values*, 2d ed. (New York: John Wiley and Sons, 1963). The second edition contains a new concluding chapter, in which Arrow reviews the literature produced after the original publication of the book in 1951 and makes further comments on the implications of the argument. Arrow's argument is formal, technical, and ingenious, but it is so elegantly presented and so clearly explained that it is accessible to a reader with a modest knowledge of logic and an immodest amount of patience.

In a recent and very important book, Howard DeLong tries to refute Arrow's reasoning. See DeLong, *A Refutation of Arrow's Theorem* (Latham, N.Y.: University Press of America, 1991). DeLong examines the assumptions Arrow makes about democracy and finds them highly questionable. This is not the place to provide a rejoinder to DeLong's argument, though in the spirit of scholarship, DeLong says that he hopes his book will stimulate others to correct any deficiencies (52). Suffice it to say that the bulk of DeLong's argument turns on disagreements between his interpretation of democracy and Arrow's. DeLong says that he "takes Athenian and American democracies to be the paradigms of democracy" (2). He then attempts to show that Arrow's assumptions about democratic procedure do not conform to the political procedures of either society. As a consequence, DeLong concludes that Arrow has not provided the fundamental assumptions of democracy, though DeLong never identifies the kind of government to which those assumptions might apply. Since an important part of the argument of this book is that neither ancient Athens nor the modern United States are democratic (or capitalist or socialist), the bulk of DeLong's argument could more appropriately be characterized as a disputation with Arrow's reasoning rather than a refutation of it. In his chapter 6, DeLong does try to show that Arrow's reasoning is invalid in the logical sense, but once again, far from showing that its conclusions do not follow from its premises, DeLong shows that alternative interpretations are at least possible. As DeLong recognizes, however, both Arrow's proposed proof and a possible refutation of it are critically important to democracy. We can hope that, perhaps, building on DeLong's pioneering work, a refutation may be found and we may not have to continue to confront this deeply troubling issue.

I believe the problems identified by Arrow have not been solved to date, nor has anyone found substantial flaws in his reasoning. I have myself presented some technical papers in which I have argued that what we have before us in democratic theory is perhaps analogous to the paradoxes of set theory in mathematics. In addition, I have presented papers attempting to find ways around the problem, but as a result of generous comments of respondents, I have realized they have not been successful. As a consequence, I am inclined to believe that the kind of crisis which the paradoxes of set theory set off in mathematics in the early part of this century is now due atomistic ideological theory.

9. Those familiar with Arrow's work on this topic and the extensive literature which followed will note two changes I have made from the standard presentation. First, instead of the common presentation of a society with three members facing three alternatives, I have used a case with seven members and three choices. I do so because in the literature there is a temptation to treat the only troublesome 3×3 case as analogous to a tie vote in a situation in which there are an even number of voters. Even DeLong yields to this temptation (see *Refutation*, 10, 11). As the matrix expands in numbers of voters and numbers of alternatives, however, the number of troublesome combinations increases. Duncan Black has shown that the proportion of troublesome cases levels out to be about 11 percent of the possibilities as the parameters of the matrix grow but the final vote of the society remains the same. See Black, "On the Rationality of Group Decision-Making," *Journal of Political Economy* 56 (1948): 23–34; and idem, *The Theory of Committees and Elections* (Cambridge: Cambridge University Press, 1963). Of course, in any somewhat complicated setting, while the final vote may

remain the same, when the votes are analyzed individually, it is clear that the voters are attempting to express different social results. The second change from the standard presentation I have made is to move ahead and have the committee members explicitly vote on all possibilities even though the final vote in each case may seem irrelevant. One of Arrow's assumptions which has been subjected to the greatest amount of attack by DeLong (see his chapter 4) and others is the so-called independence of irrelevant alternatives assumption. My purpose is to show that the assumption is not necessary to get Arrow's result. Obviously, if the premise is unnecessary, as the case cited shows, then even if DeLong's critique of the premise is successful, it is itself irrelevant.

10. This is just the claim DeLong disputes. He believes that irrational and immoral choices should not be granted to the voters. Obviously, someone must then decide a priori which alternatives are irrational or immoral. In many important political debates, each side considers the other(s) to be irrational and immoral. Democracy is designed to enable the society to make a *political* decision in the face of such disagreements. Of course, if some "enlightened" third party decides before the vote that rationality and morality belong only on one side and that is the only alternative presented, then there may be no contradictions, but there is no democracy either.

11. John Stuart Mill, *On Liberty,* ed. David Spitz (New York: W. W. Norton, 1975), 3–4.

12. One wants to ask where there is a governmental system in which some group cannot be tyrannized. Mill's second chapter of *On Liberty* develops the famous defense of the free press which is often quoted by press advocates. It is difficult to read it without cheering and thinking of the ways in which totalitarian regimes control the press. A moment's reflection, however, will make us realize that we pay a price for freedom of the press. Many innocent people have felt victimized by the press. Consider, for example, the tendency of reporters to push microphones and cameras in the faces of grieving people at the scene of an accident when they have just found that a loved one has been killed or seriously injured. Let us suppose, for the moment, that the majority were to pass legislation saying that for seventy-two hours, the press could not contact or otherwise intrude in the life of someone whose relative had died or been seriously injured. Democratic? By supposition. Restriction on the freedom of the press? Clearly. Unacceptable? Not so clear.

13. In order to be judicious, we should note that no one has yet been able to develop a foolproof or even a foolishness-proof system of governance, so it may be unfair to ask democracy to do what no other system has done. In any event, the purpose of democracy is not to provide better governance but to provide governance which is responsive to the people. Thus, to criticize it for not doing something it is not designed to do is a little like criticizing automobiles because they do not provide good means of transportation across the ocean or criticizing airplanes because they are inefficient means of going to the corner grocery store.

In spite of wide differences, Plato and Aristotle both thought that the ideal state would be run by people of the highest intelligence. Perhaps we can excuse Plato and Aristotle for their lack of experience and, thus, for their naive faith in intelligence. It is much more difficult to make similar excuses for Mill, since he had the benefit of the intervening two thousand years of experience. There is nothing about majority rule which means that the majority will rule sensibly, sensitively, or justly. The majority can be as stupid and shortsighted as any minority.

14. Mill, *On Liberty,* 5–6.

15. Mill had no empirical base from which to arrive at his conclusion because the opponents of democracy have always been successful in preventing its implementation.

16. Robert Paul Wolff, *In Defense of Anarchism* (New York: Harper and Row, 1970).

17. Apparently, their motives were not really pure in this effort. They wanted to garner the votes of the poor.

18. Robert A. Dahl, *A Preface to Democratic Theory* (Chicago: University of Chicago Press, 1956), 133.

19. Ibid., 31.

20. Ibid., 36.

21. The caveat is that in contrast with the case of ice cream, Dahl believes populist democracy does not exist. Thus, rather than pointing to an actual instance of ice cream, the presenter would have to give only a theoretical description of it and add that no one thinks it should exist.

22. Actually, Madison was terminologically more consistent than Dahl. Madison, like Franklin, preferred the term *republican.*

23. Dahl, *Preface to Democratic Theory,* 37.

24. Ibid.

25. Ibid., 38.

26. Ibid., 50.

27. Ibid., 51.

28. Ibid., 52.

29. Ibid., 55.

30. Ibid., 56.

31. Ibid., 133.

32. Ibid., 63.

33. Ibid., 74.

34. Ibid., 69.

35. The person who wishes to follow up this chapter with a thorough reading on democracy which incorporates the most recent thinking and also offers a careful analysis of earlier writings is well advised to examine Sartori's *Theory of Democracy Revisited.* It will require close reading—Sartori does not pander to his readers—but the effort will be rewarded.

36. Sartori, *Theory of Democracy Revisited,* 24.

37. One cannot help but think about the filibuster provisions in the United States Senate, no doubt designed to check headlong decision making by a majority of senators, that was used effectively for generations to block civil rights legislation.

38. Sartori, *Theory of Democracy Revisited,* 31. This is essentially the same point made by DeLong in his dispute with Arrow's axiomatic definition of democracy.

39. Aristotle, *Politics* 7.4.1326b25, in Richard McKeon, ed., *The Basic Works of Aristotle* (New York: Random House, 1941), 1284.

40. Sartori, *Theory of Democracy Revisited,* 115.

41. Ibid., 116.

42. Ibid., 117, 118.

43. Ibid., 108. The quotes from Dahl are from his *Preface to Democratic Theory,* 125–27.

44. Sartori, *Theory of Democracy Revisited,* 165, 166–67, 169, 171.

Chapter 6. Democratic Socialism and Democratic Capitalism

1. In the section of this chapter on democratic capitalism, I will discuss the meaning of the term *liberal.*

2. Marx died in 1883, and Engels died in 1895 after overseeing—with Bernstein's help—the publication of the third volume of *Das Kapital.* Though I do not know of any direct biographical reference, it seems likely that Bernstein delayed publication of his work out of respect for Marx and Engels.

3. To the end, Engels denied those differences. A close reading of the explicit editing Engels did of the second and third volumes of *Das Kapital,* however, show a shift. Engels allowed himself to appear explicitly in the two volumes while claiming all the time that he was merely re-presenting Marx. Engels was no more a mere transcriber of Marx than Plato was a mere transcriber of Socrates. By the time of Engels' death, he had taken part in the founding of the Second International and had been made honorary president of the International Socialist Workers' Congress.

4. For the sake of historical accuracy, it is worth pointing out that these are economists who succeeded, but did not follow, Adam Smith.

5. Milton Friedman, *Essays in Positive Economics* (Chicago: University of Chicago Press, 1953), 4, 5.

6. Seeing people pay for junk food with food stamps drives this point home directly.

7. Friedman, *Essays in Positive Economics,* 14.

8. Friedrich A. Hayek, *The Road to Serfdom* (Chicago: University of Chicago Press, 1944), xi.

9. There are even deeper historical ironies. If we associate *conservative* historically with people like Edmund Burke, the modern self-proclaimed conservatives are actually the historical liberals, and the modern liberals are the conservatives. I have not developed a theory of conservatism in this book, because Burke's approach to conservatism deserves respect. In that context, *conservative* is not a noun standing for a distinct ideology, but an adjective modifying ideologies. To understand Burke, one needs to understand how the same person could have consistently supported the American Revolution and opposed the French Revolution. By and large, modern journalists have gotten the meaning of *conservative* right. They refer to conservative Russian Communists and conservative Chinese Communists while recognizing that those people are some of the most dedicated Communists. *Conservative* is a qualification which makes sense only if we know what is being qualified. The fact that modern self-proclaimed conservatives in the United States do not recognize this and try to use the word as if it were a noun is simply further evidence of the poverty of their vocabulary after they have given so much of it away.

10. Hayek, *Road to Serfdom*, xi.

11. Ludwig von Mises, *Human Action: A Treatise on Economics*, 3d ed. (Chicago: Henry Regnery Co., 1966), v.

12. Milton Friedman, *Capitalism and Freedom* (Chicago: University of Chicago Press, 1962), 6.

13. It may surprise some readers to notice Friedman's name missing from this list. Friedman must not be as interested in democracy as the others. It is not that Friedman tries to restrain democracy, as so many democratic theoreticians have done. Rather, Friedman thinks the crucial question is not how citizens vote but whether they are free. *Capitalism and Freedom* does not treat democracy in any substantial way, nor does the book Milton and Rose Friedman wrote to explain their views to a lay audience, *Free to Choose* (New York: Avon Books, 1980).

14. Von Mises, *Human Action*, 150, 193.

15. Ibid., 193, 652n7.

16. Hayek, *Road to Serfdom*, 70.

17. Ibid.; Friedman, *Capitalism and Freedom*, 10, 24.

18. Hayek, *Road to Serfdom*, ix.

19. Ibid., 61, 64, 67. In the second passage, Hayek comes very close to the issues which would later be developed by Arrow. Hayek, however, thinks the problems are empirical, and Arrow shows they are in theory itself.

20. Hayek, *Road to Serfdom*, 67.

21. Variations of the case itself are reproduced in many texts on business ethics. See, for example, W. Michael Hoffman and Jennifer Mills Moore, *Business Ethics: Readings and Cases in Corporate Morality* (New York: McGraw-Hill, 1984), 412–20; John B. Matthews, Kenneth E. Goodpaster, and Laura L. Nash, *Policies and Persons: A Casebook in Business Ethics* (New York: McGraw-Hill, 1985), 301–9; Grover Starling and Otis W. Baskin, *Issues in Business and Society: Capitalism and Public Purpose* (Boston: Kent Publishing Co., 1985), 434–40.

22. Von Mises, *Human Action*, 715.

23. I have added the reference to integral equations here because it is not only the economic area—space—which needs calculating, but also individual change over time. This point is, in a sense, a merely technical one and does not threaten von Mises' general point, since differential and integral calculus are mathematically linked. For a further discussion of the issue of time in economics, see the section on economics in chapter 8.

24. Hayek, *Road to Serfdom*, viii; Friedman, *Capitalism and Freedom*, 8; von Mises, *Human Action*, 682; Robert Benne, *The Ethic of Democratic Capitalism: A Moral Reassessment* (Philadelphia: Fortress Press, 1981), 93.

25. It is also strange that Benne never refers to Niebuhr's *Leaves from the Notebook of a Tamed Cynic*, in which Niebuhr develops a direct socialist argument. Admittedly, that tract was written early in Niebuhr's career, but Niebuhr referred to it in his later works and did not recant it.

26. Friedman, *Capitalism and Freedom*, 34.

27. Ibid., 13.

28. V. I. Lenin, *The State and Revolution*, in *Marx, Engels, Marxism*, by V. I. Lenin (Moscow: Foreign Languages Publishing House, 1946), chap. 5, sec. 4, p. 429.

29. Friedman, *Capitalism and Freedom*, 10.

30. It should be acknowledged that one could do market research, but it is primarily marketing professors and market research consulting firms who believe such efforts yield truly reliable information. Even in the American economy, most reliable market research is done in the market. The Susan B. Anthony dollar resulted from centralized market research, as did the Edsel.

Chapter 7. Managerialism

1. Robert L. Heilbroner, *Between Capitalism and Socialism: Essays in Political Economics* (New York: Random House, 1970), xv.

2. See Thomas S. Kuhn, *The Structure of Scientific Revolutions*, 2d ed. (Chicago: University of Chicago Press, 1970), chaps. 5 and 2, and pp. vii–viii. It is at least possible that the willingness of social scientists to adopt the language of paradigms is further evidence of what some wags have called their physics envy. In teaching philosophy of science and philosophy of social science, I have sometimes suggested to students that they can take it as a generalization that when a discipline includes *science* in its title, it is not really a science, as in Christian science, library science, political science, and so forth. Indeed, what may be happening is an attempt to gain semantically what cannot be gained in reality.

3. Perhaps I shall be accused of promulgating an eternal verity here, but that is not so: if Gödel's discoveries were found wanting and other similar issues, such as the paradoxes of set theory, were found empty of force, then that would bring my conclusion about the nonattainability of eternal verities into question, and it might need to be abandoned. An excellent, accessible book on Gödel's work is Ernest Nagel and James R. Newman, *Gödel's Proof* (New York: New York University Press, 1958). Another accessible treatment occurs at the end of a book mentioned in chapter 2: Raymond M. Smullyan, *What Is the Name of This Book?* (Englewood Cliffs, N.J.: Prentice-Hall, 1978), 225–41. Has the reader answered the question yet?

4. Charles C. Heckscher, *The New Unionism* (New York: Basic Books, 1988).

5. Leonard Tivey and Anthony Wright, eds., *Political Thought since 1945* (Aldershot, Eng.: Edward Elgar Publishing, 1992), introduction, esp. 30–33. See James Burnham, *The Managerial Revolution* (New York: John Day, 1941).

6. That may explain why political rhetoricians often cry "crisis" in an attempt to unite the society into an organic whole.

7. This leaves out the considerable problems discovered by Arrow. See chapter 5.

8. Following the presidential election of 1992 in the United States, perhaps this statement should be qualified. H. Ross Perot may have shown that certain individuals can achieve substantial influence. Perot's popularity may have sprung from America's lingering romantic attachment to an earlier era of rugged individualism. Thus, perhaps we need to qualify the claim made here by saying that individualism is alive and well in the United States for billionaires. The advantage to such a qualification is that it gives managerialism a kind of symmetry with capitalism and socialism. Recall that in

discussing those ideologies we made minor exceptions for people who did not have to be consumers or did not have to work for a living.

9. As I am writing this section, one of the periodic fads is sweeping management circles. Like other fads, it is especially aggressively promoted by the numerous consulting organizations as something they must teach members of the corporation. It goes under a variety of names, but perhaps the most popular is Total Quality Management. The shorter expression is Quality Management, and the shortest is TQM. The latter threatens to become a mantra for good management in the 1990s. Central to TQM is a team approach to resolving corporate issues. In our own terminology, the effort is to construct organic teams out of atomistic elements. In short, for an up-front price, the management consultants promise to take people whose selfish instincts have been nurtured and developed even in their educational programs and convert them into team members ready to sublimate their self-interests to the interests of the team. By the time it is clear that this fad is not the universal panacea sought by senior management, the consultants will have found a new mantra to teach all to pronounce, and their patrons will have forgotten about the unfulfilled earlier promises. In an impudent aside at a conference on higher education, I once suggested that since higher education was now getting on the TQM bandwagon, it should be clear that it had probably run its course in business management. The TQM consultants, seeing the end of the market, were trying to integrate horizontally. It is difficult to imagine an organizational structure less conducive to the real principles of TQM than the university.

10. I have stated this point rather baldly. In a fully organic organization, managers might put organizational goals ahead of their own.

11. It should be noted that this statement is normative, not descriptive. One of the unexamined dogmas of managers favors what is called merit pay. Since corporate managers attempt to control information about the corporation and thus make it almost impossible to determine how effective their merit pay systems are, it may be instructive to look at a business sector in which it is difficult to hide the relevant data: investment management for publicly held funds, such as mutual funds. An examination of the public reports of investment managers reveals how much these managers tend to manipulate the concept of merit pay. When the market—or their sector—is doing well, they suggest that positive performance of the portfolio is the result of their capable management. When their portfolio performs poorly, they often blame general economic conditions rather than their bad decisions. We can see similar pronouncements if we examine general corporate annual reports in good times and bad. The presumption is that managerial talent is the independent variable when things are going well, but the general state of the economy is the independent variable when things are going poorly. Conveniently from management's perspective, managers "deserve" their high compensation in either case.

As any sophomore statistics student could attest, the real relations are likely multivariate, and identifying the contribution of a particular variable is somewhere between extremely difficult and impossible. To say that management *should* be evaluated on the basis of management discretion identifies the solution of the problem without identifying how to get to the solution and without stating the difficulties involved. A further element confuses the situation even more. Discretion is not merely a dependent variable. Management can help increase the amount of discretion. Identifying the complexities does not solve the problem, but hypocrisy does not either.

12. James MacGregor Burns, *Leadership* (New York: Harper and Row, 1978), esp. pts. 3 and 4.

13. While this section takes a different approach, I want to give recognition to a recent chapter by Joseph L. Badaracco, Jr.: "The Boundaries of the Firm," in *Socio-Economics: Toward a New Synthesis*, ed. Amitai Etzioni and Paul Lawrence (Armonk, N.Y.: M. E. Sharpe, 1991), 293–327. Badaracco also recognizes the limitations of the theory of the firm, and he suggests that historically the theory assumed that firms had identifiable boundaries, an assumption he argues is retained in economic theory even to the present. Badaracco suggests, however, that the boundary metaphor is significantly overworked and that it is time to recognize that firms do not have the boundaries theory assumes. Badaracco seems to want to continue to distinguish business firms from other kinds, a distinction managerialism challenges. He also does not seem to recognize the central role incorporation has had in destroying the boundaries. Nevertheless, Badaracco's exciting analysis and the one suggested here share much in common.

14. See, for example, the so-called Lester-Machlup debates: R. A. Lester, "Shortcomings of Marginal Analysis for Wage-Employment Problems," *American Economic Review* 36 (March 1946): 62–82; and Fritz Machlup, "Marginal Analysis and Empirical Research," *American Economic Review* 36 (Sept. 1946): 519–54. These articles started the debate which went on for a long time and eventually drew in luminaries such as Milton Friedman, Paul Samuelson, George Stigler, R. A. Gordon, Ernest Nagel, and H. M. Oliver. The parties never convinced each other and eventually retired from the fray, apparently exhausted. There was a peace, but it was a peace without a victory, and occasionally there are further incursions. The debate became one between empiricists and theoreticians. The former argued that the hypothesis of profit maximization did not correspond to reality. The latter argued that the empirical evidence is insufficient to justify abandoning the hypothesis. Some even argued that no empirical evidence could possibly be brought forward to refute the hypothesis. Obviously, the hypothesis is deeply embedded in contemporary capitalist economic theory.

15. Ironically, some senior managers who have relied on extensive organizational decentralization have come to realize that subordinate executives can quite adeptly manipulate the accounting systems in order to exceed profit goals set by central senior management. Exceeding the goals is a way to promotion. The subordinate then leaves to a successor the problem of picking up the pieces.

16. In telling this story, I am conscious of the fact that Weiner may have been making his point humorously. I do not suggest that the views presented here were Weiner's considered conclusions on the topic. Even if his point was meant to be humorous, it is that point to which our attention is addressed here.

17. Peter F. Drucker, *The Concept of the Corporation* (New York: John Day Co., 1946).

18. See, for example, Peter F. Drucker, *The Practice of Management* (New York: Harper, 1954). See also Peter F. Drucker, *Management: Tasks, Responsibilities, Prac-*

tices (New York: Harper and Row, 1973): "the fallacy of Profit Maximization" (58); "the concept of profit maximization is, in fact, meaningless. . . . A theorem that can be maintained only when qualified out of existence has surely ceased to have meaning or usefulness" (59); "the rhetoric of 'profit maximization' and 'profit motive' are not only antisocial. They are immoral" (810).

19. Peter F. Drucker, *The End of Economic Man* (New York: John Day Co., 1939), 242.

20. To show the argument is persuasive, consider what would happen if it were discovered later that I set the whole thing up, bribing the driver of the car to hit me so I would hit that person. Under those changed circumstances, people would sensibly hold me responsible.

21. John Ladd, "Morality and the Ideal of Rationality in Formal Organizations," *The Monist* 54, no. 4 (Oct. 1970): 489, 488.

22. Ibid., 488, 507.

23. Ibid., 495.

24. Ibid., 494.

25. Ibid., 500.

26. Ibid., 490.

27. Ibid., 500.

28. *Boss:* "Didn't you know that if we raised prices when we did we would lose too many customers to justify the action?"

Subordinate: "Well, I suspected that might happen."

Boss: "Why didn't you tell me so?"

Subordinate: "You didn't ask."

29. Ladd, "Morality," 508, 494.

30. Milton Friedman, *Essays in Positive Economics* (Chicago: University of Chicago Press, 1953), 14.

31. Milton Friedman, "The Social Responsibility of Business Is to Increase Its Profits," *New York Times Magazine,* Sept. 13, 1970; Milton Friedman, *Capitalism and Freedom* (Chicago: University of Chicago Press, 1962), 133.

32. Friedman, *Capitalism and Freedom,* 133. As I am writing this section, a curious instant case is being debated in the popular press. Some self-identified conservative politicians discovered that the popular rapper Ice-T included a song titled "Cop Killer" in his album *Body Count*. As the song's title indicates, its lyrics advocate the killing of police. The recording is mass-produced and distributed by Time Warner, which is, of course, a major corporation. The conservative politicians argued strenuously, publicly, and successfully that Time Warner was being irresponsible in producing the album and in allowing its distribution. The irony of the situation is that even though the conservative politicians find their allegiance with Friedman and are the same people who once insisted that corporations should not get involved in doing things such as divesting South African stock because corporations should strive only to make a profit (as Friedman argued), when they find it politically convenient, they abandon their former "principles" for new ones. And their newfound principles are just like those which they criticize their adversaries for holding on other topics. Friedman usually does not shy

from facing the logical consequences of his own views, nor does he moderate his views to suit current political fashions. To the best of my knowledge, however, he has not weighed in on this topic.

Ice-T has withdrawn the song from future issues of the album. (That produced a new irony: the "original" album became a collector's item, and true to capitalism's dictates, many individuals rushed out to buy the album in case its later value should increase. Real collectors, of course, will never listen to the album or even remove it from its shrink wrap. In all likelihood, Time Warner and Ice-T are the major holders of the original album still shrink wrapped, thus increasing their return on investment.)

33. Friedman, *Capitalism and Freedom*, 135.

34. Ibid., 34.

35. Ladd, "Morality," 508.

36. Peter A. French, "The Corporation as a Moral Person," *American Philosophical Quarterly* 13 (July 1979): 207. See also W. Michael Hoffman and Jennifer Mills Moore, *Business Ethics: Readings and Cases in Corporate Morality* (New York: McGraw Hill, 1984), 171.

37. John R. Danley, "Corporate Moral Agency: The Case for Anthropological Bigotry," in Hoffman and Moore, *Business Ethics*, 173.

38. See, for example, Carol Gilligan, *In a Different Voice* (Cambridge: Harvard University Press, 1982).

39. Larry May, *The Morality of Groups* (Notre Dame, Ind.: University of Notre Dame Press, 1987). It is important to emphasize that May's title uses the more generic term *group*. This is in some ways preferable to my frequent reference to *corporation*. I do not mean to confine attention merely to those groups which have approved articles of incorporation and, thus, are recognized by some government agency as such. There are groups, associations, gatherings, and so forth which have not been legally incorporated and which I include in my analyses. Similarly, there are corporations in the technical and legal sense which are only included in a broad sense. For example, in the process of acquisition and merger activities, lawyers and investment bankers may set up shell corporations to receive assets in order to carry out the transfers. These entities are corporations in a technical sense, though their effective lifetimes may be counted in seconds. They are not of much interest to me in this section except as illustrations of one of the extremities of the concept. In spite of its limitations and its potential for misunderstanding, however, I shall continue to use the term *corporation*, in part because it reflects the literature and in part because I believe the granting of incorporation privileges was an act of singular importance in creating the new ideology. The fact that many nonprofit groups have become incorporated is not a result of some deep commitment to incorporation on their part, but a response to some practical issues which arise out of the general corporate context. Thus, I include nonprofit corporations as well as business corporations. In addition, I include a wide range of associations, groups, organizations, corporations, and so on in this analysis.

40. Once again, *atomism* is my term. May uses the term *individualism*, but for the sake of consistency, in this book I shall stay with my terms. May's preferred term for organicism is *collectivism*.

41. May, *Morality of Groups,* 13, 17.

42. Ibid., 24.

43. Ibid., 29.

44. For clarity's sake, I would not want to be committed to the notion that this is a unidimensional continuum. Numerous factors may need to be considered.

45. I am emboldened by recalling the fact that the analytic philosopher and anti-metaphysician Arthur Pap is said to have admitted in the last days of his life that while immortality is logically possible, it is not empirically probable. See Brand Blanshard, epilogue to *An Introduction to the Philosophy of Science,* by Arthur Pap (New York: Free Press of Glencoe, 1962), 430. If Pap could find nothing logically inconsistent with the doctrine of immortality, I am prepared to believe, until shown otherwise, that there is nothing logically inconsistent with the organic doctrine.

46. Of course, the apologists of latter-day capitalism continue to teach their listeners that government should not be involved in business!

47. "The Stateless Corporation: Forget Multinationals—Today's Giants Are Really Leaping Boundaries," *Business Week,* May 14, 1990, pp. 98–105.

48. Charles Peirce, the founder of pragmatism, once became so disturbed at the popular misuse of the term *pragmatism* that he tried to relabel his view *pragmaticism,* which he said might be an ugly enough word to keep it from popularizers. Perhaps the pluralists should retreat to the use of *polyarchism,* since it is ugly enough to insure that it will not be taken up by others. *Pluralism,* however, can be made to do the job in this book if we remember that something quite specific is meant by it.

49. This is especially true in the case of candidates. The issue with regard to referenda is not as clear. It may be that in the United States the electorate is responding in the only way it can: by not voting. Thus it verifies its recognition of the trivialization of the electoral process.

50. See, for example, the pathbreaking American article, P. C. Schmitter, "Still the Century of Corporatism," *Review of Politics* 36 (1974): 85–131, and the excellent review volume, Alan Cawson, *Corporatism and Political Theory* (New York: Basil Blackwell, 1986).

51. The basic presumptions of government personnel policies seem to come directly from McGregor's theory X. See Douglas M. McGregor, *The Human Side of Enterprise* (New York: McGraw-Hill, 1960).

52. Considering AFL-CIO membership alone, those unions represent about 12 percent of the business work force. Much of it is in struggling industries such as automobiles, steel, and electric power. At the same time, they represent about 35 percent of public employees. The conceptual impact of public unions still has not been acknowledged. By the received theories, there should be no public unions, because the public sector, by definition, has no profit to share with the workers and public management has no self-interest in hard bargaining.

53. The problems are not easy ones to solve, especially in the context of the rhetoric of taxpayer revolt, which increases the suspicion that government workers are lazy and uninterested in doing a good job. There is a useful aphorism which hangs around labor policy discussions, however, to the effect that in the long run, management gets

the labor relations it deserves. There is considerable room for improvement and for saving money.

54. Cawson, *Corporatism and Political Theory*, 3.

55. Ibid., 145; Alan Cawson, *Corporatism and Social Welfare: Social Policy and State Intervention in Britain* (London: Heinemann Educational Books, 1982).

56. George C. Lodge, *The New American Ideology* (New York: New York University Press, 1975); idem, *The American Disease* (New York: New York University Press, 1986); and George C. Lodge and Ezra F. Vogel, eds., *Ideology and National Competitiveness: An Analysis of Nine Countries* (Boston: Harvard Business School Press, 1987). The latter is a collection of papers from a conference which examined the impact of ideology on different cultures, with special attention to business communities. It includes an instructive introduction and a chapter by Lodge.

57. Lodge, *American Disease*, 43, 197.

58. George C. Lodge, "Introduction: Ideology and Country Analysis," in *Ideology and National Competitiveness*, ed. Lodge and Vogel, 14–23.

59. Lodge, *American Disease*, 209.

60. Lodge, "Introduction," in *Ideology and National Competitiveness*, ed. Lodge and Vogel, 23.

Chapter 8. Ethics, Economics, and Business

1. Harold Arthur Prichard, "Does Moral Philosophy Rest on a Mistake?" *Mind* 21 (1912): 4.

2. The sense of moral dilemma can be induced in the student, and I, at least, often start my courses by trying to get students to experience vicariously dilemmas which have led people to intellectualize as they have.

3. Perhaps the judge decided that forcing someone to listen to philosophy would be a good form of punishment! If so, we cannot gainsay the decision, though Frankel's class was almost surely interesting and challenging.

4. I once taught philosophy in a prison. It was interesting to me that the students almost always elected to discuss topics in epistemology and metaphysics rather than ethics. Perhaps they simply had little interest in doing what ethics might require them to do.

5. A survey of various dimensions of this topic can be found in Willard F. Enteman, ed., *The Problem of Free Will* (New York: Charles Scribner's Sons, 1967).

6. See William James, "Dilemma of Determinism," in *The Will to Believe* (1896; New York: Dover, 1956), 145–83.

7. Richard Taylor, "Fatalism," *Philosophical Review* 71 (1962): 55–66.

8. Enteman, *Problem of Free Will*, 86.

9. Democracy escaped the debate by staying with its commitment to a process approach. It does not matter in democracy whether we assume that people are determined to vote as they do or that people freely choose to vote as they do. Thus democracy could survive without becoming embroiled in the issue. When people advocating their version of democracy allied it with capitalism or socialism, democracy simply absorbed the determinism of those views.

10. See, for example, Carol Gilligan, *In a Different Voice* (Cambridge: Harvard University Press, 1982).

11. I have left aside the institutionalists who have also examined the facts carefully. Their interest, however, has been largely empirical and not seriously theoretical. Veblen, Hobson, Ayers, Berle, Means, Minsky, Kindelberger, Hirschman, Galbraith, Leibenstein, and the two great historians Gras and Chandler have made enormous contributions to our understanding of the institutional conditions. Chandler comes close to what I am trying to articulate when he refers to the development of "managerial capitalism." He recognizes that somehow whatever we have is not standard capitalism, but even his phraseology gives away the problem: he does not see how these developments have posed a major challenge to the foundations of capitalism. His presumption remains that since whatever he is observing is not socialist, it must be some variation on capitalism. Speaking semantically, Chandler's expression *managerial capitalism* makes some progress toward managerialism, but it does not move far enough. The semantic qualifications for *capitalism* go back at least to Gras, who spoke of prebusiness capitalism, petty capitalism, mercantile capitalism, industrial capitalism, and finance capitalism See N. S. B. Gras, *Business and Capitalism: An Introduction to Business History* (New York: F. S. Crofts and Co., 1939). Gras believed that all were variations on the basic capitalism, so the noun *capitalism* remained, and it was qualified with the adjectives. Chandler added a new adjective, *managerial*. The view of managerialism, however, is that what was once a noun (i.e., *capitalism*) gradually became an adjective. It might make some kind of sense to talk of capitalist managerialism and differentiate that from socialist managerialism, where the former would be essentially oriented around the consumer through competitive markets and the latter would be essentially oriented around workers through worker alliances. Even the adjective, however, has gone and been replaced by the noun, *managerialism,* itself. Perhaps *managerialism* will disappear when it is first qualified with adjectives and then moves to an adjectival state itself, but that has not happened yet.

12. G. L. S. Shackle, *Decision, Order and Time* (Cambridge: Cambridge University Press, 1961), 272–73.

13. C. A. Campbell, "Is 'Free Will' a Pseudo Problem?" *Mind* 60 (1951): 29–45.

14. For example, when I teach this subject matter to introductory students, in order to induce a sense of the intellectual itch I referred to earlier, I start by taking a hard-line deterministic position. Invariably, the majority of the students start on the side of free will. That seems to be true irrespective of the background or age of the students.

15. J. Ralph Lindgren, ed., *The Early Writings of Adam Smith* (New York: Augustus M. Kelley, 1967). This quoted passage comes after Smith explains Newton's system in admirable detail. The whole essay is worth reading.

16. Milič Čapek, *The Philosophical Impact of Contemporary Physics* (Princeton, N.J.: D. Van Nostrand Co., 1961), 121.

17. Ibid., 122.

18. G. L. S. Shackle, *Time in Economics* (Amsterdam: North Holland, 1958), 23.

19. I need to issue a caution. Einstein's tensor calculus is just as deterministic in its own way as Newton's infinitesimal calculus was. It is useful to recall that Einstein

identified Spinoza as the philosopher he admired most. I have already quoted Spinoza's deterministic explanation of the illusion of free will. The abandonment of the illusion of time really follows Heisenberg's uncertainty principle. Heisenberg's principle did not shake Einstein's faith in determinism. He is said to have declared, "God does not play with dice."

20. GM seems fully capable of shooting itself in the foot without the media's holding the gun.

21. Willard F. Enteman, "The Ideology of Corporate Restructuring," in *The Ethics of Organizational Transformation,* ed. W. Michael Hoffman, Robert Frederick, and Edward S. Petry, Jr. (New York: Quorum Books, 1989), 237–44.

22. Of course, the real adjustment is to stop contorting capitalism in order to try to account for these changes. The real adjustment, as I have argued throughout the book, is to recognize the commitment of the bifurcation fallacy and to abandon capitalism as either accurately descriptive or reasonably prescriptive.

23. If some professedly conservative people have their way, government will overturn the Griswold decision, by which it restrained itself from telling us whether we could use contraceptives.

24. Willard F. Enteman, "Economics, Ethics, and the Environment," in *The Corporation, Ethics, and the Environment,* ed. W. Michael Hoffman, Robert Frederick, and Edward S. Petry, Jr. (New York: Quorum Books, 1990), 217–26.

25. Peter F. Drucker, "Ethical Chic," *Public Interest* 63 (Spring 1981): 18–36.

26. Kenneth E. Goodpaster and John B. Matthews, Jr., "Can a Corporation Have a Conscience?" *Harvard Business Review* 60 (Jan.–Feb. 1982): 145–54; Peter F. Drucker, *Management: Tasks, Responsibilities, Practices* (New York: Harper and Row, 1973), 307.

27. I have heard James Burke, the CEO of Johnson and Johnson during the Tylenol scare, say that representatives of Johnson and Johnson went into retail outlets on their own and removed Tylenol from the shelves before he gave the order to do so. Presumably, the representatives knew what kind of corporation they represented and did not have to wait to be told about the ethically appropriate action. That was clear to them by the nature of Johnson and Johnson. Of course, we all know of other corporations whose representatives would have taken much different actions.

28. Willard F. Enteman, "Ethical Responsibility in a Corporation," in *Corporate Governance and Institutionalizing Ethics,* ed. W. Michael Hoffman, Jennifer Mills Moore, and David Fedo (Lexington, Mass.: D. C. Heath Co., 1984), 237–47.

29. Of course, democratic managerialism is not necessarily the only possibility in *O,* any more than managerialism itself is the only possibility in *U.* We need to guard against further instances of the bifurcation fallacy.

Index

Adorno, T. W.: on alienation, 234*n6*
AFL-CIO: management of, 162; mentioned, 248*n52*
Alice: mentioned, 7
Alienation: of worker in Marx, 79–81
Apartheid: ideology of, 16
Apter, David: editor of *Ideology and Discontent,* 228*n3*
Aristotle: *On Rhetoric: A Theory of Civil Discourse,* ix, 227*n1;* on Plato, 20; constitutions of Greek states, 21; *Politics,* 21, 240*n39;* democracy, 101, 110, 116; size of state, 125; women in politics, 229*n18*
Arrow, Kenneth: inconsistencies in democracy, 105–8, 118; social choice, 155, 157, 159; paradox avoided, 221; *Social Choice and Individual Values,* 237*n8,* mentioned, 209, 243*n7. See also* Duncan Black, Robert Dahl, Howard DeLong, and Robert Paul Wolff
Atomism: ideological division, 30–34; and capitalism, 44–71 *passim*

Babeuf, François: socialist rejection of capitalism, 87
Badaracco, Joseph: limits of theory of the firm, 245*n13*
Baseball: atomistic sport, 236*n26*
Belenky, Mary Field: *Women's Ways of Knowing: The Development of Self, Voice and Mind,* 230*n7. See also* Blythe McVicker Clinchy, Nancy Rule Goldberger and Jill Mattuck Tarule

Bell, Daniel: on the end of ideology, 8–9; *The End of Ideology Debate,* 228*n3*
Benne, Robert: on private property, 144
Berger, Peter: on capitalism, private property and corporations, 69–70; *The Capitalist Revolution: Fifty Propositions about Prosperity, Equality and Liberty,* 232*n26*
Berlin Wall: destruction and ideology, 95
Bernstein, Eduard: disciple of Marx, 89; evolutionary socialism, 132; *Evolutionary Socialism,* 236*n17;* collaborator of Marx and Engels, 241*n2*
Bifurcation fallacy: described and defined 41–45; socialism and capitalism, 132; supporting democratic socialism, 137; supporting democratic capitalism, 141–42; democracy *versus* totalitarianism, 147; matrix analysis, 149–51; Heilbroner, 152; nature of corporation, 178–79; George Lodge, 187; mentioned, 30
Black, Duncan: on Arrow's theorem, 238*n9*
Blalock, Hubert M.: *The Behavioral Persuasion,* 228*n3. See also* J. G. Miller and Heinz Eulau
Blefuscuians: and bifurcation fallacy, 43
Bloomsbury Group: mentioned, 228*n2*
Brown, Charlie: duped again, 212
Burke, Edmund: as conservative, 241*n9*
Burke, James: Tylenol scare, 251*n27*
Burnham, James: and mangerialism, 155; *The Managerial Revolution,* 155–56, 243*n5*
Burns, James MacGregor: transactional *vs.* transformational leadership, 165, 220; followership, 194; *Leadership,* 245*n12*